the New Radicals

the New Radicals

A Report with Documents

by Paul Jacobs
and Saul Landau

Sponsored by the Center for the Study
of Democratic Institutions

RANDOM HOUSE

New York

Second printing

© *Copyright, 1966, by Paul Jacobs and Saul Landau*
All rights reserved under International and Pan American Copyright
Conventions. Published in New York by Random House, Inc., and
simultaneously in Toronto, Canada, by Random House of Canada Limited.

The authors are grateful to the following for permission to reprint:
Randy Battle for "Letter from an Americus Jail";
Barbara Brandt for "Why People Become Corrupt";
City Lights Books for excerpts from "Howl" by Allen Ginsberg, © Copyright 1956, 1959, by Allen Ginsberg;
Bradley Cleaveland for "A Letter to Undergraduates" from SLATE supplement;
Commentary and Bayard Rustin for "From Protest to Politics," © Copyright 1965 by the American Jewish Committee;
Dissent and Irving Howe for "New Styles in Leftism," April 1965;
FSM for "FSM's Joy to U.C.—Free Speech Carols";
Paul Goodman and Alvin Duskin for excerpts from their dialogue "How to Make a College";
Hall Syndicate, Inc., for the cartoon by Jules Feiffer, © Copyright 1965 by Jules Feiffer. All Rights Reserved;
Insurgent for the May–June 1965 Editorial;
Liberation for "Generational Revolt and the Free Speech Movement" by Gerald Rosenfeld, December 1965–January 1966, and "Coalition Politics or Nonviolent Revolution" by Staughton Lynd, June–July 1965;
Charles McLaurin for "Notes on Organizing";
The Movement for "Questions Raised by Moses," April 1965, and "Nonviolence in the Ghetto," September 1965;
PL for "Preamble and Introduction to the Constitution," May–June 1965, and "Perspectives for the Left" by Ed Clark, January 1965;
Ramparts and Michael Rossman for "Barefoot in a Marshmallow World," January 1966;
The Realist for the cartoon by Dick Guindon;
Jane Stembridge for selected poems;
Students for a Democratic Society for excerpts from "A Strategy for University Reform" by Paul Booth, "The Port Huron Statement" by Tom Hayden, "Some Problems, Issues, Proposals" by Dick Flacks, "Liberalism and the Corporate State" by Carl Oglesby;
Studies on the Left for the editorial "The Radicalism of Disclosure," Fall 1959, "On the Ideology of the Campus Revolution" by Dale Johnson, 1961, "On the New Left" by C. Wright Mills, 1961, "Newark: Community Union" by Jesse Allen, Winter 1965, and "Up From Irrelevance" and "Reply," Spring 1965;
The Young Socialist for "In Tribute to Malcolm X" by Jack Barnes, May–June 1965.

Library of Congress Catalog Card Number: 66–18328

Manufactured in the United States of America

to A. J. Muste   *from P. J.*

and the late C. Wright Mills   *from S. L.*

Our youth today love luxury. They have bad manners, contempt for authority, disrespect for older people. Children nowadays are tyrants. They contradict their parents, gobble their food and tyrannize their teachers.

—SOCRATES, 5 B.C.

Cuando Merda Tiver Valor, Pobre Nasce Sem Cu . . . .

—PORTUGUESE PROVERB

Acknowledgments

Much of the impetus for this book came from the authors' participation in a seminar at the Center for the Study of Law and Society at the University of California, Berkeley. We wish to thank our colleagues in the seminar for their advice and criticism. Joan Bowman helped us greatly in bringing together the documents and in the preparation of the chronology. Barbara La Morticella carried out the tedious secretarial work with better spirits than we thought possible.

Caroline Craven and Ken McEldowney offered detailed criticism of the SDS chapter, for which we are most grateful. Elizabeth Southerland performed a similar role with the section on SNCC. Many people in The Movement allowed themselves to be interviewed, giving honest and often painful answers to our often impertinent questions. We thank them, too. As always, the authors are to be held solely responsible for the opinions expressed, and any errors or omissions that have been made.

Finally, our thanks and gratitude to Nina Serrano Landau and Ruth Rosenfield Jacobs, who helped, as always, in so many ways.

Contents

the New Radicals

1. The Movement's Themes

The Movement is a mélange of people, mostly young; organizations, mostly new; and ideals, mostly American. In 1960 and 1961 the Freedom Riders and Negro college students who sat-in in the South were acting in the spirit of The Movement. Most of those who protested against President Kennedy's Cuban policy in 1962 were responding to the impulse of The Movement. That same impulse took them south for the Student Nonviolent Coordinating Committee (SNCC) in 1963, got them arrested in Sproul Hall at the University of California in 1964, and marched them to Washington in 1965 to demonstrate their opposition to the war. Movement youth can be found today in the San Joaquin Valley of California, helping striking farm workers; some will become organizers in the slum communities of Northern cities; others will try to change the university system in America.

These young people believe that they must make something happen, that they are part of a movement stirring just below the surface of life hitherto accepted all over the world. So they identify with the Zengakuren students whose snake-dance demonstrations prevented President Eisenhower from visiting Japan, and wince at the photos of the young rebel shot by a policeman in Santo Domingo. They empathize with the young Soviet poets who read their poetry at the statue of Mayakovsky in Moscow until the police break up the meeting.

How many people are in the American Movement? Certainly, it is possible to count those who are members of the organizations within The Movement, but that would be to misunderstand one of the basic facts of its nature: The Movement is organizations plus unaffiliated supporters, who outnumber by the thousands, and perhaps even hundreds of thousands, those committed to specific groups. The Movement's basic strength rests on those unaffiliated reserves, who are just as much a part of it as the organization youth.

The leitmotifs that dominate The Movement extend far beyond politics. The Movement is much more than anti-Vietnam marches, civil rights demonstrations, and student sit-ins. To be in The Movement is to search for a psychic community, in which one's own identity can be defined, social and personal relationships based on love can be established and can grow, unfettered by the cramping pressures of the careers and life styles so characteristic of America today.

The Movement rejects the careers and life styles of the American liberal, too, for to The Movement it is the liberal way of life and frame of mind that represent the evil of America. Those in The Movement feel that modern American liberals have substituted empty rhetoric for significant content, obscured the principles of justice by administrative bureaucracy, sacrificed human values for efficiency, and hypocritically justified a brutal attempt to establish American hegemony over the world with sterile anti-Communism. The Movement sees the liberals righteously proclaiming faith in American democracy from their comfortable suburban homes or offices, while the United States Air Force drops napalm on villages and poisons the rice paddies.

So, those in The Movement see not only the openly authoritarian or totalitarian society as an enemy but the administered, bureaucratic, dehumanized, rhetorical-liberal one as well. They reject liberal authority. They were stirred, momentarily, by President Kennedy's call for a commitment to freedom, but were so disappointed by his actions in Cuba and Vietnam that they turned on him with bitterness. And the Johnson Administration's foreign policy reinforces their view that America flouts, in action, the traditions of freedom and justifies the use of military instruments associated with the Nazis.

The new movement is also a revolt against the postwar "over-developed society," with its large bureaucracies in government, corporations, trade unions, and universities. To those in The Movement the new technologies of automation and cybernation, with their computers and memory-bank machines, are instruments of alienation, depersonalizing human relations to a frightening degree. The brain machines and the translation of human qualities into holes punched into a card are viewed as devices that break down communication and destroy community in the interests of efficiency. Technology's emphasis on routine efficiency has created a set of values, rationalized by its supporters as representing "the facts of modern life." But The Movement sees these values as false, imposed on the whole society without "the consent of the governed." Even worse, the decision-making over which the governed no longer have control extends far beyond politics: in the technological order every aspect of the people's lives is under the control of administrators far removed from responsibility to the governed. And the elders of those in The Movement have exchanged their decision-making right for the comforts of American affluence. All that remains is nineteenth-century rhetoric about democracy and freedom, and technology has drained the words of their content.

In their personal life style, their aesthetic sense, many in The Movement reject affluence and its associated symbols. The ambition to escape from poverty is no spur to action in their lives, for many are children of America's post-Depression *nouveau* middle class. Their parents are the once-poor scholars who head rich academic institutes; the ex-union organizers who run their own large businesses; the former slum dwellers who develop segregated real-estate tracts; the families once on the WPA who live in suburbia—all those who have made it. But their parents' desire to own, to accumulate, to achieve the status and prestige which go with material wealth, are meaningless goals to the children. To them television is not a wonder but a commonplace, and they see the $5,000 a year their parents spend on the analyst as too high a price to pay for the loss of human values.

The marvels of the space age are commonplace to them, too,

and the voices to which they listen are not those of the orbiting astronauts exchanging banalities. They respond instead to the sense and sound of friendship and community, to the exultation they feel when thousands of people link hands and sing "We Shall Overcome." And to achieve that feeling of community, of life, they have been willing to sacrifice most middle-class comforts.

They are willing to do this, for until they enter The Movement their inability to affect the quality of their own lives disturbs them profoundly. Those of the upper middle class were trapped, protected to the point of coddling through their childhood and early teens, sated with *nouveau* affluence by the time they were twenty. They knew they could achieve a place in the society of their parents, but it was not a society in which they wanted a place; it offered little beyond physical comfort. They believed the ideals they were taught, and felt miserable when the ideals were exposed as empty words. Their awareness that Negroes and millions of poor have been left out of the society moved them to act rather than depend on the persuasion techniques advocated by their elders.

Many of them were born in the year of The Bomb, and so their history begins with the history of nuclear destruction. The twenties and even the thirties are almost prehistory to them, and the burning issues which agitated the older generation's radicals and liberals are devoid of meaning. Some know of the mid-fifties' McCarthyism and the House Un-American Activities Committee (HUAC), but the internecine wars of the thirties have little personal significance for them.

In some measure, too, the modes of extreme personal behavior adopted by this group—their permissive view of marijuana or hallucinogenics like LSD, their matter-of-fact acceptance of sexual freedom and their habitual profanity—are part of their search for identity. That search assumes a rejection of everything connected with their old identity and of the technological, bureaucratic values they see as dominant in American life. It is also possible that their difficulties in finding personal meaning in the routine politics of the civil rights struggle and their anguish in seeing the country carry out a foreign policy they believe to be totally bad force these young people into seeking meaning in experiences. They think the ivory-towered men of ideas have cheated them, lied to them, and that action and spontaneous experience will show them truth.

Above all, those in The Movement now restlessly seek to find a new politics and a new ideology that will permit them to link existential humanism with morally acceptable modes of achieving radical social change.

2. The Movement's Origins

*T*he Movement's origins are elusive and have many strands. In the 1930s and 1940s the radical movement encompassed a broad spectrum of organizations and political beliefs: the Communists and their front groups; the socialists, Trotskyists, and other anti-Stalinist organizations; sections of the CIO and a few other unions. The Communist groups, drawing worldwide support, dominated Amercian radicalism, since their size and prestige were greater than any of the other political tendencies. And although the American Communist Party was shaken in 1939 by the Stalin-Hitler nonaggression pact, the Nazi attack on the Soviet Union returned them to political acceptability.

But by the mid-fifties the old movement was nearly dead. The Communist Party had declined badly in the postwar period, because of government persecution and its own internal weaknesses. The trade unions were no longer crusading, many once radical anti-Communists had become supporters of the Establishment, and the socialists were barely distinguishable from the liberal Democrats.

Then, when today's young radicals were still in junior high school, the entire Communist world was shaken by the revelations about Stalin made at the 20th Party Congress. The Com-

munist movement soon suffered further blows from the uprisings
in Hungary and Poland. The Labor Youth League (LYL), the
Communist Party youth group, was disbanded shortly after the
shock of 1956, but it would have declined from internal stress
anyway. At the very time the American Marxists were being
disillusioned by the actions of Soviet socialism, England, France,
and Israel joined in an invasion of Egypt. A few intellectuals,
faced with Western imperialism and brutal Soviet Marxism,
began seeking a fresh way out of the crisis, developing what
C. Wright Mills described as The New Left.

It started in England, where in 1957 a group of university
intellectuals published two new journals, *Universities and Left
Review* and *The New Reasoner*. In 1959 they merged into the
New Left Review. Many of the editors had been members of
or had been close to the Communist Party at Oxford. For them
the failure of Marxism was more a failure of the vulgar Communist Marxists than of the theory. In the new journals the
ideals of socialism were rediscovered, and the kind of humanist
analysis that had been forgotten through purges, war, and Cold
War was revived. Often, too, *New Left Review* debated ideas
that could not comfortably be talked about within the framework of Soviet Marxism: alienation and humanism.

New Left political clubs of college and working-class youth
followed the magazine's formation, and through 1959 this small
group lit a new spark under dormant English radicalism—Aldermaston marches in support of peace and against nuclear testing
grew larger each year, and the Labour Party swung to the New
Left position on nuclear weapons, for one year.

By the end of the fifties concern for racial justice was developing among American students. A strong reaction to the indigni-
ties of fear and anxiety heaped on the country by McCarthy
and a general rejection of the symbols of American affluence
were growing. Some youth responded with the "beat" mood;
others developed an interest in the new British intellectual radicalism; still others rejected the style of life practiced by J. D.
Salinger's characters.

Simultaneously, a group in the American pacifist movement,
strongly influenced by pacifist leader A. J. Muste, was developing a "third camp" position, which rejected both the American

and Soviet Cold War positions, concentrating instead on attempting to create a third force to resist all militarism. Many "third camp" pacifists had been involved in the civil rights struggle, to which they had brought the nonviolent techniques that they had been studying and practicing since the outbreak of World War II. And although their original interest and commitment had an informal religious base, they moved over easily to politics.

As McCarthyism waned in the late fifties a group of university intellectuals, much like the British New Left although less vigorous and certain, began to develop around the universities of Wisconsin, California at Berkeley, and Chicago. At Wisconsin the Socialist Club was formed by ex-LYLers and younger undergraduates who had never experienced Communist Party schooling; at Berkeley a similar group called SLATE formed a student political party; at Chicago a student political party founded in the early fifties was revived.

At Wisconsin the success of the Socialist Club and the inspiration of the British New Left were combined with the teaching of William Appleman Williams, the historian, who attempted to use Marxism creatively to understand American history. The result was the publication of *Studies on the Left,* "a journal of research, social theory and review." Several months later at the University of Chicago a group of graduate students began to publish *New University Thought.*

The difference between the magazines was essentially over the use of the word "left." At a meeting held in Madison, Wisconsin, in 1960 to discuss merging the two magazines, the Chicago group, most of whom had had some experience with Communist youth groups as had the Wisconsin editors', argued that the word "left" and certainly the word "socialism" was so discredited as to be useless. The *Studies* editors argued that since they were socialists and Marxists, they should say so. One of their regrets was that during the McCarthy period they had been forced to mask their true political beliefs.

The advent of *Studies* and *New University Thought* marked the transition from old left Marxist dogma to a new period, even though most of the editors were Marxists who retained some loyalty to the Soviet Union, at least as a force for peace and reason. But the editors were also deeply concerned with scholarship, and saw themselves not so much as professional Movement people but as a new breed of university professor.

Meanwhile new journals appeared at Columbia, at Harvard, at campuses all over the country, reflecting the increased activity among intellectual radicals. These publications and the discussions over their contents were not limited to politics but covered every aspect of life from sexual freedom and pornography to civil rights and peace issues.

"It's his turn now and then me again . . ."

Copyright, 1962, by The Realist Association, Inc.

Another generation graduated from high school, and the colleges and universities became breeding grounds for campus political activity and the civil rights drive. Some of the young people in The Movement began to exhibit an inclination for activism and a spirit of anti-intellectualism, in part a rejection of the very university system in which they were involved. "The University" came to be regarded as part of the Establishment, and as the point of immediate contact, the most oppressive part.

Unlike their immediate predecessors, who had published magazines like *Studies* and *New University Thought,* this new group of youth activists knew little about the debates of the thirties. They learned about Stalinism, Trotskyism, and Social Democracy only in an academic context. Outside the classroom they referred with a sneer to the "old days"—the thirties, forties, and now the fifties. Like the rest of American society, the old left, they believed, had in some way "betrayed" them: they had "sold out" or else were "hung up" on old and dead battles. To most of these young people Marx, Lenin, and Trotsky had little relevance for what they understood to be America's problems. They simultaneously refused to identify with the Soviet Union or to be greatly concerned about injustice in any of the Communist societies. Their enemy was the American society and its Establishment.

Many of the young people in this activist generation were the children of parents who had been the radicals and left liberals of the thirties and the forties. At home they had heard the discussions about civil rights, and they knew of the political pall that hung over the country during the McCarthy era. They had learned a set of ideals from their parents and now, much to their parents' discomfiture, they were trying to put those ideals into practice.

And so by 1960 this new generation was throwing itself against American society, literally and figuratively. They found a new hero in Castro, the man of action, the man without an ideology, whose only interest seemed to be bettering the life of the Cuban people. They responded to the youthful Castro with enthusiasm and demanded "fair play" for the Cuban Revolution.

In May 1960 they were ready for an action of their own, and the opportunity was provided by the House Un-American Activities Committee. Hundreds of students from the campuses of the University of California at Berkeley and San Francisco State College, joined by some of the people who were moving away from the inactivity of the "beat" coffee houses, demonstrated physically against the Committee's San Francisco hearing. And after the demonstration, which received enormous publicity, they scorned the allegation that they had been led or inspired by the Communists. That charge, which they knew to be untrue, only reinforced their feelings of distrust for the celebrants of American society.

They identified, too, with the Freedom Riders who went South in 1960 and 1961; for this again meant taking direct action with their own bodies against segregation. They were not interested in theory, and so the long historical articles even in such left journals as *Studies* were not seen by them as being relevant.

This new activist Movement influenced even those who thought of themselves as being outside of society. As the apolitical "beats"—almost alone as symbols of protest in the fifties —turned their concern to concrete issues of racial equality and peace, their style, dress, and decor affected the activists. Arguments about politics began to include discussions of sexual freedom and marijuana. The language of the Negro poet-hipster permeated analyses of the Cuban Revolution. Protests over the execution of Caryl Chessman ultimately brought together students and some Bohemians—the loose and overlapping segments of what was to become known as The Movement.

President Kennedy gauged accurately the need of many youth to participate in programs for justice, and a few of the new activists were attracted to the Peace Corps. The Peace Corps stressed, at least in its appeal, a non-paternalistic, activist program in which people would be helped to help themselves, but most activists rejected the Peace Corps or any other government program. They felt American society supported rascism, oppressive institutions, capital punishment, and wars against popular movements in underdeveloped countries. "Alienation" was used to describe the society's effects on its citizens, and American society was seen as the source of injustice and suffering everywhere. While opposed to injustice and suppression of liberty in general, the activists did not feel the same outrage against Castro or Mao or Khrushchev that they could against their own rulers. It was "our" fault. Brought up and nurtured on the United Nations and liberal political values, hearing them articulated so well by President Kennedy and Adlai Stevenson, they demanded purity at home first, and when it was not forthcoming, quickly became convinced that it was impossible, that there was something rotten at the core of American society.

This dashing of hopes, the feeling that they had succumbed to what turned out to be only rhetoric on the part of Kennedy and Stevenson, was an important part of their turning so bitterly against the Establishment.

And while the older ones among them had been able to articulate their views in a speech or a pamphlet, some of the younger ones, those who came into The Movement later and rejected politics—a small but growing number of middle-class youth—made a virtue of their inability to articulate and analyze coherently. They talked "from the gut," stumblingly, haltingly, using the language of the new folksingers, deliberately adopting a style that was the antithesis of what they had heard from their professors.

In their revulsion against the liberal intellectuals who were celebrating America and the end of ideology, the young activists rejected all ideology and traditional party politics, turning instead to where the action was, to SNCC, formed in 1960 by Negroes and whites, Southern and Northern. SNCC wasn't political; it was concerned with right and wrong, with people. The SNCC ideal of morality in action also provided the spur for the Students for a Democratic Society (SDS) and its community and campus programs: the decision to act was reinforced by the role of the liberal intellectuals in the 1961 Bay of Pigs episode and the 1962 missile crisis.

What began perhaps as a rebellion against affluence and liberal hyprocrisy grew in a few years into a radical activism that protested injustice at the very core of the society. But when even this was tolerated by the structures that were under attack, some of the young radicals began to think about something beyond rebellion or radical protest. The Movement now is struggling to develop an ideology that will guide them toward building an organization that can compete for political power.

3. SNCC—One Man, One Vote

*T*he kind of anguish that SNCC, the Student Nonviolent Coordinating Committee, produces in its staff and among it supporters has not existed since the Abolitionist groups nagged at the conscience of American society.

SNCC was formed in April 1960 at an Easter Week conference in Raleigh, North Carolina, from a group of Negro college students who had been brought together by some of the civil rights leaders interested in coordinating the student sit-in movement that was spreading so rapidly through the South. In June 1960 SNCC had a staff of only two but by now it has reached more Southern Negroes on a personal level than has been done since Radical Reconstruction. "This battered brotherhood of organizers, poets, hipsters and visionaries," as Jack Newfield characterized them in *The Nation* (July 19, 1965), "has grown up to have a staff of 200 full-time paid workers in the field, plus 250 full-time volunteers; an annual budget of $800,000, and an evolving philosophy unburdened by obsolete blueprints of utopia from other generations or other countries."

All through the fall of 1960 into the winter of 1961 SNCC founders planned and conferred. Several hundred delegates, from organizations as far apart as CORE and the YWCA, and unaffiliated Negroes and whites met in October 1960 in Atlanta and agreed that the various student activities needed coordinating. So SNCC became an official institution although without a bureaucracy or hierarchy. "We seek a community," said Fisk University graduate Marion Barry at the conference, "in which man can realize the full meaning of the self which demands open relationships with others."

Other Negro college students and youth who had organized and participated in sit-ins, independently, through CORE or SCLC, began to "get the SNCC spirit." Sit-ins continued throughout the South all winter. New blood joined The Movement in the spring of 1961 when the Freedom Riders came down from the North on integrated buses. Some of them, like twenty-year-old Stokely Carmichael, a Howard University student arrested in Jackson, Mississippi, left jail radicalized and committed to work as full-time SNCC staff. The sit-ins and Freedom Rides provided the students with education in action. They had won some victories and were ready for a full confrontation with white supremacy. By the end of the summer of 1961 the sit-ins and Freedom Rides, wrote Howard Zinn in his book on SNCC, "ground to a bloody halt in the Deep South, leaving the participants wounded but determined. . . ."

In August 1961 SNCC invaded Mississippi, led by Robert (Moses) Parris, who quit his teaching job at a private school in New York. SNCC was in McComb in 1961, in Greenwood in 1962, all over the state in 1963 and 1964. Another group of SNCC workers began a separate organizing campaign in southwest Georgia in late 1961 and the name Albany came to mean cracker terror instead of the capital of New York State.

In 1963 SNCC began organizing Selma, Alabama, later to become the scene of the historic march that led directly to the adoption of new civil rights legislation, and in a sense the symbol of the last strong stand of open white supremacy.

SNCC's short history has literally been written in the blood of its staff and supporters.

Ironically, just as books and articles heralding these young visionaries are appearing everywhere, their Movement itself faces a crisis. The weary veterans of harassment, arrests, beatings, and the psychological torture of living in the South, have begun to re-examine their objectives at the very time they confront the full and often subtle power of the American economic and political system.

SNCC was formed to make a revolution in the South—what kind of revolution they did not know, and they only *felt* how they would do it: they would go out to meet the people, talk with them, share their needs. They would help Negroes to organize themselves so that each individual could gain dignity through participatory democracy, by participating in the decisions that affected his life. But more recently those who came to the SNCC staff have seen needs in bread-and-butter terms. Yet these differences do not adequately represent the shades of diverse thinking that characterize this unorganized organization. One Negro staff member has said that the SNCC ideal was different for different people. Then, after stating his ideal—a society in which the people truly decide—he admitted to some disillusionment and to a questioning of his own basic premise. Like other SNCC veterans he still wants to make a revolution, but his faith that organization can be built through openness, honesty, and personal contact is no longer as firm as it once was.

Like SDS leaders, many SNCC veterans see the liberal corporate Establishment as the main but often faraway enemy. SNCC has worked almost exclusively in the South, where it has had to face the Southern police system and vigilante terror. It views America as if it were one large Mississippi. (Friends of SNCC groups in the North serve mainly as money-raising branches and recruiting offices, although they initiated and participated in Northern community projects and protests.) The majority of the SNCC staff is Negro, Northern and Southern. Unlike SDS, SNCC's major successes have been in rural southern Georgia or in Delta cities like Greenwood, Mississippi.

The general affluence that characterizes SDS members is not true of SNCC staff. They do not usually come from wealthy or middle-class backgrounds, and their subsistence salaries are not glorified as an example of their purity—they take some pride in their spirited poverty—but rather are seen as necessary: if SNCC could pay more, it would. When an individual volunteers for SNCC service in the South, he quickly dons the uniform: blue jeans, blue jean-Ike jacket, and sunglasses. The language and norms of SNCC workers are quickly learned by newcomers because the values have already been accepted.

SNCC is very much a Negro organization, unlike SDS which is predominantly white. Although the two groups' political philosophy is similar and their approach to politics and organizing reflects the same mode of openness and honesty, a strong strain of black nationalism links the SNCC staff to a tradition of Negro nationalism and to contemporary revolutionary nationalists like the late Malcolm X. Some black nationalist feelings take the form of "anti-white" language and behavior—understandable if unpleasant.

Further bad feeling stems from the appearance on the scene of young skilled whites who do not understand the educational and social differences between themselves and the Southern Negroes. The young whites proceed to do things for the Negroes, to handle secretarial and office jobs routinely, rather than teach local SNCC workers how to do them. In the view of the local people these whites also take away jobs in the black people's movement from a black person.

The enormous racial sensitivity The Movement has produced makes interracial cooperation difficult, since each innuendo, every poorly chosen word or facial expression is the subject for criticism and discussion, on the spot or at staff meetings. Either the Northern volunteer "makes it," learns to acknowledge deeply buried feelings and come to grips with them, functions with them and tries to overcome them, or he must go home.

But The Movement has developed positive aspects that reveal an awakening consciousness and a new-found pride in Negro identity. "Question," a poem by W. W. Long, former SNCC coordinator who worked in Selma, Alabama, exemplifies this spirit:

> Where am i
> in our history books
>
> i built the
> ark that
> saved you
> from the sun

and nursed
your babies
with black
milk laughter
everywhere

so where

am I

oh where
am i

The concept of community organization that SDS has tried
to practice in Northern cities developed in part from SNCC's
successful community programs in the Mississippi Delta and
other Black Belt areas. There was no urgency in SNCC's approach, for its premise was that to be an effective organizer one
had to be involved in the daily lives of the people. Sometimes
this meant, as one SNCC staffer wrote, "We just might sit here
and build a base in the community. It doesn't mean anything
that we don't have an active program going yet. We're not concerned with time. We're just going to let the people in the community know we're here, become involved in their daily lives,
and find out what it is they want us to do."

So, unlike the Marxist-Leninist vanguard party vision, the
SNCC ethos doesn't assume it knows what is good for the people.
It would rather help people to organize around their needs. But
leadership then becomes a difficult problem which produces in
the talented and intelligent staffers an anguish that often fright-
ens and threatens outsiders, even sympathetic ones. This psychological anguish, coupled with the tensions of a civil rights
worker's harassed life in the South, creates a quality of suffering that leads these young people to openness, occasional reck-
lessness, and to some exclusiveness.

Northern reporters and observers often encounter hostility
when they try to interview SNCC staff: "Why do you come to
us?" "Why don't you ask the people? They're the ones that are
making this movement. We can't speak for them." Even sympathetic correspondents are asked: "If you want to help us and
you say that you are committed, then why don't you write for

The Movement? Why don't you investigate areas that The Movement needs researched and written up?" In McComb, Mississippi, a young Negro SNCC staff member rebuffed a question about the statement issued by the McComb Freedom Democratic Party (MFDP), condemning American involvement in Vietnam and calling for Negroes to refuse to fight, because to her anyone from outside would stir up trouble, no matter how valid his credentials. Had SNCC workers asked the question, it would have been different; at a SNCC meeting it would have been discussed. But outsiders—even sympathetic ones, who take the time of staff people or leaders—are resented.

The personalism of Martin Luther King, James Farmer, or Roy Wilkins is shunned by SNCC and its "leaders." This difference—a symptom of deep ideological discord—has led to serious disagreement within the militant or left wing of the civil rights movement. When, in 1962, SNCC, the Southern Christian Leadership Conference (SCLC) and the Congress of Racial Equality (CORE) formed the Council of Federated Organizations (COFO) to carry on a unified voted registration drive, COFO was SNCC-dominated. But it was difficult to reconcile the three groups' differences in goals and style: the bread-and-butter objectives of King, Farmer, and Wilkins, their view that integration was possible within the existing society and that Negroes could share in American affluence, clashed continuously with the SNCC notion that no matter how much welfare was provided, the society was rotten because men could not achieve dignity.

The conflict between SNCC and SCLC was dramatized in 1965 by the events in Selma, where after two years of painful SNCC organization, Dr. King decided that a march would help speed passage of the voting rights bill. SNCC believes that the people had no opportunity to decide on the merits of the march although the SNCC staff had educated them to believe that they had that right. So when the march was announced, SNCC could do little except support it unless they were willing to wreck a tenuously based coalition.

The decisions about the ways and means of the march were then left to King. Whether or not the rumors about his "deal" with President Johnson to limit the demonstrations were accurate, the stories had their effect on the SNCC staff, especially the younger ones. King was privately denounced, and the obscene label with which he was tagged is still used by "Snick kids" from Georgia to Mississippi. While some of the older SNCC staff are worried about maintaining the truce and continue to deny that any rift exists between SNCC and SCLC—at the top, not among the community organizers—the younger ones believe that the difference in goals cannot be ignored. But Dr. King's militant statements after the Watts riots, as well as SNCC's own inability to organize in the Los Angeles ghetto, have sobered some of the young critics who have come to realize that purity is no longer easily achieved.

The honesty and openness that characterized SNCC through the summer of 1963 and into early 1964, were necessarily diluted as the staff was forced to confront complexities of power, in and out of the civil rights movement. The straightforward veracity of Robert Moses, when he oriented the volunteer summer staff that went to Mississippi in 1963 and 1964 and helped to break the stranglehold of fanatical segregationists, no longer seems possible. Indeed, Moses, one of SNCC's guiding spirits, has left it and become active in other radical activities. He was being treated as *the* leader, and he saw this as an obstacle to SNCC's fiercely democratic goal.

And, at the very time SNCC was being praised for its honesty and openness, it found it very difficult to practice these traits. Its radicalism, based in part on its opposition to American affluence and manipulative and unrepresentative politics, became somewhat compromised by its need to get liberal money, to preserve unity among civil rights groups in the South, and to have a public face different from its private soul. Thus, a SNCC spokesman in San Francisco was recently forced to deny the truth when he said: "There have been rumors of a rift between the Student Nonviolent Coordinating Committee and the Southern Christian Leadership Conference. Not so. SNCC and SCLC have never been closer." True, the spokesman was fund raising in San Francisco, and the liberals who donate to SNCC might have been upset by reports of a rift between the national hero, King, and SNCC. Honesty was no longer practical.

The necessity of raising funds for SNCC's work has had organizational consequences, too. In Los Angeles the SNCC office in Watts which had been concentrating on organizing the Negro ghetto was closed and a new office was opened in Hollywood, where money is more available. The "horror story" became part of the stock in trade of the SNCC fund raisers who quickly discovered that the amount of money given is in direct ratio to how much blood and how many beatings are conjured up in the minds of those who donate.

SNCC's entrance into national politics—its participation in, if not initiation of, the MFDP and the Challenge, both at the Atlantic City Democratic Convention and in Congress—has also created new problems. The liberal and radical cocktail set, which supplies money but is privately derided by SNCC, urged compromise at the Convention. The MFDP rejected compromises, but there was no hope of unseating the Mississippi delegates or the Congressmen without liberal support. The MFDP's attempt to gain support from the liberal community had inevitable consequences, especially after a Washington office was opened. In Washington the organization had to depend on the liberal polity and its lobbyists for access to the larger political community; and it had to face making decisions involving some compromise with the principled positions it had been able to maintain while it was still only a Mississippi protest organization. Thus, for example, in order to retain the MFDP's Washington relationships with liberals whose support was being sought for the Challenge, Lawrence Guyot, the MFDP's principal spokesman, had to say that the McComb statement on Vietnam did not represent the MFDP, although all who knew Guyot were certain that his views were in accord with the statement.

Several SNCC staff veterans are aware of these dilemmas, and have little hope that the old spirit of SNCC can be revived. "I would leave Mississippi now and forever," a twenty-seven-year-old veteran says, "except that I owe something to the people I got involved."

Compared to the earlier, spirited days, 1965 produced a letdown. The freedom songs and the active life in The Movement no longer hide the political and organizational problems these young revolutionaries must confront: how to operate openly and keep the ideal pure; how not to get "coopted" into the American system and yet gain victories meaningful to the ideal, not just to President Johnson's notion of the "great society."

SNCC work continues in rural areas, from Georgia to Arkansas, and indeed has branched out to some of the cities, but the early optimism is diluted. Transcendent experiences continue for the SNCC staff, which was nourished by the awakening of an illiterate sharecropper or by Fanny Lou Hamer's new-found articulateness, but now they must also cope with the movement bums. Around the MFDP offices in Jackson, McComb, and other cities there are young Negro hangers-on, "junior flips," who have nothing to do except harass white women, mooch money, drink, and sing, demoralizing the office staff and making it difficult for the spirit of Negro-white unity to mean more than words. These unemployed youth shout "Freedom Now" and get arrested at demonstrations, but their driving force is often hate rather than love, bitterness rather than understanding and sensitivity. Robert (Moses) Parris had great faith in the potential of many of these young Negroes. But without proper direction and orientation they are unable to cope with unstructured times. Now under the leadership of MFDP Chairman Fannie Lou Hamer, and James Forman, and Stokely Carmichael, who are "trying to make order out of chaos," more practical and in a sense realistic goals have replaced the poetic ideals that Moses personified.

In SNCC the normal growing pains endured by any organization shifting from loose informality to a more structured concept have been accompanied by a sense of anguish. The attempt of the SNCC leaders to create a more bureaucratic or efficient structure has met with resistance from the activists who resent the time they are expected to spend at staff meetings, training seminars, and educational sessions. As the organization has grown it has attracted Peace Corps rejectees or people seeking to solve their personal problems by a trip South. The coming into the South of a new group of well-educated Northern students has created tension among the older, less educated, less articulate SNCC members and staff people. Finally, the growth of black nationalism in SNCC has made some white SNCC veterans uncomfortable.

Other SNCC veterans have confessed that they feel SNCC has

performed its function, even though that function may have been different than intended by its founders. They know that if not for SNCC, the Selma march and the voting rights bill might have been years away; the anti-poverty program that employs some ex-SNCC staff people might not have taken the shape it did if not for SNCC activity. Yet other SNCC staffers are extremely disturbed by what has happened. "Who will get the votes?" they ask, and answer, bitterly, "LBJ." The MFDP's challenge failed. They wonder what will become of the grass-roots party they envisioned now that the Mississippi Democratic Party will be integrated. How can they prevent the divide-and-rule strategy of the power structure from working, while being true to their ideals and attempting to win power for the people?

And in 1968, they say resentfully, President Johnson will claim that he "gave" the Negroes the vote and the anti-poverty program. They point out that "the people" are not really deciding how they are going to spend the money—although occasionally they do—but that rather the white man and the Uncle Toms, now tuned in to the rich wind, will tell them how to spend it. Instead of dignity from a vote and an anti-poverty program they control, the people are more humiliated, further removed from basic decisions, more indebted and debilitated by welfare capitalism.

What can they do about it? The difficulty in answering that question is the source of deep frustration in SNCC. Yet few are willing to quit, and none of them fear hard, frustrating work. But the temptation to be "coopted" is strong, especially when added to the money is the real opportunity to help people in a basic way—with medical care, preschool training, job upgrading —at least in theory.

SNCC staff people are in a process of painful evaluation. "What to do next" and "Why" are the questions. There are few answers. In predominantly black Lowndes County, Alabama, SNCC has helped organize a political association to elect Negroes to county and state offices. Such a policy is possible in other Black Belt counties as well.

But what about the revolution in the South or the goals of rescuing the individual from the rush of a phony political system and the false values of affluence? "Well, in recent months," said a Friends of SNCC secretary, "the generals have replaced the poets." The romantics, the idealists like Moses and other veterans, are no longer directing SNCC practically or spiritually.

At staff meetings there is no longer the certainty of where they are going. John Lewis, James Forman, Stokely Carmichael, and others who have "stayed with it" are talking and thinking and even demonstrating against the war in Vietnam. Many, at first wary about "confusing" civil rights and other issues, have concluded that Vietnam and segregation are part of the same system. They no longer believe, however, that by meeting and organizing people a revolution can be made. Many wish Malcolm X were still alive, and they advocate the use of weapons; others talk of guerrilla war—but that is from frustration. SNCC, its veterans and newcomers, no longer have the romantic faith of just two years ago.

SNCC was never merely a starry-eyed group of romantics even though the SNCC activists were romantic about the potential of the Negro poor and their ability to effect changes. They were correct about both, but in the past five years the Negro's economic and cultural plight has worsened. In addition, the rapid escalation of the Vietnam war outraged the sensibilities of the SNCC staff both because the war itself is barbarous and because Negro troops were doing a disproportionate share of the fighting—and dying. Stokely Carmichael, newly elected SNCC chairman, viewed the black troops as essentially mercenaries, men without a cause, for whom society could not provide regular jobs.

SNCC's increasing militancy was a change not so much in quality as in degree and tactics. Carmichael and the other leaders were surprised neither by the character of the Vietnam war nor the Great Society's failure to throw even a measurable tidbit to the mass of Negroes. But the cumulative frustration built up within SNCC led to the announcement of a new goal: Black Power. This position marked the end of SNCC's liberal alliance, for no matter how liberal intellectuals debated or berated the phrase, they could not remove its racial sting. Black power was to be the rallying cry for millions of poor blacks—they, not the liberals, would define it as they used it. Racial integration— SNCC staff never believed in integration into society as it was—

was abandoned as a not impossible but foolish and undesirable goal, one which Reverend King, not SNCC, could continue to suffer for.

At the same time, SNCC dropped its previous, at least tactical, commitment to non-violence. In a series of speeches Carmichael excited SNCC's black radicals and depressed many white liberals. If the new militancy in SNCC can develop black power in the swelling urban slums, it may channel centuries of discontent into the most explosive period in American history. Thus far, however, black power is a slogan that has produced little beyond some excitement and a minor riot in Atlanta. The masses of poor Negroes remain an unorganized minority in swelling urban ghettos, and neither SNCC nor any other group has found a form of political organization that can convert the energy of the slums into political power. Meanwhile, despite SNCC's courageous position on the Vietnam war, Negroes continue to live in poverty at home and fight in bloody battles in Vietnam. SNCC's task is to translate its angry consciousness of the shame of America into a mass movement. Its members, after all, are the only troops that have had extensive battle experience.

The SNCC ideal will continue to nag and haunt all liberals and liberal organizations, for SNCC has made it much more difficult to manipulate Southern Negroes. Even if this alone were all that SNCC has so far accomplished—which is far from true—"Snick kids" would be entitled to a significant place in the history of American democracy. Their ideal and their approach may yet serve to form a broader based movement that will make serious changes in American society.

4. Students for a Democratic Society

*I*n June 1965 between four and five hundred young people gathered at a camp in Upper Michigan for the fourth convention of Students for a Democratic Society. By car and bus they came from all over the country, although the Eastern contingent was larger than those from the West and South. All SDS projects were represented at the convention, and other left groups—including the League for Industrial Democracy (LID), the uneasy and unhappy ex-parent of SDS—sent observers.

Most of the delegates—college students, college dropouts, graduates, and graduate dropouts—were relaxed and eager to talk. They exchanged comradely greetings, although some had met only once before. Everyone referred to "The Movement" rather than to SDS. They spoke of their allies, SNCC, as the "Snick kids."

Living conditions at the camp were primitive: sleeping bags were crowded together in small rooms or on the cold ground outside. The food was cheap, badly cooked, and insufficient to feed the crowd. But no one expected anything better. Despite the lure of the lake, the warm sun, the empty tennis courts, most of the people spent their energy in workshops, discussing the issues that had brought them to the convention: program, policy, and strategy, the election of officers and the exchange of information.

The exchange of information was probably the most important function of the week-long convention, for although SDS has printed pamphlets about its work, the primary source of information among the members is conversation. And since they travel about the country continually to regional and national meetings or talk to each other by phone, they and their SNCC allies are very well informed about The Movement's activities. They pass on to each other whatever they have learned about community organizing, the dos and don'ts of working in the South, the why and how of setting up a campus chapter, the tactics and theory, or non-theory, of their movement.

"Theory" or even "ideology" are uncomfortable words. Most SDS members are anti-ideological, not so much because they have learned and rejected ideology, but because they are suspicious of it before they know it. In conversation they "put down" the generations of the thirties, forties, and fifties, not for what they did, for that is unknown to them, but for what they didn't and don't do.

In the formal sense SDS is a direct descendant of the Student League for Industrial Democracy (SLID), organized in 1930 by the League for Industrial Democracy, a Fabian group closely linked to the Socialist Party. During the thirties, SLID had been a Socialist opposition to the Communist-dominated National Student Union (NSU). SLID and the NSU merged to form the American Student Union, which died a few years later, torn apart by an internal struggle betwen the Socialists and Communists.

After the end of World War II, SLID was revived, under the leadership of James Farmer, who later became national chairman of CORE. But the new SLID suffered from the deadening effect of McCarthyism on the campus, and by the end of the fifties its membership had dwindled. It was revived by the new activist radicals, mostly from the University of Michigan campus, who took it over in 1960 and gave it an action orientation.

SDS maintained a formal but steadily weakening link with the LID, for purposes of tax exemption and for an aura of respectability, not from any common ideology, but on January 1, 1966, there was a break. SDS is a new radical group with few ties to any of the older left groups in America. In the view of SDS, LID, once an active and vital socialist education organization, is now dominated by aging trade unionists whose anti-Communism outweighs old commitments to socialism. In turn, SDS's radical critique of American policy goes too far for most of the LID board, especially since SDS does not frame its analysis from an anti-Communist premise.

The majority of the newer SDS members, unlike the founders, are not well read in Marxism or in other radical literature. Most of them—middle-class born and bred, not oriented toward careers—are moved to action primarily by events in their own lives, and they see themselves as active public men.

Few relate themselves to the Soviet Union, China, or even Cuba, although they would probably give visceral support to the Cuban Revolution, without knowing too much about it. The SDS founders recall the Bay of Pigs and the missile crisis, and their critique of American foreign policy was stimulated in part by those events.

For many members and leaders SDS is more than an organization; it is a community of friends. Both the national office staff and the local campus and community chapters stress openness in their personal lives and in their political roles. They try to understand the motives for their actions, although this often results in parlor psychologizing. "But how else do you get to know each other?" asked a Chicago SDSer. There is no "criticism and self-criticism" in the Leninist tradition, but particularly at the community projects some discussions resemble group therapy. Meetings as therapy are not rejected, for self- and group-knowledge enhance relationships on all levels. Personal relationships are often inseparable from political life, since the community projects involve group living in the same house, sharing the experiences and matériel of sustenance. Movement marriages and Movement divorces are not uncommon; love affairs abound, but they are unfrivolous and usually involve a deep commitment. For many SDS staff the distinction between marriage and relationship is questioned: "Why do you need a legal sanction for a relationship?" asked the West Coast SDS organizer.

The SDS attitude is "anti-cool," for the essence of their activity is serious commitment to other people, in the community, in the project houses, and in campus chapters. Their response to questions about marijuana and promiscuous sex is that if the interviewer understood them, the questions would not be asked. While all agree that marijuana smokers should not be penalized, many feel it pitiable that people need artificial stimulants to "turn on." Sex should be linked with love, and many SDSers, both men and women, state emphatically that they cannot accept sex without a deeper commitment to the other partner.

Their vocabulary reiterates words like "initiate," "participate," "community," "hang-ups," "movement," and, especially, "people" (poor people, middle-class people). Those who work in community projects develop an almost oversimple speech. "How many blank stares and 'What does that mean?' does it take to make an organizer realize that the shorthand he learned in college won't do in the poor community?" asks an SDS official.

The vocabulary and community life are part of the SDS style. Many staff members talk more than they read, but this is not necessarily anti-intellectual. It is partly a result of the new experiment: living in a communal project while trying to organize a poor community around social and economic issues.

In Cleveland, where an SDS community project is more than a year old, the organizers are considering leaving their communal house and moving into small apartments in the neighborhood. The urban *kibbutz* produces great satisfaction for young people whose quest for community is answered by SDS projects: there is security in a community and intimacy in the friendships that develop. But new people are often more attracted by the group's communal life than by their neighborhood activities. This places the SDSers who live in the project house in the position of being exclusionist when they allow or refuse someone entrance to their *kibbutz*.

They are aware of this, and at group meetings their openness is apparent. They exhibit great tolerance, and no speaker is silenced, no matter how irrelevant or repetitious. And it is difficult to single out those who hold authority. Leaders, elected or *de facto,* hem and haw when they are called leaders, for traditional authority and arbitrary decision-making are incompatible with the values of the SDS staff.

Leaders mean organization, organization means hierarchy, and hierarchy is undemocratic. It connotes bureaucracy and impersonality, said one of the speakers at the plenary session of the Kewadin, Michigan, convention. He described his project, in Hoboken, New Jersey, as a non-project. One of his speeches, about forty-five minutes long, was an example of a kind of spasmodic sincerity, an inarticulate, highly gesticulating presentation which emphasized "gutting with people." For him, and for many in his audience, the fine line between leader and organizer must remain clear: an organizer does not impose his ideas on the community.

Leadership *per se* is viewed with apprehension. Tom Hayden, past SDS president, writing in *Studies on the Left,* warned of "maintaining a dependency on fixed leaders, who inevitably develop interests in maintaining the organization (or themselves) and lose touch with the immediate aspirations of the rank and file."

True leadership, in the SDS ethos, must avoid imposing ideas and values on the people. If there was to be a transformation in values, the spokesman for the Hoboken non-project felt, it had to come through personal relationships. Throughout his speech he spoke of alienation, the quality of human life produced by the bureaucratized society. It was not Marxist alienation, however, since it did not relate directly to the economic structure.

SDS approached economics more through the eyes of C. Wright Mills than Karl Marx. Some early SDS members with Marxist backgrounds contributed a kind of reality to SDS politics and analyses. Nevertheless, the labor metaphysic, a belief that the working class had a historic mission to transform capitalism into socialism, was rejected. In the Port Huron Statement of 1962, in which SDS outlined its ideals, the largest section analyzed the economy, but in terms of elites, not classes.

It was SDS that injected economics into the early civil rights movement, and underlined the role of private American capitalism in supporting foreign as well as American racism. To demonstrate this point SDS led pickets on the Chase Manhattan

Bank, which had large investments in South Africa. In its community organizing and education programs SDS stressed employment, control of anti-poverty funds, and even conversion from wartime to peacetime industry. But in the Port Huron Statement there is no talk of workers' power. Rather, the SDS vision is "the establishment of a democracy of individual participation governed by two central aims: that the individual share in those social decisions determining the quality and direction of his life; that society be organized to encourage independence in men and provide a medium for their common participation."

What SDS founders were groping for in their early statements and pamphlets was a theory or narrow ideology that could simultaneously encompass their ideals of democracy and serve as a guide for social change. The rejection of Marxism, the only ideology that revolutionaries have had for a hundred years, placed an enormous burden on the shoulders of young men like Al Haber, Tom Hayden, Robb Burlage, and Dick Flacks.

Just as SDS injected some concept of economics into the civil rights movement, so too did it begin ideological discussion among the young intellectuals. But the majority of SDS members, then and today, are anti-ideological, and are in SDS because that's where the action is. In 1962 and 1963, however, the staff and leadership began to debate whether SDS's analysis was developed enough to go into the community, where the ideology would grow from experience, or whether the answer was to be found in universities and libraries.

In 1966 SDS is still uneasy and undecided about an ideology. An SDS member from the University of Texas chapter expressed this in a mimeographed communication: "Someone said, 'ideology disunites, action unites.' And there is a good deal of truth in this. I also recognize the desire of SDS to stay away from rigid dogma. However, it has been my experience that, to persons not intimately connected with radicalism, a lack of ideology in some form is misleading."

In fact, SDS has several partially developed ideologies, but they converge around the importance of the individual and his ability to make meaningful decisions. In turn, this assumes that individuals must have the resources, other than empty forms of institutions parading as democratic, to make these decisions.

Within this over-all concern for the individual SDS leaders and members differ over how to achieve the good society, in which the individual will be able to function freely. At this point choices must be made among agencies of change, and these choices in turn involve an analysis of society, a theory of how it works, where it is going, and who will bring it there.

SDS now has two major sections reflecting its continuous internal debate: one deals with the campus and related work around education and political issues; the other, Economic Research and Action Project (ERAP), involves community organizing, mainly of the poor. ERAP began with a $5,000 grant from the United Auto Workers in 1963. The most active community project in 1964-65 was in Newark, and it was directed— although the word would be rejected—by Tom Hayden, past president of SDS and the drafter of the Port Huron Statement. Hayden is the most articulate spokesman for a strong position in SDS. His charisma and energy attract people, and of all the activists in community organizing he has the most coherent ideology.

To this group the enemy is "corporate liberalism." Existing institutions, from Cold War to home welfare, have been framed and are administered by political liberals who assume that the large corporation is the most desirable unit for organizing social and economic life. These liberals try to effect a smooth and efficient meshing of all levels of society by distributing enough rewards to keep even the lowest segments from disrupting the harmonious balance. But because this cannot be done, argue SDS activists, large numbers of poor people remain. Therefore, the revolutionary thrust toward restructuring society should be through organizing the poor, for they are the force that shakes up all institutions.

In this SDS view the leadership of the liberal community is responsible for all the barbaric aspects of American society: Southern segregation, the war in Vietnam, and to some extent apartheid in South Africa. (The largest depositor in the Chase Manhattan Bank, whose interests in South Africa are enormous, is the ILGWU, claims an SDS publication.) In addition, this SDS group is convinced that these liberals do not want to help young radicals, but rather wish to hold them back as they did the Mississippi Freedom Democratic Party at Atlantic City by urging a compromise of principles, or as they opposed the recent SDS March on Washington, where ideological disputes over Communists and the contents of posters drew strong criticism.

In addition, says this SDS faction, the corporate liberals seek to "keep the lid on local insurgency" to prevent an alliance developing between the poor and the workers that might defy the existing trade union or civil rights leadership. According to this group, the traditional liberal leadership always takes into account the needs of the President as chief representative of the national interest, and gives these needs the highest priority.

To this large segment of SDS barbarism and war are at the very center of the nation, supported by the liberals who have helped merge respectability with pseudo-fascism and have played a large and conscious role in defending the barbarism. At one of the workshops at the Michigan convention Tom Hayden explained: "My own disenchantment with the U.S. didn't really come because of its failures in Negro rights and foreign policy, but with the realization, which has grown within the last year, that responsibility for these things lies with the most respectable people in society . . . people in the North with connections with the foundations, corporations and banks and the Democratic Party, who parade in their own suburban communities as liberals, but who happen to own, lock, stock and barrel, the major enterprises in Mississippi."

Hayden's thesis, then, that the politics of the poor is the way to revolutionary change, relates to his critique of liberalism. The poor have no organization, not even the forms, and since they are outside the pale of organized liberalism, not only because of the failures of the social and economic system, but often because of designed exclusion, they are the forces who, with allies, can be organized with their own ideology and values. In this perspective organizing the organized working class and middle class are not excluded, but the middle-class alienated professionals must discover that their salvation also lies with organizing the poor.

Obviously, the poor must be organized around and for something. To meet these needs, not just tactically but philosophically, the ideas of "counter-organization" or "counter-government" were developed. And because means and ends must not be separated in SDS's good society, the concept of "participatory democracy" has evolved, where every man has an equal voice in decision-making. With "participatory democracy" the poor can achieve political realignment, but from the bottom up, not from the liberal middle class that imposes conditions: "If we support you, you must promise to do such and such, or not to do it." Hayden explained:

> The emphasis in the movement on "letting the people decide," on decentralized decision-making, on refusing alliances with top leaders, stems from the need to create a personal and group identity that can survive both the temptations and the crippling effects of this society. Power in America is abdicated by individuals to top-down organizational units, and it is in the recovery of this power that the movement becomes distinct from the rest of the country and a new kind of man emerges.

"Counter-community" was discussed at a spring, 1965, ERAP meeting, but many felt Hayden's notion was not developed enough to use. According to past SDS President Paul Potter, a community organization must develop "to a point where it has enough strength and cohesiveness to withdraw support and respect from existing government agencies." The counter-organization, perhaps a clearer term than counter-community, opposes and challenges the established organizations, for example "the building of a free university to confront the existing university structure." The counter-organization is both a tool for challenge and a demonstration of an alternative that hopes to attract or win people away from passive commitment to established forms.

The SDS counter-organization would allow the poor to participate in the control of their own lives. Because these SDS activists are convinced that the important needs are personal, the immediate goal in organizing among the poor is to help each person feel his own sense of dignity and worth. Before the poor can achieve political independence and act as an insurgent force they must have a sense of independence, a sense of identity, a sense of being able to make decisions in a nation of bureaucracies that has usurped all decision-making. The men who administer these bodies are part of a system that regards the poor as unqualified to make their own decisions. SDS projects often begin organizing around such issues as housing and urban renewal, or jobs and welfare, or school lunch programs, taking on local governing bodies.

In political terms, this loose SDS faction thinks a new kind of independent politics should begin in Northern cities, but not related to the traditional third party which runs candidates before it has a constituency. Instead, independent politics means finding a Northern parallel to Southern freedom politics, so that the Northern poor have a real means of political expression, a means of choosing their own representatives to challenge the Establishment at local levels.

Such new politics means organizing perhaps a parallel to the Mississippi Freedom Labor Union in or out of the AFL-CIO, or even some type of business that would support a "counter-society." It might mean attempting to control the anti-poverty allocations, the economic resources, in the community. This search is for a form through which a constituency can be developed based on a radical program and analysis.

Since the Establishment, through its official and unofficial control mechanisms (trade unions or many civil rights groups, for example), will not recognize the organized poor's claim, a counter-government might be set up, in Hayden's words, "to compete with the existing structure for legitimacy." This legitimacy only comes, however, when the counter-government becomes a real threat or gets enough allies, when large numbers lose their respect for "law and order."

The ideas of this grouping in SDS attempt to bypass the concepts of reform versus revolution, or realignment versus independent political action. It is Hayden's belief that the support for the new politics, like the MFDP, must come from "local people's movements elsewhere," or else, as the failure of the MFDP to win its Challenge showed, it will have to depend on the liberal reformers and the Democratic machines. Even a realigned Party that would bend more to the demands of the poor would be "committed still to elite domination of politics, industry and war."

Thus it is not the far right that poses the great threat, but the broad liberal consensus that has developed present American society into the most "flexible of totalitarianisms," paralyzing human activity by its dependence on welfare capitalism and the Cold War.

These SDSers believe that the new movements are still in their infancy and that a great amount of work has to be done at the base. Hayden and most of the ERAP workers are not deluded by articles in *Life* or the left-wing *National Guardian* about the strength of the insurgencies. The war in Vietnam continues despite marches and draft card burning; Southern civil rights workers are murdered despite vigils and challenges. They hope that the civil rights movement, plus riots in Watts, will expose the limits of the American political and economic systems' ability to provide social justice and democratic participation. Yet talk of breaking all ties with liberal Establishment institutions is meaningless because at times such groups are needed, with the result that no "choice" of political alternatives really exists: in civil rights, SCLC needs SNCC and vice versa, and both need the NAACP. Nevertheless, Hayden and others in ERAP and on campuses believe real tensions can be created inside the Democratic Party which would be helpful for new movements and perhaps for those liberal Democrats who could accept meaningful realignment. In Hayden's view, "The new movements . . . *are* realigning the Democratic Party even though they often work outside the Party and their values go far beyond those of the Democratic leadership." For example, SNCC did more to realign the Democratic Party than the coalitionists could hope to do.

The real task visualized by this group, a vision which most of the SDS shares, is to gain freedom from the "one-dimensional society" which controls by terror, welfare, and vested interests.

Almost all SDS members are convinced that in order to survive the might of the Establishment, the emphasis of new politics must be on letting the people choose, on decentralizing decision-making. Thus, the citizen will recover his power and emerge as a civic person who will not be lured from his responsibilities. Concomitantly, in their concept, the movement must differ from older left and liberal ones in retaining a long-range commitment from its rank-and-file members, so that no organizational shells with only leaders develop. The old left is irrelevant to them largely because they believe it is rendered ineffective by Communist-anti-Communist arguments, is committed to overly bureaucratic organizing, and is limited by its adherents' family ties and jobs. For some of the militants in ERAP it is all or nothing: work full time for The Movement if you wish to be accepted by the committed revolutionaries on a personal basis.

Always, while organizing the poor, the belief that the poor must lead themselves is uppermost in the organizers' minds, with all decisions to be made democratically, and not just in the formal sense. An organizer, for example, might organize but has no right to make decisions for those he organizes. His job is to help them make their own decisions, even though in practice this does not always work. The organizer must reach people, talk to them, involve them in action which would radicalize them. The young college graduate must communicate to poor people that they are worthy, potentially powerful, and capable of fighting for rights and ideals. It is understandable that many SDSers cannot accomplish this formidable task.

SDSers do feel rewarded when they influence people and enlarge the social consciousness, but theory or even long-range strategy is a fuzzy notion to them. The question of how to link the various projects is unanswered, not only by SDS but by all the new radicals. A radical political movement does not necessarily mean socialist to them, for only a few of them could explain what "socialist" means. They have faith that through sincere and determined organizing the people's essential goodness will transform itself into effective politics. That faith remains with them, despite the frustrations and hardships endured in many projects, and despite the internal conflicts between the SDS members who worked so closely on a day-to-day basis. Typically, Judy Bernstein of the Chicago project replied to the question of whether she believed that all this activity would get anything done, with: "I have to believe it. . . . I want to eventually go back to school . . . but I will end up talking to students about how to organize a community."

Another trend in SDS does support involvement with the institutionalized labor movement and liberal reformers. The goals of this group, centered in New York and deriving from a more traditional left background, are increased material benefits and a greater share of the national income for the poor. For them human dignity and decision-making are dependent upon better material rewards and can be accomplished through a modification of pacifist Bayard Rustin's idea of a coalition with unions, religious groups, and the liberal political forces.

Another faction feels the middle classes can be organized and that they too can form a change agency, not from material stress but because they are the most alienated. According to this group, the middle classes can be shown that they are able to control their own lives and that the sham of affluence, symbolized by conspicuous gadgets and services, is less meaningful than experiencing more profound human feelings and needs. It is an offering of the possibility of joy or even sorrow in place of fun, fun, fun.

Combinations of these approaches exist in SDS, too, as does a group of "leaders" who feel it essential to develop a new political philosophy that can encompass the general need for social justice with concern for the individual. This philosophy calls for "existential humanism" in personal life and behavior coordinated with the social goal of a "radical transformation" in society.

The two sections of SDS, the campus and the poor neighborhood, organized the twenty-five-thousand-man March on Washington in April 1965 to protest the war in Vietnam. The role of SDS in stimulating and organizing anti-war sentiment, especially at the universities, has been given wide attention by the press and government. Newspapers have reported and analyzed SDS's role, while right-wing columnists have labeled them Reds. After the October 15-17 protests Senate speeches abounded, and the Attorney General and the FBI promised an investigation. SDS membership rose rapidly, and there are now chapters in most states.

It has been SDS's emphasis on foreign policy, particularly on Vietnam and the Dominican Republic, that has gained them new supporters from the campuses, the center of SDS strength. Often the new recruits become interested in the community projects, and after working on campus for a semester, move into a project house.

The national teach-ins were organized at Michigan, the birthplace of SDS, and much of the impetus for the teach-ins came from SDS. Strong chapters developed at Swarthmore, the University of Texas, Johns Hopkins, and in the Boston colleges. Some SDS campus chapters have singlehandedly begun anti-Vietnam movements, while at other campuses like Berkeley, where SDS is weaker, they have either joined or worked with existing organizations.

The SDS community projects, linked in the loose organization of ERAP, have had more difficult experiences than the campus chapters. Even the successful ERAP projects in Newark, Chicago, New Haven, Boston, and Cleveland, some in existence for more than a year, have gone through a very trying period. The Baltimore and Oakland projects have gone out of existence, despite the enthusiasm with which they began. SDS leaders believe the failures are due to the organization having overextended its staff resources; in some of the projects the staff had great vigor but little knowledge, while in others no clear conception existed of the project's role in the community.

It is amazing that the SDSers did possess the determination to carry on in the face of the difficulties they confronted, and did succeed in organizing some communities, in Newark, Cleveland, and Boston, both on issues and around ideas. Changes in the lives of the communities did take place which would not have occurred without ERAP and SDS: in Newark, an urban renewal plan that was in effect Negro removal was defeated by a solid organization that included local people as organizers. Community services around welfare, schools, and legal aid have been provided by other projects, and some of the poor have become involved in attempting to direct their own lives, even in communities where projects have failed.

Many who have been active in SDS for a sustained period see an urgent need for The Movement to develop an effective new politics based on a sound ideology; this need has become the main concern of some of the older leaders, all in their late twenties or early thirties. Paul Pipkin of the Texas chapter wrote: "It is time to stop fearing ideology and lay the basis for a new one, more suitable for our times, as well as a more stable guide for our own policies. This is what C. Wright Mills was working towards at his death, and I feel that the task falls to us."

So it is that perhaps SDS in its short life has come almost full circle. Created partly as a response to the lack of radical ideology in America, some segments of it then attempted to carry out operations based on an ideology of simple activism, of getting people in motion; but now, once again, the question is being asked: Motion toward what?

Paul Potter analyzed the experience of the last two years of SDS as an experiment in which organizing strategy was substituted for program. But it was discovered that the mere rejection of old ideologies, such as social democracy or Bolshevism, did not provide a new one that could effectively destroy Cold War and welfare liberalism and also serve as a guide for future alternatives and programs.

SDS came into existence, according to Potter, "because of a concern for the lack of ideological thinking in the developing civil rights movement and out of a reaction to the anti-ideological ideology of the universities and the society. Initially, its founders hoped SDS would fill the vacuum of thought for the new left movements." It then moved into activism, and according to Potter, "The experience . . . particularly in the communities has shaken people loose from their once facilely constructed analytic constructs," forcing them to think anew. Many in SDS now feel they must get back into the habit of reading and writing so that they can confront the university not with anti-intellectualism, as many have, but with radical scholarship and sound polemics that can be transformed into action. In the minds of these SDSers, it is their obligation to show broad segments of American society that the misery suffered by the domestic poor is part of a system of over-all deprivation that threatens the individuality and potential of most Americans; that American foreign policy is hindering world peace rather than building it.

5. The Leftovers

*F*or the new radicals the political sects of the old left of the thirties and forties are for the most part irrelevant. Political echoes and resonances of the past can be heard within the new radical movement; but the Communist, Trotskyist, Lovestoneite, and Socialist groups who once fought capitalism, fascism, and each other with equal ferocity either have disappeared or exist more in name than strength. The Communist Party is only a shadow of the organization which once dominated the left; the Trotskyists are a series of tiny sects still fighting ideological battles devoid of real meaning; Jay Lovestone, once the American delegate to the Communist International, is now the savage advocate of unlimited war on his former comrades; and the Socialist Party is without significant influence.

This old left was destroyed by its own internal failures, by the Cold War and McCarthy era, and by American affluence. Many of the millions who had passed through the ranks of radicalism were absorbed into prosperous, middle-class America. Only a handful of groups survived through the fifties into the sixties, tenaciously carrying on in the traditions and dogmas of Marxism and publishing doctrinaire newspapers like *The Worker, People's World,* and *The Militant.*

As political men and ideologues, the older radicals were initially regarded by The Movement as no more than leftovers from the thirties, but with the widening interest of youth in civil rights, civil liberties, and peace issues, the older versions of Marxism began to have a new appeal. It provided some coherent explanation of capitalism, together with a method for changing it; to those unfamiliar with the dismal history of failure that characterized the American Communist movement the Marxist program seemed even attractive. And so the concept that the working class could be an agency of effective change was revived and became a frame of reference for the new Marxist groups within The Movement, linked either to the Soviet Union or China.

But these new Marxist groups are also children of the spirit found among the new radicals in the sixties; like those who joined SNCC and SDS, the young Marxists are also members of the sit-in generation, proudly defying authority. When the W. E. B. DuBois Club members shouted "Freedom Now" in the lobby of a San Francisco hotel and a Progressive Labor group chanted the same slogan in Harlem streets, many were speaking in the same spirit as the SNCC people in Mississippi. But unlike SNCC or SDS members the DuBois Clubs and Progressive Labor Party reflected Soviet and Chinese influence. The debates and struggles inside the world Communist movement had consequences for them, and in fact the two groups emerged as they are today as a result of the Sino-Soviet split.

The DuBois Clubs and Progressive Labor Party are the most influential of the Marxist groups associated with The Movement; the Young Socialist Alliance (YSA), which is the Trotskyist youth group, and the Young People's Socialist League (YPSL), the Socialist Party's youth organization, are smaller and less prestigious. But the four groupings together have only minimal strength within The Movement.

The Progressive Labor Party

In 1962 the Chinese Communist Party openly attacked the Soviet line, and the Communist parties of almost every country split.

In the United States the old Communist Party had followed the Soviet position; the group which split from it, Progressive Labor (PL), supported the Chinese position. Initially, PL was composed of young people who had been in the Communist Party, but by April 1965, when it formed itself as the Progressive Labor Party, it had won over many students and other youth possessed by the same spirit that compelled others to join SNCC and SDS. PL promised action—Revolution Now: "The people's needs require *revolution,*" stated an editorial in PL's *Marxist-Leninist Quarterly* (Vol. 2, No. 2), and they underscored revolution. "The people's dreams demand *revolution.* But revolution needs organization, an organization of revolution—a *revolutionary* organization."

In its 1964 Constitution, PL resolved

> to build a revolutionary organization with the participation and support of millions of working men and women as well as those students, artists and intellectuals who will join with the working class to end the profit system. . . . We will build a socialist U.S.A., with all power in the hands of the working people and their allies.

PL's commitment to the revolution carried them into action during the 1964 Harlem riots, and several of them are still in jail as a result of PL activity during that summer in New York. They frightened not only the city officials, but other groups on the left, for PLers stated openly that they were Communists trying to create and lead a revolution. When Bill Epton, a Harlem PL leader, was indicted and convicted of "criminal anarchy" he found little support for his defense efforts from other Harlem groups although there was protest and aid from various civil liberties groups. PL leader Milt Rosen explained: "Because our work and ideas give us a great potential, the ruling class singled us out for sharp attack." Yet such statements, so reminiscent of the early Bolshevik tradition, are not a total reflection of PL's spirit. "We have as much in common with the new groups as with the old," says an Oakland PL leader. "For a lot of us, PL was our first commitment, a wild leap into total commitment, the great leap forward, as we say."

Some PLers admit that they had been "beatniks" before be-

coming aware that the answer to their anguish was not in escape
but in commitment. "Before I joined PL, I was a head, nothing
but a head, copping out," said one young man. "I didn't really
start to groove until I joined PL," said a twenty-five-year-old
woman. These PLers speak the "hip" or "beat" language, but do
not have the "beat" mentality, for PLers are the most disciplined
of all the youth groups. There has been some public discussion
of PLers using marijuana, and a few admit that they occasionally
"turn on." "But it would not be good for the Party if we were
caught. You know, the press and the DA and judges would
probably accuse us of using smuggled Chinese opium." More
important, they believe that smoking marijuana is inconsistent
with PL work. "You just can't do revolutionary work if you're
smashed all the time."

PLers feel that they must set examples for others. "Our culture is in such decay it's a nightmare. If we can straighten out
our own lives and be strong, it would draw people to our way
of life." PL members share the SDSers' quest for community.
"It's important to have a family and be in a family, and live
closely with other people," said one PL girl.

And just as SDS and SNCC went into the communities of
the North and South, so too PL is involved in community organizing. In New York, in Harlem and on the Lower East Side,
PL has set up offices; PL organizers are in San Francisco's
Spanish-speaking Mission District and in other urban ghettos,
attempting to start revolutionary activity, educating and agitating for their ideals.

Neither PL ideals nor methods are new: the United States
should become a workers' state after going through the steps
that lead to revoluiton. Sooner or later, the PL analysis goes,
a severe economic depression will come, and pressure in and out
of America will combine to topple the ruling class. As Milt
Rosen wrote in *Progressive Labor* (May–June 1965):

> Only by destroying the political power of a small greedy
> ruling class, can our people achieve their aspirations. By
> traveling the road to revolution we will learn the strategy
> and tactics necessary to transfer political power to those
> who build and create the wealth and genius of our coun-

try. . . . The perspective of the ruling class, for oppression, war, and cultural and moral decay, is totally at odds with the aspirations of the world's people. The people will win.

To achieve the people's victory, PL based its Party on the Leninist principles of democratic centralism. Policy discussion includes all members, but once a decision is reached, criticism must cease. Most of PL's leaders are youth from a Communist Party heritage—like Fred Jerome, Jake Rosen, Milt Rosen, and Mort Scheer—but the organization also includes youth who joined because, as Yvonne Bond has said, "While we share the same reasons for political involvement as SDS and all the new left groups, this burning moral thing, we have adopted a realistic means of changing society. To make a revolution in the U.S. you can't be just good guys who want to relate to people. You need a correct analysis." This analysis has led PL to work with minority groups and to establish a Black Liberation Committee. The disturbances in Harlem and in Los Angeles, while not initiated by PL, were viewed by them as signs of revolutionary potential which PL must direct "in the interests of the people."

"The main aim of community work," explains *Progressive Labor* (May–June 1964), "must be the organization and radicalization of the working people in the community. The clubs must identify intimately and warmly with the life and work of the community, and maintain consistent day-to-day, door-to-door organizing and propagandizing. We can move people into direct confrontation with the class enemy in the form of landlords, cops and city agencies."

In community work PL, like SDS and some of the committees to end the war in Vietnam, has just begun. They are optimistic that by following their ideology, using Marxism with the refinement of Chinese thought, they can become the vanguard of the revolution. "We are a new kind of Communist," said a young San Francisco PL poet. "We are not bound by the paranoia and secrecy of the old Communist Party."

PL openly admires Chinese revolutionary thought. One of them, reflecting the organization's thinking, explains: "PL is

accused of being Maoist and that is true, but we don't want to
tail after the Chinese like the CPs tailed after the Soviet Union.
We look to the Chinese for illumination. Our aim is to develop
a truly American, not a Chinese Communist movement." PL
has a rigorous education program for its own members, on the
fundamentals of Marxism and analyses of current struggles.
Education is partly a way of working out the Party line and
partly a preparation of the membership for leadership roles in
the community, and among workers, students, and minority
groups.

On college campuses PL initiated, with some non-PLers, the
May 2nd Movement, designed to radicalize campuses around
the issue of the Vietnam war. "As it developed," explained a
PL leader, "the non-PLers dropped out and it was essentially
taken over by PL people. Everyone knows this. We don't hide
what we are." PL itself has chapters on several major campuses,
and these student groups work not only in the university community but are also assigned to "mass work" in the larger metropolitan areas. In PL's San Francisco office students and non-
students work, handing out leaflets, ringing doorbells, attempting
to organize the neighborhood on economic and social issues that
press all poor communities.

PL has been active in the anti-war demonstrations, too, but
like most new radicals, they feel little hope that they will succeed
in changing policy. According to a New York PL leader, the Chinese have "a slightly unrealistic view of the demonstrations." But
he added, "They might do this to encourage their own people."

Thus far, PL has worked with other youth groups for civil
rights and civil liberties and in peace organizations. But PLers
say that SDS is ideologically confused, "which is why their community work has been a flop"; that SNCC cannot succeed, although it has done good work, unless they see their way to
adopting the Marxist ideology; that YSA "still harangues you
about Stalin and the betrayal of all the revolutions"; that YPSL
"is hung up on anti-Communism and Red baiting."

PL, of all the Marxist groups, attracts to its cause some of
the most dedicated, hard-working, and serious youth, who believe that socialism will come only through revolution, through
the armed struggle of the masses. Therefore, PL believes the

masses must arm themselves. This emphasis on revolutionary action separates them most clearly from the Communist Party-oriented youth group, the DuBois Clubs.

The W. E. B. DuBois Clubs of America*

When in 1964 the local DuBois Clubs called a convention to form a national organization, the result was an active youth group close to but not organizationally tied to the Communist Party. Despite the Justice Department's charges, the DuBois Clubs are not controlled by the Communist Party as were the Labor Youth League (LYL) of the 1950s or the American Youth for Democracy (AYD) before it.

Like PL, some of the DuBois Clubs' leaders come from Communist Party backgrounds or those sympathetic to the Party. And like PL it is new—of the sixties—in important ways. For one thing, the Communist Party is greatly changed, apart from its organizational weakness, due to the major changes in the world Communist movement. The kind of discipline, of following a clear Party line on most issues, as did the old youth groups or as does PL today, is not possible in the DuBois Clubs. Conditions for membership were stated in the Berkeley chapter's *Mailer* (November 30, 1964):

> *Who May Join the DuBois Club?* Mr. Hoover notwithstanding, a Communist Party card is not prerequisite for membership. Generally the club consists of young people who are actively pro-civil rights, who are opposed to HUAC, the war in Vietnam, and the ultra-right, etc. There is probably a long though limited list of single issues on which the members are unanimous in their views. Again generally, we believe that the composite of the multi-various

* W.E.B. DuBois was an American Negro historian who became a Communist at age ninety. He wrote many books on American history and on Negro and African life. He was honored by Kwame Nkrumah, who awarded him the first citizenship of Ghana. At ninety-two, DuBois renounced America and went to live in Ghana, where he died in 1963.

demands being made by labor, civil rights organizations and peace groups can only be fully realized under socialism.

Generally, the DuBois Clubs favor coalition with the liberal forces inside the Democratic Party and other liberal institutions, especially the trade union movement. They believe in working for liberals electorally and on behalf of specific issues, and to do this effectively, they often moderate their socialist ambitions. They believe, too, that as more liberal gains are won and kept, from the onslaught of the far right, America comes nearer to becoming a good society. Their good society would be an extension of these reforms, with the working class controlling the means of production, whatever that might mean in the United States. The DuBois Clubs explain their tactical position as it relates to their ultimate goals:

> . . . how are we different from other socialist groups? The answer to this question also relates to the reason we are under fire from Hoover and the right wing. We are the only socialist youth organization which participates in coalitions and mass struggles and at the same time seriously approaches Marxist theory. We call ourselves an action-based organization, and that means that hopefully our ideology will grow in large part out of political action. Strong in our opposition to red-baiting, we do not exclude *anyone* who fits in the above category. It is this combination (mass politics, coalitions, Marxist theory, and no red-baiting) which scares the ultra-right. Probably they know it is a successful combination.

In its language, style, and goals the DuBois Clubs, are reminiscent of the American Communists' People's Front Activities in the thirties. And an article by two PLers, analyzing the DuBois Clubs' founding convention in 1964, makes clear the differences between the two wings, essentially the Russian and Chinese:

> . . . The leadership surrounding the founding of this youth group feel that they can gain socialism in this country through the ballot and through reforms. They seriously

believe that a reformist movement will produce socialism. Of course, on this point, they are dead wrong. . . .

PL has also criticized the camouflage and undemocratic procedures that belied the DuBois Clubs' promises, and scorned the foundation of the DuBois Clubs as a national organization. How could a socialist youth group be formed without advocating socialism? How could a socialist youth group fail to criticize Johnson, and even advocate working inside the Democratic Party? But, as expected, the delegates at the DuBois Clubs convention adopted the non-revolutionary programs and resolutions the leadership wanted.

In an interview in a Berkeley magazine, a DuBois Club member characterized himself and the members of his club as part of "the Pepsi generation—those who think young." Characteristically, the DuBois Clubs celebrate James Dean, the Beatles, "beat" poets and Bob Dylan, in a modern extension of the Communist Party's popular front admiration for baseball and bowling clubs. But the DuBois Clubs strive to be "in" far more than did any other Communist Party-oriented group in the past. Underlying their admiration of James Dean and the Beatles is the assumption that these entertainers are good because they express the feelings and needs of the masses.

Far greater personal and political liberty exists in the DuBois Clubs than was allowed by their predecessors: long hair, rock 'n' roll, "beat" dress, and the other "hipster" norms, including smoking marijuana, are often found. Partially this behavior is designed to show how "in" the Clubs are and to attract Negroes who hate "squares." But many DuBois Clubs members are "in" and find their political activity compatible with their "psychedelic" activity.

The DuBois Clubs are involved in the same types of activity as are other New Left and radical groups. Campus chapters have been supplemented by community projects in Cleveland, Chicago, and Oakland. Despite a common Marxist tradition, the DuBois Clubs are no closer to PL than to SDS and SNCC. SDS, according to a young woman activist in the DuBois Clubs, just tries to find out what the people are thinking and then somehow organize them. "We believe that you have to concentrate on working-class youth, not everyone in the community as SDS does, and you must have a program that concentrates on the struggle for jobs."

The DuBois Clubs' future policies are not as clearly defined as PL's. Some leaders are pushing for a clearer socialist orientation; others argue that the DuBois Clubs should remain a broad organization that can attract masses of working-class youth and students.

The leadership is also discussing the old tactic of infiltration, for DuBois Clubs members have been active not only in *ad hoc* committees on peace and civil rights, but in a few cities have joined the Young Democrats. These popular front tactics cause some dismay among the less ideologically-oriented membership, who believe "we should be open and tell everyone who we are."

Because of the DuBois Clubs' belief in broad coalition organization, the inner discipline is lax. Ideological deviation is often very wide, partly because, unlike formal Communist Party youth groups, there is little ideological education in the DuBois Clubs. Although the Los Angeles DuBois Club has a school offering courses in the Theory of Surplus Value or the History of the Negro People in America since 1630, the general educational level of both leaders and members is lower than that of PL or even the LYLers of ten and fifteen years ago, still lower than the Young Communist League of the thirties.

The Berkeley DuBois Club states that:

> The DuBois Club has a representative in many organizations. We try to participate in all facets of democratic struggles. We have a representative of the executive and steering committees of the FSM on the *Ad Hoc Committee to End Discrimination* and on the permanent committee in the area to abolish HUAC. In fact, although he doesn't give reports at meetings, we are probably represented in the FBI. Our base is getting broader all the time.*

This ideological laxness is also found today among the DuBois Clubs' elders in the Communist Party. Bettina Aptheker,

---

* This statement represents another phenomenon new on the left: the Communist Party never joked openly about the FBI.

a student leader at the University of California who announced her membership in the Communist Party before running for student office, recently wrote a letter to the student newspaper, criticizing the Soviet Union for its arrest of the writer Andrei Sinyavsky, who was convicted by a Soviet court of publishing in the West under the name of Abram Tertz. Even though her criticism was qualified, the difference between the old-style Communist and the current generation appears when a well-known Communist student leader states, as she did, "I wish to reaffirm the fundamental principle of opposing unequivocally the arrest of an author for what he writes. Socialism requires and encourages creativity. Certain writings may contain ideas which hinder the growth of Socialism. But the stifling atmosphere created by prohibition is a much greater hindrance to the building of Socialism. The way to fight ideas is with better ideas."

Most of the DuBois Clubbers who are not in the Communist Party, and even some who are, do not idealize the Soviet Union, although they do feel it is a good socialist state with a foreign policy that might lead to world peace. The existence of anti-Semitism in the Soviet Union is conceded by many DuBois Clubbers who feel that "by this time they should have coped with it better." Characteristically, they say, "We supported Khrushchev, but also think it's good that there is a division between Party and government leadership. The way they did it though. . . . Soviet public relations are terrible."

DuBois Clubs leaders emphasize the practical as opposed to the utopian. To a San Francisco club officer, PL is completely unrealistic. "They see the Watts and Harlem riots as revolutionary. They want people to engage in armed struggle now. They encourage that. But nothing concrete has changed in the people's lives in Harlem or Watts. In order to make changes you need the organization of a political movement."

Some competition exists between the DuBois Clubs and SDS on campuses and in communities, but relations between them are generally amicable. The leadership of the DuBois Clubs adopts the same approach to The Movement as does the Communist Party. In the December 1965 issue of *Political Affairs,* the Party's theoretical organ, the line of the cautious Communists is stated:

. . . For too long we have avoided contact with the New Left and held them in contempt.

Our new policy should be to join in struggle with the New Left whenever it is possible and prudent for us to do so. This does not mean that we can give a blanket guarantee to the New Left that we will always join their activities, but it does mean that we must not automatically pull out of every operation when a disagreement arises.

In our disagreements with the New Left, we are confident that we are right, and that history will prove us right. But truth in a vacuum is no truth at all. In order to be able to criticize the New Left effectively, and to teach it what we know, we must be accepted and admired by it. This can only happen when Communists are known to be on the picket lines and in the jails.

By joining with the New Left, I also suspect that our young comrades will learn something too: a boldness of action and a directness of approach that has been lacking in our party for some time.

Naturally, we cannot limit ourselves to joining with the New Left; we must also initiate activities of all kinds, both on the Left, and in the broadest people's movements. We must also play the role of trying to bring the New Left closer to other Left groups and to help them to an understanding of the need for cooperation with non-Left forces. We must also do battle with ultra-Left ideas and win from it members of the New Left who are there by mistake.

Both PL and the DuBois Clubs have had victories and failures in their short history, and they were encouraged by the successful sit-ins at the Sheraton Palace Hotel in San Francisco and some of the community efforts. Both feel that their versions of Marxism will convince large numbers of people that political action, electoral or revolutionary, will solve America's problems.

The Trotskyites and Social Democrats

The Young Socialist Alliance and the Young People's Socialist League are less important than PL or the DuBois Clubs. YSA is the youth group of the Socialist Workers Party, the Trotskyist Party, and like its parent group it sticks adamantly to the guns of the 1930s; its ammunition is revolutionary purity based on the thinking of Leon Trotsky.

YSA's faith is in the historic mission of the working class, which, it believes, was betrayed both in the Soviet Union and in China, although to different degrees. It has campus chapters and clubs in the community, and like PL, it stresses internal education, leaning heavily on classical Marxism. YSA fought a free speech issue in 1963 at Indiana University, where three YSAers were charged with sedition. In addition, it joins in local peace groups, often providing much of the drudge labor for coalition groups, and pushes its own line.

Recently, YSA was accused by the new radicals of attempting, unsuccessfully, to "take over" an organization being formed to coordinate The Movement's anti-war activities. In roles like this, the YSA, of all the youth groups, is most reminiscent of the thirties, for Trotskyism has changed very little. American capitalism and Soviet bureaucracy remain anathema; Marxism-Leninism-Trotskyism remain the answer. But it would be incorrect to describe the bulk of the YSA members as being different from those in other groups: YSA members are also involved in "that burning moral thing."

Many YSA members are committed to militant social protest because of deep feelings for the people and against injustice. Some admit that there is something comical about a Trotskyist organization that has lingered on long after the deaths of Trotsky and Stalin, and after the Bolshevik conflicts of the twenties and thirties have been relegated to historians' files. Yet there is a comradely spirit, a sense of community and a satisfying reference group in YSA that keeps them committed.

And to YSA the working class remains America's hope. The

organization admired the late Malcolm X, and is in general awe
of Negroes and workers who show sign of "revolutionary consciousness." But unlike PL and the DuBois Clubs, the YSA
seems to have little potential for expanding its membership or
its importance. It does educate its members and sympathizers
in Marxism, however, and its members, like all young radicals,
have put their bodies on the line for peace and civil rights.

The Young People's Socialist League is, in reality, outside
the Marxist orbit, functioning primarily as the anti-Communist
socialist opposition. In the past few years YPSL has not grown
or developed, and its politics and style lack energy and spirit.
YPSL characterizes other Marxist groups as "totalitarian,"
charging them with hypocrisy for not being as concerned about
freedom in the Soviet Union and China as they are about freedom in America. Ironically, too, the dominant group in YPSL
is close to the DuBois Clubs' position on political action: it
does not foresee possibilities of revolution, and therefore hopes
to accomplish what it can through coalition with, and inside of,
liberal and progressive Democratic Party or union institutions,
or with the civil rights leadership. YPSL believes that in this
way important social legislation can be passed and, hopefully,
that the Hawks can be made slightly less influential and bellicose.

The most important meeting places for the new radicals and
the groups still connected ancestrally to the old left have been
the *ad hoc* committees, formed for such specific purposes as
organizing a demonstration against HUAC or a protest march
against the Vietnam war. Initially the committees predominantly
tended to reflect, as did the FSM, the spirit of the new radicals
with their emphasis on individual freedom. But the lack or
fuzziness of ideology and the failure of sensational tactics to
achieve anything more than publicity has led members of these
ad hoc committees to frustration. At these junctures the Marxist-
Leninist members often gain moral ascendancy, but like the new
radicals they are not able to mobilize masses or even be taken
very seriously by local and national power structures. With or
without ideology the *ad hoc* committees are short-lived, for no
matter what they call their organization, no matter how divergent

their thinking, young people have not found effective methods of dealing with power, much less changing such key policies as the war in Vietnam.

The principal conflicts between the Marxist-Leninist groups and the structureless radical organization focus on methods and goals. In the tradition of Communist movements the DuBois Clubs and PL are concerned with one major factor: power. They are in awe of it and work to touch it; they organize the big meeting, rally, or demonstration in order, as one DuBois Club leader put it, to "expose the raw nerve of the power structure." The DuBois Clubbers defend their tactics by appealing to pragmatism. "It worked," they said after a successful sit-in, but shortly afterward the demonstrators were tried, convicted, and given stiff sentences.

The tactical differences separating the Marxist-Leninist youth groups internally are the same as those found in SNCC and SDS, for any discussion over methods is necessarily related to goals. The traditional debate continues in radical movements on coalition versus independence, reform versus revolution, exclusion of Communists versus cooperation with them by non- or anti-Communist radicals.

But despite the differences among the groups, it is impossible from looks or style to differentiate among them. Chants like "Freedom Now" or the various slogans derived from civil rights experience are used by all groups. Only when it involves irritating the Democratic Party does a dispute arise over the "correctness" of poster slogans, with the DuBois Clubs guarding their language carefully lest it antagonize "progressive" elements in the Democratic Party.

So, too, any differences in policy among the DuBois Clubs, PL, and YSA are always seen as based on an incorrect understanding of Marxism-Leninism, for all three groups are committed to fundamental Marxist themes. Even more than having faith in materialism or dialectics as a guiding force, the leadership of the Progressive Labor Party, the YSA, and the DuBois Clubs possess faith in the historic mission of the working class. This belief in the working class as the agency of change then subsumes the role of intellectuals. According to PL: "Intellectuals should be convinced to relate their work and their future to the future of the working people. . . ." The DuBois Clubs declare: "It is the working people of our country through their organizations, whatever their present difficulties, who will ultimately be the decisive force in meeting our pressing social and economic needs."

Thus, the ancestral ties of these groups, especially in the leadership, have not been lost: the concern with Marxicology, the hairsplitting, and the dependence on Marx or one of the disciples as proof, authority, and footnote. The dialectic is still a subject of importance, the insider's crown; and the groups' internal organs or theoretical journals are still engrossed with this kind of subject.

Finally, the Marxist-Leninist groups share a truly dialectical cosmic optimism: as Marxists they know that socialism is inevitable, while as Americans they are pessimistic about the future of their country under capitalism. Every contemporary event is weighed on the socialist-capitalist balance scale, on a worldwide basis. A bomber shot down in Vietnam, a race riot in Los Angeles, a water shortage in New York, or a Soviet victory in the Olympics, all point to the inevitable fall of capitalism and triumph of socialism.

Yet it is unlikely that foreign Communist funds support any of these groups. Even if such funds were available, it would be very difficult to control Marxist-Leninist youth today, for in addition to the spirit of openness which the experience of civil rights and free speech movements has engendered, there is no longer a Comintern or Cominform to enforce discipline and ideological purity.

The membership of the groups cannot be accurately estimated. Records are not available and changes are rapid: gains may be made after spectacular successes or in one metropolitan area, and within a year these gains may be depleted. In different parts of the country different groups have been successful in carrying out the big event, the sit-in, the rally, the trip to Cuba. These activities have usually led to a temporary increase in membership, but no lasting energizing has resulted: the ebb and flow that has always characterized small-sect radicalism in America continues to operate. Centers of activity gravitate from New York to San Francisco, with an occasional year or two at some campus in between (Wisconsin, for example).

It is unlikely that any of the three Marxist-Leninist groups have more than two thousand members nationally, but their effectiveness or importance should not be gauged by their size. The DuBois Clubs, PL, and YSA have attracted young people because they have shown that they provide a vital and militant spirit, a sensitivity to the problems of politically aware youth, and organizations that have the courage to act upon their convictions despite severe penalties. When freedom songs are sung or slogans shouted, the members of the Marxist-Leninist groups endow them with just as much meaning as do SNCC or SDS or independent young radicals. Ideological differences and variations in style and language are important only at the top; for most of the members it is a matter of which group attracted them first and can fill their immediate social and political needs. Thus, the ancestrally-linked left continues, no matter its small size or influence, to recruit new members and leaders. Most of them eventually leave, of course, but others remain as tireless, lifelong workers for their cause.

What is consistently true about them is that wherever they are, issues will be raised. They create debate, conflict, tests and trials about the nature of liberty. The Marxist-Leninist left will be found challenging society on questions of speech, travel, assembly, or anything related to due process. They are instrumental in organizing communities, gadflies which resist smashing. They also keep Marxism from an academic burial.

An enormous amount of publicity in national newspapers and magazines, from *Saturday Evening Post* to the *National Guardian,* has spotlighted Marxist-oriented youth. Although they are few in number and unsuccessful in achieving their goals, except national publicity—and this through no fault of theirs—their energy and activity should be recognized. Their failure to build organizations or attract "masses" should not obscure the role that they do play in American politics.

6. The FSM—Revolt
Against Liberal
Bureaucracy

Do Not Fold or Mutilate

*T*he clearest expression of what The Movement means to Northern students was found in the grievances of the Free Speech Movement at Berkeley and in the methods and styles it devised to redress their complaints.

The FSM was neither controlled nor formed by any of the organized political groups, yet it was far more than a coalition of organizations. It drew a deep commitment from thousands of students, recent graduates, and dropouts in the San Francisco Bay Area. It attracted older radicals, who saw it as providing an opportunity to be where the action was, and throughout the nation's campuses, it became *the* model for student organization.

As some of its critics point out the FSM was not primarily concerned with free speech or even advocacy, although these were the immediate reasons for its formation and provided the impetus for rallying support, as well as the justification for its continuance. But the FSM, as many of its spokesmen carefully explained, was a revolt against a liberal bureaucracy.

To the FSM the multiversity of California, the world's largest educational corporation, was the most immediate symbol of a way of life. It was the oppressor, the faceless monster that produced graduates and professionals; its faculty were engineers and trainers, who cared little about teaching but much about production. Furthermore, the university was the embodiment of liberalism. President Clark Kerr was the winner of the Meiklejohn Freedom Award, and its faculty had a corps of professional liberal social scientists who wrote about freedom and democracy, praising the United States and the university itself as the most noble embodiment of freedom. To the FSM the university appeared to be the living example of the integration of liberalism with actual policy, for its physical scientists do research on behalf of the military, and the social scientists provide the government with vast amounts of material designed to implement foreign and domestic policies.

The university has also achieved a fruitful integration with large corporations throughout the nation. Its agricultural science departments are tied closely to the large growers; university graduates are placed in corporations; and the university provides basic research for every level of corporate needs.

At the political level, the students felt, the university pretends to liberal democracy while providing material and men for barbarism, both in the California agricultural valleys and in Vietnam. It seemed to have defined its educational function as one of producing for society's needs as defined by government and the large corporations; it was no longer concerned with educating students.

Yet, paradoxically, the university offered its students the freedom to say much of what they wanted, as members of campus political clubs, and even to bring to the campus Communists and Nazis. But the FSMers felt patronized by this approach, for to them it appeared that the university tolerated all of this talk as long as it did not interfere with the production of the educational corporation. To the students the freedom of speech they were granted was primarily a way of keeping them amused, within the concept of education for democracy and citizenship, and within a framework of "listen to all sides, etc.," lest they be distracted by the content of their own lives, by their places in the university, and by world events.

The FSM revolt against bureaucracy was a revolt against liberalism, against the rhetoric of freedom and democracy. It was a revolt against the inhumanity of actual American practices the students believed were disguised by eloquent clichés in the speeches of liberal political leaders and in the writings of noted university professors. Throughout their educational lives students had heard these ideals articulated, but had watched society carry out the very opposite of the ideals. Finally, the students in The Movement rose in revolt to make the society live up to its professed ideals.

Prior to the FSM the students had been involved in movements focused on civil rights, peace, anti-capital punishment, anti-HUAC, community organizing, and even long-range revolutionary activity. And nowhere were the feeling and thinking of The Movement so clearly articulated as on the Berkeley campus.

It was not that Berkeley students were groping to find a place in society; on the contrary, many were children of the affluent. They wanted to change society, not because they had no place assured to them but because they did not want a place in it as it existed, for it had become so oppressive that they could no longer function acquiescently within it. Mario Savio's dramatic speech prior to the sit-in that resulted in the arrest of eight hundred expressed the idea that having a place in this society is far less important than creating a society in which one would want to have a place. And Savio also said that at a certain point the bureaucracy's rhetoric must be challenged. "There is a time," he explained from the steps of the university administration building, "when the operations of the machine become so odious, make you so sick at heart, that you can't take part, you can't even tacitly take part. And you've got to put your bodies upon the gears and upon the wheels, upon the levers, upon all the apparatus, and you've got to make it stop. And you've got to indicate to the people who run it, to the people who own it, that unless you're free the machine will be prevented from working at all."

By their acceptance of Savio as FSM's key spokesman, the

students acknowledged that at the heart of The Movement was the challenge to the quality of life, to the essence of modern American values, and to the social system itself. Most students who had been attracted to civil rights activities believed, from their experience, that racism and discrimination were not an aberration or a mutant of an otherwise normal and healthy society; so, too, they thought, American policies toward Cuba, Vietnam, or the Dominican Republic were not unfortunate excesses but rather the logical results of a basically wrong and rotten system.

On December 8, 1964, the University of California administration conceded the major demands of several thousand students who were supported by the majority of the faculty at Berkeley: there would be free speech and advocacy with only the most limited and necessary restrictions, and the students and faculty would have a loud voice in determining future policy based on these new rules.

But when a liberal judge tried and convicted students of trespassing and resisting arrest, their ideas and feelings about the nature of the enemy were reinforced. To those students who thought their actions had been legitimate if not noble expressions of freedom the convictions demonstrated that they had to enter the world of politics now, because the fervor and spirit of the mass meeting on the campus could not be simply applied to other areas and issues. Finally, they became convinced that although the faculty had given important support to the FSM, the professors were not willing to make the total commitment to change the world which the FSM leaders had made.

Soon after the December 8, 1964, agreement, the students suffered a sense of malaise when President Clark Kerr, with faculty support, expelled and suspended those few FSMers who took part in the so-called "Filthy Speech Movement." These FSMers, convinced that society was oppressive to the sexual needs or to the need of artists to write, paint, and film, had openly attempted to push the December 8 agreement to its limits by giving support to a young man who had been arrested for holding up a sign, on campus, saying "fuck." They believed their actions were properly in the realm of speech, and they assumed that under the December 8 agreement only the civil authorities would have jurisdiction to discipline them. But Kerr imposed the penalty, and the FSM leadership debated whether they could again call upon the eight hundred to protest and risk arrest, ultimately deciding, uneasily, against such action.

The total experience of the FSM was a radicalizing one for many of the students. Most of the FSM leadership is now involved in the Vietnam Day Committee, the grape strike in Delano, California, and other radical activities; many, as they put it, are permanently "turned off" the university. They have left the classrooms to work as full-time revolutionaries with SDS, the VDC, or The Movement in the South.

Few of the thousands involved in the FSM trust the university administration or any Establishment body to keep its word; thus, despite the frantic unmolested daily political activity on the campus, tension continues. A good many faculty members, fearful of political repercussions in the state, express their concern that another FSM situation may arise, again bringing the machinery of the university to a halt.

On campuses all over the nation faculties and administrations have combined to prevent themselves from becoming Berkeleys. The FSM succeeded in bringing the key feelings, ideas, and moods of The Movement to the attention of the entire national student body. At Berkeley the democracy that was practiced inside the FSM, the long hours of debates and discussion, the tedious decision-making procedure that involved thousands, each free to speak on the issues and forms of protest, has been carried over to other arenas.

But this same FSM-type democracy, once so attractive to many faculty members, is now viewed apprehensively when it is practiced in the VDC. The lack of formal organization and leadership, so acceptable in the FSM, has become unacceptable in the VDC, where such lacks are described as "irresponsible." But the flavor and style of the FSM in Berkeley has been so defined that faculty members, whether agreeing or disagreeing with the VDC, are compelled to take a stand on their rights to protest. Thus the FSM continues and will continue to link protests on foreign policy or civil rights with elementary freedom, keeping the faculty in a continuous state of tension.

Many issues raised by the FSM are unresolved and will remain unfulfilled. The students' demands for a good education, rather than only the form of an education; for linking, in some way, the university education with affairs of students as public men; for students having some control over curriculum; for insuring excellence of teaching; for the right to become full and equal members of an intellectual community—these issues continue to be aired and discussed. Talk of establishing a free university, based on models offered by Paul Goodman and others, has led to the formation in San Francisco and New York of Movement schools, with university professors and active radicals on the faculty.

But the failure or inability of the FSM to follow up on its promises has not gone unnoticed. An FSMer now active in the VDC wrote recently:

> After having spent the greater part of last year deeply involved in campus politics as a member of the Steering Committee of the Free Speech Movement, I looked forward with great anticipation to the future of Berkeley. Now, however, I am both saddened and angered by the course of events on our campus and in our politics. For most of us the "new university" has become a phrase we smugly give to the press. Our creative political potential has degenerated into a short-sighted repetition of demonstrations. . . . People waited in vain for others to voice the new values which were never to appear. . . . The "politics of apocalypse" became the "politics of despair." *

The real contribution made by the FSM is implicit in that statement: the students aroused by the FSM maintain their vigil over America's promises and ideals. They are a constant reminder that the struggle must continue so that the energy and idealism expressed through the FSM will be a constant, haunting force within the liberal intellectual community and at its institutions.

* Letter of Martin Roysher.

7. The Vietnam Anti-War Campaign

Make Love, Not War

*D*uring the past year Vietnam Day Committees or *ad hoc* groups protesting the war in Vietnam have been organized all over the country to protest American military involvement in Southeast Asia. In each of these committees the new radicals, affiliated and unaffiliated, join with the members of the Marxist-Leninist groups for endless discussions about the proper course for the anti-war campaign, invariably followed by anti-war demonstrations. Of all the groups in the country the Madison, New York, and Berkeley committees are the most active, with Berkeley, as usual, gaining the most attention.

In Berkeley the Vietnam Day Committee has shifted the focus of radical student activity from concern with the university as bureaucracy or the relation of the student to society (the university) to the arena of foreign policy. Although basically an off-campus organization headed by university dropouts, the constituency of the VDC is the few thousand students, plus others in and around the university community, that made up the Free Speech Movement.

Campus controversy and activity have switched in two semesters from the FSM to the VDC; the new issues are centered around the structure of the society that produces what the VDC believes to be a barbarous foreign policy.

Describing and analyzing the VDC presents many of the same problems encountered in making an analysis of the FSM. No controlling ideologies or clear political factions exist in the VDC; no consistent policy or practice is apparent; no clear structure or procedures exist for activities or conducting meetings. In the VDC office, a rented house near campus, a working staff is continually busy phoning, typing, making posters, organizing fund-raising parties, directing community education and organization, or working on a play commissioned for the VDC. PLers, May 2nd people, DuBois Clubbers, YSAers, SDS and SNCC members all hang around the headquarters or are on the staff. But the majority of VDC activists are unaffiliated, although not uninitiated, with campus politics or civil rights, peace, anti-HUAC, and the other causes popular on the Berkeley campus.

VDC meetings are characterized by a great deal of talk and discussion and as a rule are dull. Most of the words fly about tactics, which are mistaken for theory. The desire to do something, especially something sensational, is not easily talked down, for no one in the VDC would dare—rightly so—to stand up and offer answers to the specific problem of changing American foreign policy.

At the October 15–16 rallies in 1965 spokesmen from traditional left groups made traditional speeches about the alliance of progressive forces throughout the world, projecting a vast movement of Negroes, the poor, and students who will be knocking, any day, at the White House door. But at VDC meetings, either the general ones or the daily 6 P.M. kitchen committees, there is little of the old-time ideological talk.

The absence of ideological discussion is not because the membership does not have political views or leanings; they do, but they are based on impulsive right-wrong feelings as much as on reasoned analyses. At a general meeting an older ideologue proposed an end to the planning of large and militant demonstrations, with strong left demands, and a substitution of a petition with milder wording to be circulated throughout the country, like the Stockholm peace petition. In his view such a petition could get perhaps a million signatures and would therefore carry more weight than a demonstration. A spokesman for the May 2nd Movement, one of the new ideological left groups, answered him in an emotional speech, concluding with, "History, it won't absolve you." The audience laughed but sympathetically, for although they do not agree with some of the May 2nd leader's ideas, they did agree with the spirit of his remarks, with his call for dramatic action now, based on undiluted demands.

The FSM spirit of acting directly and openly on immediate needs remains the VDC's dynamic. But the State Department is not the same kind of enemy as the university. It has become apparent that strings of actions or demonstrations, marches, rallies, troop train stoppings, and so on, are leading to diminishing returns or are not very effective. The group inside the VDC that sees it as a militant demonstrating organization, emphasizing public exposure of strong demands, is competing with groups and individuals who feel that the peace movement must also engage in political struggle: community organizing; alliance with other radical groups and issues; ultimately a drive for political power.

The VDC has been the center of Berkeley political activity since the FSM period, and this places its informal leaders in an uncomfortable position. The objective of getting twenty thousand people to the November 20, 1965, March often blurred the question: After you get such a commitment from twenty thousand, what will they do the next day?

Other VDC activists are concerned with community organizing, in relation to Vietnam and as a device to help build an independent political movement on radical principles. But their ideas are confused by many things, including their daily involvement in the VDC. They have discovered that it is difficult to discuss basic principles, goals, and objectives *after* the general membership has agreed to have another march; they feel obligated to work for a march even though they believe it to be futile. At least a march is concrete, they rationalize, while community organizing or building a grass-roots political movement offers little theory and little concrete satisfaction, either to students or dropouts who have only recently begun to think in political or even social terms. And participation in the events radicalizes

The Hall Syndicate, Inc.

and commits new people to The Movement, but for what they are not sure.

The VDC is an example and a victim of the new radicalism. Some of its members are groping for an ideology, for clear links between their daily personal activity and the war in Vietnam or the institutions of American society. Its commitment to participatory democracy falters when it confronts a crisis of immediate seriousness or because it has not created a machinery which allows large groups of people to take part in the decision-making process.

Its view of political action is shifting from the chanting of action slogans at demonstrations to running a candidate in the Democratic Party's primary against a liberal Congressman. After the November anti-war March in Oakland, some VDC leaders proposed still a third march in December; this was rejected because marches didn't seem to accomplish anything. When the idea of running a candidate was proposed, some breathed a sigh of relief, for a campaign is a place for radical energy.

The VDC ran out of gas, much as many SDS and SNCC projects did. The search is for "what to do next." With that approach they will find gimmicks, not ideology or strategy, and a new focus will be needed for radical campus energy.

The anti-war movement will continue. But without the search for a guiding ideology the anti-war movement will remain "protest," always reacting to government policy rather than initiating radical alternatives.

8. Community Organizing

"Out There"

"*T*he future of the student movement," according to a Berkeley Vietnam Day Committee flyer written in language reminiscent of the thirties, "lies 'out there'—in Berkeley and Oakland—and we cannot succeed without your active participation—in writing, designing and distributing leaflets and posters, manning tables, door-to-door work, contacting other groups (churches, civil rights organizations, etc.)."

"Out there" is a big place, as the new radicals are discovering, and the problems they are encountering in it are formidable. As it becomes more difficult to carry The Movement with freedom songs and slogans, and as the complexities of social change in the overdeveloped society become apparent, the early idealistic non-political thrust has been blunted. To function "out there" demands the use of politics.

Initially, the new radicals did not have a clear political alternative to offer to their potential constituencies in place of the government's civil rights act and anti-poverty program. The passage of the civil rights legislation plus the revolt of the Negro poor in Los Angeles gave a sense of frustration to the new radicals, for the Los Angeles events demonstrated, dramatically, The Movement's lack of contact with the urban black masses. The simultaneous rapid escalation of the war in Vietnam allowed many to turn their energy and attention from civil rights to peace, an issue providing sustenance for their own intellectual and emotional needs but not requiring the kind of political program needed by domestic problems.

Attempts to link civil rights and peace have been made by some new radicals, especially those in the community organizing projects. More talk of The Movement's involvement in independent electoral politics is being heard, too, in which local issues of poverty and police brutality are to be combined with an anti-war stance; and there are a few infant community projects with a political focus. SDS, SNCC, PL, and the DuBois Clubs have initiated some projects concerned with electoral power, but other than SNCC worker Julian Bond's election to the Georgia legislature in 1965* and a large minority vote polled by a Cleveland insurgent, The Movement's independent political efforts have been frustrated.

H. Stuart Hughes' campaign for the U. S. Senate in Massachusetts and Noel Day's for state Congress in Boston drew upon The Movement for activist support, but their failure to win more than a minuscule percentage of the vote demoralized young precinct workers. And The Movement people felt betrayed in New York City by the reform politicians' continual forsaking of principle for a sniff of power; in San Francisco, where a liberal mayor elected with the help of Movement people lost his liberalism when it came to sit-ins in "his" city, while "he" was mayor; by the failure of other "peace candidates," after they were elected, to speak out as strongly as they had promised.

Independent community organizing in New York by *Studies On the Left* editors and in Oakland by youth from the anti-Vietnam and local grievance groups attracts those whose urge

* The Georgia state legislature subsequently refused to seat Bond because of his support for SNCC's position against our involvement in Vietnam. The legislature's action was widely criticized, and Bond is appealing his exclusion in the federal courts.

to demonstrate and act now has been replaced by a more sober perspective. They seek to educate a constituency rather than to concentrate on "the number of votes." Such education takes patience to wait while working out a program and a radical ideology.

An exciting idea like community organizing usually ends in disillusionment if it lacks an ideological base. The notion of purity of action inside the community is inevitably diluted, when the students face the realities of community life among the poor. Without a long-range commitment or ideology community organizing is rarely more than an experiment in frustration.

Meanwhile, some of the new radicals tried to ease their ideological frustration by joining the government's War on Poverty and participating in programs sponsored by the Office of Economic Opportunity. But once inside the government-sponsored programs they found only new frustrations in the red tape and the officials' fear about the demands or methods—not in the government manuals—which the new radical staff considered legitimate. Those people in The Movement who believed that they could use government funds for the needs of the poor found that this process was far more difficult than they had imagined.

The SNCC and MFDP staff also resented what they felt was the government's attempt to steal their program. They are convinced that the Administration's motivation was insincere and that the government could not deliver the major part of the goods: government could not produce a sense of dignity, but could only reinforce the feelings of drift and helplessness sponsored by the giant Washington-centered bureaucracies. Some SNCC veterans also felt that the government was buying off its potential enemies by paying salaries, especially to Negroes, that they could never hope to get in The Movement or in any kind of work that would be emotionally satisfying.

The government's offer to do good deeds sounded a false note in The Movement, and in fact did produce divisiveness and considerable chaos in many Movement offices. The staff of the summer 1965 Child Development Group of Mississippi (CDGM) project threatened to revolt when Washington intervened in its project and pressured the project leader. And when the Office of Economic Opportunity was faced with determined opposition from Mississippi Senator Stennis about CDGM, it was forced to crack down on it, quarreling over loose administrative procedures and improper bookkeeping. To many in The Movement such problems, which demoralize the staff and take up time and energy that should go into field work, are endemic to any government-sponsored project.

Today the less sophisticated people in The Movement view the anti-poverty program as simply an attempt to divide and destroy. The veterans view the program as growing from the needs of corporate liberalism to make some necessary adjustments when the business system's defects become glaring. In either case, the more experience those in The Movement have with government projects, the more most of them adhere to the position of Robert (Moses) Parris that our society cannot be patched or even regain health through major surgery.

But no one in The Movement is even vaguely sure of what should replace the rotten system. Within The Movement there is a crisis of ideology, of where to go, of how to deal politically with "the power structure" so that it can be weakened. There is confusion about tactics and strategy, and often an inability to distinguish between them. There is an inability to organize, except in a few Southern communities, a base of support outside the university. There is radical activity on many issues, but as yet no coherent intellectual force has replaced the moral obligation to put one's body and mind on the line in order to oppose large-scale and deep-rooted injustice and inhumanity.

9. Ideology, Communism, and Coalition

*T*he young radicals have been criticized and even criticize themselves for their lack of ideology. But perhaps their critics are overly harsh, for they have developed, if not an ideology, at least guidelines for their thought and action. In their writings and conversation they describe American society as "one-dimensional," or "operational only" in Herbert Marcuse's sense: it cannot be reformed, and in fact successful reform actually strengthens and widens its flexible periphery. Successful reform movements demonstrate for the liberal and radical pluralists that change can be brought about, that "the people" do have power. But the young radicals hold that such change does not give control to individuals over basic political, social, and economic decisions. Instead, they are convinced that these major decisions and the necessary resources for making them are in the hands of small elite groups which function as a ruling circle within the framework of "corporate liberalism."

In the new radical view corporate liberalism began under the New Deal and has developed steadily since then. It features the government as the dispenser of welfare services and doles for those whom the private sector cannot include. In the corporate liberal state the government even tries to find a place for those who cannot fit readily into the society.

To the new radicals a flexible political system is another essential feature of corporate liberalism. Almost any kind of dissent can be tolerated within it, and the society even rewards its critics. In communications anything that is well-written and readable can be published, publicized, and sold on the market. This "freedom" was another example of pluralism, the young radicals had learned in college. But ultimately they discovered that dissent within the system was meaningless in terms of building a political opposition.

The young activists have seen that today as in the past it is the older radicals and liberals who put the pressure on governing bodies, who spearhead the poverty program or the campaign for legalized abortion. And in time the political system shows that it responds to pressure and makes reforms. But, argue the young radicals, these reforms do not change the "one-dimensional" quality of life.

Since they believe society to be unreformable at its core, the young radicals are ambiguous about reforms like the voting rights bill and the anti-poverty program. On the one hand the laws *do* give immediate rights and services to those previously deprived. But these "rights" are not clearly won, and they are not exactly the goals so bitterly fought for. And they think that what is given is not the right to make decisions meaningful to life, but the right to vote, which may or may not be meaningful.

In this sense the new radicals have begun an ideological critique of the American system, but it is more a negative than a positive guide to action. Positive ideology did end in America during the fifties, as Daniel Bell asserted: in the political arena radicals have not presented new alternative programs and policies since the thirties. They have not educated constituencies around new ideas and they have not entered electoral politics with radical programs. (This excludes the dogmatic Marxist parties, which have not changed significantly since the thirties.) Radical activity has focused instead on achieving justice in individual causes, on a policy of protest, not politics. And this course has provided evidence that pluralism is king because "protest" did help to change inequities, in civil rights and civil liberties, in welfare and wages, in countless other reform programs; and to that extent it *has* strengthened American society, the very society that the new radicals say is evil at its core, no matter how flexible its periphery.

In some important instances serious changes in American life have been brought about through the coalition of liberals and radicals that Bayard Rustin now calls for building on a great scale. Rustin, Michael Harrington, Irving Howe, Tom Kahn, and Robert Pickus—to cite a few of the democratic socialists who hold this view—believe it *is* possible to better the lot of the American people by putting left pressure on the government from within the political system. And they believe a plurality of power *does* exist in America, that there are levels of government which can be influenced by reason or humanitarian arguments. So they participate, to varying degrees, in traditional day-to-day politics.

But in American politics and letters anti-Communism has been the litmus test for acceptability, and therefore effectiveness, 'since the Cold War began. American foreign policy may be denounced as long as equal invective is hurled at the Communists; to be equally opposed to a Viet Cong victory as to American intervention in Vietnam is within the limits of accepted patriotism and cancels out some of the irritation caused by opposition to American policy.

The concern for peace and civil rights felt by the democratic socialist supporters of coalition politics is tempered by their genuinely felt anti-Communism. And so when they picket the White House to decry the brutal war in Vietnam, they warn also that the Viet Cong will betray the South Vietnamese people. American foreign policy is criticized by the democratic socialists for being short-sighted, for not understanding that the development of Communism in pre-industrial countries can be fought better by the strength of American foreign aid coupled with a resolute commitment to democracy and social reform than it can by unilateral military intervention. Such a foreign policy, they believe, can best be advocated by a coalition with mainstream organizations that believe in reform as a general goal and also exclude Communists.

For many who were radicals in earlier periods anti-Communism is a vestigial hangover of their opposition to the Communists as betrayers of the ideals of Marxism and socialism who served only as puppets of Soviet masters. Now, although both the earlier radicals and their Communist enemies have changed, they retain the same anti-Communist posture.

These anti-Communists are The Movement's only serious outside critics, in that they question its principles and direct polemics against specific SDS or SNCC or VDC positions. The question of anti-Communism has been one of the invariable central themes for these attacks; their demand to purify the peace and civil rights movements by excluding Communists, or their demand in their policy statements that the new radicals explicitly oppose totalitarianism everywhere, recurs again and again.

The democratic socialist and liberal arguments against the inclusion of Communists in the peace and civil rights movements have several dimensions. The thesis of exclusion is based partially on the belief that The Movement can effect changes in the Johnson policy, if it proves that it is democratic and within the mainstream of American life: thus, for example, no pro-Viet Cong slogans should be raised in the peace movement. The excluders think, too, that the peace movement is now the most important part of The Movement as a whole and are worried that unless the Communists and their followers are attacked and isolated, they may take over, snowballing over the naïve young radical purists. To prevent that from happening, the anti-Communists want their group to dominate a part of the peace movement, so that if and when the time comes that the power sources are inclined to listen, their ears will remain open to the anti-Communist group.

Whatever explanation or combination of reasons is used to justify the exclusion of Communists, the issue is irrelevant to the new radicals in the contexts in which it is posed. The warnings to the younger, less-historical, less-educated radicals are viewed with distrust. The new radicals do not believe the democratic socialists are asking them to become ideological or even practical in their switch "from protest to politics." Instead they

think they are being asked to become ten or twenty years older
than they are and to take an interest in battles that are still
highly personal and carry emotional charges for the older generation but mean very little to them.

Rather than clarify their position on the Communist question,
the young radicals tend to answer the charges ambiguously.
They have confused their anti-war principles and clear understanding of America with apologies for the Viet Cong. Their
need to link themselves with the revolutions in Asia, Africa, and
Latin America often leads them to romanticize guerrilla movements. They believe that American imperialism is basically to
blame for the tragedy of Vietnam, and that American militarism
fosters anti-democratic tendencies.

The Future of the Movement

The gulf between the democratic socialists and the new radicals may widen, for the new radicals do not and will not give
adequate or convincing answers to the Communist question.
They are correct in refusing the stale arguments and acrimony
of past quarrels but they cannot avoid an ideological confrontation with the Communist position in the sixties. Although they
should not analyze Communist society today as if it were the
same model known and despised by the older radical movement,
they must still do so from their own special viewpoint.

But few young radicals are sure of themselves in terms of
ideology. They feel much more secure in postures of moral in-
transigence, using the purity of youth and action to answer their
critics' political attacks. To them Communism is an issue raised
only by those over thirty, therefore they need not be concerned
with it. They think their critics are still talking from the framework of an industrial society and they believe they are living in
the post-industrial epoch.

To the new radicals the issues are here and now, in the Dominican Republic and Vietnam, not in Hungary or Tibet. They
are uninterested in the Communist Party's vicious treatment of
Norman Thomas in 1932, but they are bitter about Norman

Thomas' criticism of SDS's inclusion of Communists in the anti-Vietnam war March on Washington. Stalin's purges are only dim history to them, something that happened before they were born; their anger is reserved for what is happening here and now.

(It is an ironic coincidence, too, that both the militant anti-Communist socialists and the Communists whom they wish to exclude from politics have essentially the same strategy for political action today—working inside the liberal or radical establishment, hoping both to influence its decision-makers and radicalize its constituency. Neither of their analyses of American society have changed, in important ways, from the days when their internecine battles partially consumed the energy of the left. Their faith in the working class has been weakened, it is true, but in lieu of a replacement for it as an agency of social change, they revert to their more traditional methods of achieving political objectives.)

It is in its fear of politics and uncertainty about political ideology that The Movement falters and often gets embroiled in sterile debates of the past. To the extent that it has entered politics in an organized and ideological way, The Movement is still victimized by the old questions. The Movement cannot resuscitate positive ideology unless it is willing to compete, ultimately, for political power.

Paradoxically, despite its internal crises and external alarms, The Movement has never been larger in numbers, and not since the first two decades of this century have so many areas of the country been involved. Civil rights and anti-war agitation, as proven by the number of demonstrations held in October and November of 1965, have spread across the country. In each case the protests have been led by the young radicals, affiliated or unaffiliated, or have been organized because of pressure from their existence.

And yet the concern with the here and now, the emphasis on action and the moral witness are the very reasons that so many Movement projects deteriorate. Enthusiasm can carry one only a short distance before a more substantial fuel is required. Community organizing (of the poor) and a faith in popular consciousness (participatory democracy), for example, are important concepts and have been used with success by radicals, but they are not enough. The questions for the new radicals are whether they are going to work out a more coherent ideology; whether they are willing to commit themselves to jail but not to twenty or thirty years of difficult political effort; whether they are willing to admit that the American political and economic system, which they describe as rotten, still has great strength.

If they admit that a revolutionary situation does not exist in America today, they can stop characterizing the coalition and reform view as a betrayal. Instead, their approach could be to build a radical constituency to educate larger and larger numbers of people in a radical framework, patiently, using the electoral process when feasible, fighting inside the Democratic Party or other political organs—but always from a strong and independent political base, recognizing the pitfalls inherent in fighting the system's strongest feature: its politics.

The increasing interest in community organizing, in building an independent radical political movement based on some form of SNCC and SDS participatory democracy, has not yet been accepted by the majority, who are more anxious to Act Now and are unwilling or unable to commit themselves to the tedious and frustrating task of political organizing outside of the universities. Instead, they believe that as students and intellectuals their basic source of power is in the examples they set, in their ability to articulate dissent and cause the government embarrassment and discomfort.

Unlike agitation for civil rights, the anti-war movement gains little sympathy in high places, and as in World War I a combination of vigilante or unofficial terror may be combined with legal moves to attempt to crush the excitement and moral force that the young radicals produce. Government repression of the anti-war demonstrations, the burning of draft cards, and the passing out of "seditious" leaflets may put The Movement on the defensive, where their battles will be for their basic rights in the courts rather than against the "one-dimensional society" in the streets.

The new radicals cannot be intimidated by threats or actual imprisonment. The self-immolation of several anti-war Americans has forced the people in The Movement to firmer commitment. Their attitude has become increasingly fatalistic, almost echoing the words of Fidel Castro in his famous trial speech: "I know that imprisonment will be as hard for me as it has ever been for anyone. . . . But I do not fear prison. . . . Sentence me. I do not mind. History will absolve me."

But history will not absolve the new radicals from their own political failures and political limitations if they do not recognize them. What is required of The Movement today is an organized search to develop an ideology for the purpose of gaining political power, to replace both its own righteous moral posture and the traditional politics of compromise.

The new ideology might establish realistic priorities so that the American system could be attacked at its weakest points—the emerging overseas empire and perhaps the flimsy social cohesion that is based on the ability to own commodities—rather than its electoral politics or powerful economy. Thus a new politics would reintroduce utopian thinking (what is possible with our technology) alongside imaginative politics (social change brought about outside of the two-party monster). If the new radicals do not give up in frustration, they can develop a perspective and a set of ideals that integrates with a sound ideology. If their utopian thinking becomes sound enough to excite people to the vision of another dimension in American society, they can begin the building of this new politics on a national scale.

10. Conclusion

*I*t is impossible to assess The Movement's long-term accomplishments now, for it is too young, and too little is known about it, despite the enormous publicity it has received. Nevertheless, it is possible to judge its immediate impact on American life and make some predictions about its future.

Immediately, Negroes' civil rights in the South have been advanced because The Movement's active presence forced the government to move more quickly than it had planned. The American universities are changing for the better, because The Movement's direct actions, or the potential of such actions taking place, have made the universities uncomfortably aware of the students' presence on the campus. In the anti-poverty drive the emphasis upon participation by the poor is partially, at least, a response to pressures stimulated by The Movement. Finally, because of The Movement, issues of foreign policy are being debated, far more intensely and by far more people in America today than since our entrance into World War II.

Yet, important as these accomplishments are, The Movement's real significance centers around other issues. Ample proof exists, for example, that The Movement attracts some of the best young people in the country, contrary to the vulgar popular notion that those who are involved are only "beats," "kooks," and "potheads." It is true that representatives of all those types can be found in The Movement, but its core is made up of those young people most committed to the values of intellectual honesty and social action rooted in the best American tradition.

That these young people reject the affluent society which produced them is one of The Movement's most startling characteristics. This generation has not grown up in a depression world, as did the youthful radicals of the thirties. Their drive is not to go from rags to riches; they know about poverty only because they adopt it as a way of life and not because they were born into it. And their repudiation of the American value system is so serious that they have forced thoughtful elements in society to re-examine their own acceptance of America, to discover what it is in American life that is so unattractive, so distasteful as to make these young people turn their backs on it and call for a revolution to replace it.

The Movement's intransigent moral posture is having consequences, too: the willingness of the participants in The Movement to translate their moral view of politics into a personal morality of action has forced others, outside The Movement, to assess their own commitment to moral positions. And The Movement's presence on the American political scene has replaced the view that ideology is dead in American politics with a revived interest in developing a new one.

We believe that this search for an ideology is at the root of the dispute between the new radicals and the traditional left. Superficially, the dispute has focused on the tactical question of whether the civil rights movement should make an alliance with the trade unions and liberal political organizations, and here we share the new radicals' disagreement with that grouping. But the real issue is that the new radicals are searching for a theory that will combine their individual, existential view of politics with the ability to carry out mass activities. We think that search is a healthy one, one that should be encouraged.

The difficulties encountered by The Movement in developing this ideology are related to its break with the past. The old left still concentrates its intellectual and activist energy on making changes in America's political and economic system on bread-and-butter issues. To many in the Marxist left, foreign policy is still explained by the simplistic view of imperialism as the stage of monopoly-capitalism's need for commodity and capital markets. On the other hand, most of the democratic left sees no pattern or systematic policy developing from the basic needs of American capitalism. This group attributes the failures of American foreign policy to a lack of understanding of Communism's dynamics and appeals; it assumes that America is capable of supporting what it describes as democratic-socialist movements in less developed countries, but has not done so from ignorance or the ill-will of a few powerful people.

In our view, both groups are wrong, and we share The Movement's determination to concentrate its basic efforts on the inadequate quality of life offered by our society. Alienation at home and intervention abroad are only different aspects of the same basic quality that results from the needs of the American corporate system. We agree with The Movement's emphasis on foreign policy: the exporting of anti-Communism has pervaded the quality, the tone, the character of our domestic life. In the name of anti-Communism the United States government has supported corrupt and totalitarian regimes that jail all dissenters.

In its attempt to create an anti-Communist empire throughout the world, America is committed to a permanent defense of and military alliance with any regime willing to share her anti-Communism. The American economy and political system have become inextricably linked to the building of the anti-Communist empire. Thus, anti-Communism has become a structural need, translated into every level of life, from Communist villains in the comic strips and TV series to the perpetual existence of the international Communist threat as a pre-condition for the permanent war economy.

Of equal seriousness is the United States government's inability to recognize the legitimacy of national revolutionary movements. In Vietnam official American policy is based on the myth that the National Liberation Front are robots being manipulated and directed from North Vietnam and/or Communist China. We applaud The Movement's efforts to explode that myth and expose the real nature of American involvement in Southeast Asia: to prevent, at all costs, the accession to power of any government influenced by the Communists, as is the National Liberation Front, whether or not it has the support of the people in the country.

The Movement has made many Americans uncomfortable, and has inspired some radicals and liberals to renew their political commitment in some form. The new radicals may not succeed in achieving the fundamental change in American society that they and we feel is necessary. Instead, perhaps, their role will be the radicalizing of two generations, who are not afraid to build a larger Movement, and who are able and willing to fight for political power. Unless Americans are awakened to action about the moral anguish they must feel, as citizens and human beings, for the victims of our society both here and abroad, then The Movement itself will become a victim of a post-industrial America, a society whose value system even George Orwell might not have imagined.

The Documents

Origins and Themes

1. An Excerpt from "Howl"

*A*merica I've given you all and now I'm nothing" is the opening line of Allen Ginsberg's poem "America," published in
1956. Ginsberg's anguish about the United States continued
with, "America when will we end the human war? Go fuck yourself with your atom bombs."

   "America" appeared in the same edition of Ginsberg's poetry
that carried "Howl." Indeed, "Howl" was the title of the whole
book, the longest poem in it, and the one which gave Ginsberg
notoriety and the serious attention his work deserved.

   Ginsberg was thirty when "Howl" was published. He had
been a student at Columbia and then drifted around the world.
In San Francisco, he was a prominent member of the group of
poets whose work was being published by poet Lawrence Ferlinghetti, also the founder of the City Lights Bookstore and Press.

   In "Howl" and most of Ginsberg's other poems there is deep
anguish and brilliant imagery. "Howl" was labeled obscene by
the San Francisco district attorney; but at the trial of Ginsberg
and Ferlinghetti the judge ruled that the poem was art. For a
large number of young people becoming socially and politically
conscious, Allen Ginsberg articulated in modern, anti-square
language their ideals of love and brotherhood. "America," he

wrote, *"I used to be a communist when I was a kid I'm not
sorry. . . . It's true I don't want to join the Army or turn
lathes in precision parts factories, I'm nearsighted and psycho-
pathic anyway./ America I'm putting my queer shoulder to the
wheel."*

II

What sphinx of cement and aluminum bashed open their skulls
  and ate up their brains and imagination?

Moloch! Solitude! Filth! Ugliness! Ashcans and unobtainable
  dollars! Children screaming under the stairways! Boys sob-
  bing in armies! Old men weeping in the parks!

Moloch! Moloch! Nightmare of Moloch! Moloch the loveless!
  Mental Moloch! Moloch the heavy judger of men!

Moloch the incomprehensible prison! Moloch the crossbone
  soulless jailhouse and Congress of sorrows! Moloch whose
  buildings are judgement! Moloch the vast stone of war!
  Moloch the stunned governments!

Moloch whose mind is pure machinery! Moloch whose blood is
  running money! Moloch whose fingers are ten armies! Moloch whose breast is a cannibal dynamo! Moloch whose ear
  is a smoking tomb!

Moloch whose eyes are a thousand blind windows! Moloch
  whose skyscrapers stand in the long streets like endless Je-
  hovahs! Moloch whose factories dream and croak in the
  fog! Moloch whose smokestacks and antennae crown the
  cities!

Moloch whose love is endless oil and stone! Moloch whose soul
  is electricity and banks! Moloch whose poverty is the spec-
  ter of genius! Moloch whose fate is a cloud of sexless hy-
  drogen! Moloch whose name is the Mind!

Moloch in whom I sit lonely! Moloch in whom I dream Angels!
  Crazy in Moloch! Cocksucker in Moloch! Lacklove and
  manless in Moloch!

Moloch who entered my soul early! Moloch in whom I am a
  consciousness without a body! Moloch who frightened me
  out of my natural ecstasy! Moloch whom I abandon! Wake
  up in Moloch! Light streaming out of the sky!

Moloch! Moloch! Robot apartments! invisible suburbs! skeleton
treasuries! blind capitals! demonic industries! spectral nations! invincible madhouses! granite cocks! monstrous
bombs!

They broke their backs lifting Moloch to Heaven! Pavements,
trees, radios, tons! lifting the city to Heaven which exists
and is everywhere about us!

Visions! omens! hallucinations! miracles! ecstasies! gone down
the American river!

Dreams! adorations! illuminations! religions! the whole boatload
of sensitive bullshit!

Breakthroughs! over the river! flips and crucifixions! gone down
the flood! High! Epiphanies! Despairs! Ten years' animal
screams and suicides! Minds! New loves! Mad generation!
down on the rocks of Time!

Real holy laughter in the river! They saw it all! the wild eyes! the
holy yells! They bade farewell! They jumped off the roof!
to solitude! waving! carrying flowers! Down to the river!
into the street!

2. *"The Radicalism of Disclosure"*

All the editors of Studies on the Left, *whose first issue was
published in the fall of 1959, were graduate students at the University of Wisconsin, mostly in history. They thought that similar groups of graduates existed at other universities and that*
Studies *would become the organ for a New Left theory. Similar
constellations, however, did not develop, and throughout the
first three years the* Studies *editors were forced to rely more on
themselves than they had anticipated. The result was a scholarly
journal that saw history as the source for a theory for an analysis of contemporary society.*

*"The Radicalism of Disclosure," the first editorial, is a call by
the* Studies *editors for radical scholars to emerge and assert the
importance of their role. When it was written, the notion that the
radicals should leave the world of the university had not yet
received the wide approval it was to get later. Instead, the*

Studies *editorial confined its attention to what should be done by
the radical scholars within the confines of the academic world.*

In academic circles, the term "objectivity" is generally used to
indicate the dispassion, the non-partisanship with which the
"true scholar" approaches his work. It is also frequently used to
indicate the prevalent, or "majority" view. For example, there
are not very many students who will stand up for their "subjective" evaluation of another scholar's work in opposition to the
supposedly objective judgment inherent in the fact that the man
has been given a professorship at a prominent Ivy League university, and a great deal of praise by established scholars. Many,
perhaps most, students will distrust their own subjective opinion
in the face of all this objective data, and they may even state that
there is no other standard of evaluation. In other words, they
have made the subtle and all-important equation between quality on the one hand, and acceptability or market value on the
other, and are well on their way to a bright academic future. The
objectivity here assumed is reducible to the weight of authority,
the viewpoint of those who are in position to enforce standards,
the value judgments of the not so metaphorical marketplace of
ideas.

Similarly, the use of the term to indicate scholarly dispassion
is, at bottom, a way of justifying acceptance (either active or
passive) of the status quo. When a man is digging up facts to
support traditional and accepted interpretations, or when he has
no interest in the significance of these facts for larger theoretical
questions, he may, without too much difficulty, prevent himself
from becoming impassioned. When he is turning out an obviously marketable piece showing that the American Constitution
is the best guarantee of freedom that man will ever come up
with, that the causes of some historical event are so complex
that they are beyond discovery, or that some poet had an aver-
sion to dogs, he may understandably remain unimpassioned. But
this does not necessarily mean that he is any less biased than his
neighbor, although it might very well mean that he cares less. On
the other hand, when a scholar arrives at a radical or unconven-

tional interpretation, he may very well become excited by what he is doing. For the act of contradiction involves emotions more tumultuous than those aroused by the state of acceptance. Scholarly dispassion is the true medium of the scholar satisfied with (or browbeaten by) things as they are.

As graduate students anticipating academic careers, we feel a very personal stake in academic life, and we feel that, as radicals, we are hampered in our work by the intrusion of prevailing standards of scholarship, which set up a screen between ourselves and our product, an automatic censoring device which trims and deflates and confines our work, under the pretext of what is supposed to be "objective scholarship," until we no longer know it as our own. Like little boys writing poems in the style of Terence, we learn the traditional, acceptable genres in our fields, and then develop the skills necssary to produce similar work, until slowly, subtly, but surely, we come to look upon our work, not as the expression of our union with man and society, but merely as our means of livelihood and security—a product for sale, neither our possession nor our creation. And the closer we come to taking our places as working people in the profession, the harder it is to remember who we are, what we have to say, and why we got into the intellectual racket in the first place.

But when we think back, we recall that at some point in our education we thought that life was interesting and challenging, and that we wanted to know more about it. We wanted to understand the phenomena which excited us: the functioning of the galaxy; the role of men in history; the creative process. And we wanted to know how we could participate creatively in life. We wanted to learn the origins of racism so that we could help to stamp it out; we wanted to know why people suffer, so that we could help to make suffering less in our time. We were not very dispassionate about our work then, because it is not easy to be dispassionate about racism, or the creative process, or the galaxy, about war and peace, and the fate of man. We did not think, at that time, that history is dull, and the search for knowledge, drudgery.

Nor do we think so yet. There is work for the radical scholar, the thinker who is committed to the investigation of the origins, purposes and limitations of institutions and concepts, as well as for the conservative or liberal scholar who is committed to their efficient maintenance and improvement. There is room in scholarship for the application of reason to the *reconstruction* of society, as well as to legalistic interpretation and reform. There is a place for the scholar who looks upon traditional formulations, theories, structures, even "facts" with a habitually critical attitude stemming from his distaste for things as they are, and from his distrust of the analyses of those who are committed to the maintenance of the status quo.

There is a place for him because, if he is a scholar as well as a malcontent, an honest researcher as well as a radical, his very partisanship, bias—call it what you will—gives him a kind of objectivity. Because he stands opposed to established institutions and conventional conceptions, the radical scholar possesses an unconcern for their safety or preservation which enables him to carry inquiry along paths where the so-called "objective" conservative or liberal scholar would not care to tread. Arnold Hauser has observed that the French bourgeoisie of the nineteenth century rejected naturalism in art from its "perfectly correct feeling that every art that describes life without bias and without restraint is in itself a revolutionary art." In 1912, Woodrow Wilson shrewdly expressed a similar feeling current within the American bourgeoisie. "The radicalism of our time," he observed, ". . . does not consist in the things that are proposed, but in the things that are disclosed." The relentless disclosure of the nature and causes of social institutions and developments is, in our own time, also radical. The Hon. Henry Cabot Lodge, Jr., unlike his more candid forbear, would even like to shroud in secrecy the now radical fact that the United States economy is capitalistic (he calls it *economic humanism*). And he has his counterparts among the scholars.

There are men and women in this country, both in and out of the academic profession, who still pursue their intellectual labor with a combination of scholarly integrity and commitment to the humanization of society. There are many more who retain a desire to do so, but who are prevented from fulfilling themselves and contributing significantly to knowledge by the paralyzing effect of forcefully maintained academic standards. The waste perhaps is tragic. It is our conviction that academic acceptance of the radical scholar's work as a contribution worthy of respect and consideration would increase both the quality and quantity of such work, and revitalize all of American intellectual life in an important way. But this respect must be earned and fought for, and it is not easy to fight alone. It is difficult for the isolated individual to maintain belief in the legitimacy of radical scholarship, even though history attests to it, and individuals in our own time demonstrate it. Even for those who believe in it, as many do, it is difficult to exercise their radicalism in individual opposition to the weight of the authorities who control our professional future. *Studies on the Left* wishes to participate in the struggles of radical scholars by existing as a meeting place where, in spite of philosophical and political differences, they can join in their common dissatisfaction with present academic standards and myths, and work harmoniously and creatively toward the future; and by helping such scholars demonstrate to the academic world the unique contribution which the radically committed thinker, by the very nature of his emotional and intellectual partisanship, is able to make. We hope that the radicalism of what is disclosed, as it increases and matures, may provide knowledge and theory for the future growth of a radicalism of what is proposed.

3. SLATE

SLATE, whose name is the shortening of "Slate of Candidates," was organized in early 1958 at the University of California at Berkeley. It was composed of students from religious groups, co-ops, independents, and political radicals like Mike Miller, now a SNCC field secretary, and Pat Hallinan, a DuBois Clubs founder. Although concerned originally with campus life and student government, SLATE soon became involved with issues of the larger community. In May 1960, for example, when the House Committee on Un-American Activities held hearings in San Francisco, SLATE members were instrumental in organizing the ad hoc *committee against HUAC, which led to demonstrations and arrests. After "Black Friday," the day the police*

*used water hoses to wash the students down the City Hall steps,
where they were arrested, activity spread to a national campaign
to abolish the Committee. Student energy spilled over into other
areas as well: political campaigns, abolition of compulsory
ROTC, civil rights, abolition of the death penalty, agricultural
labor, and "Fair Play" for the Cuban Revolution.*

I. "On the University" from the Cal Reporter, March 1958

We will be concerned with students as citizens in society—
with their involvement with national and international issues.

We will be concerned with education—with whether or not
the University helps us to be open-minded, thinking individuals.

We will be concerned with academic freedom and civil liberties.

We ask only a fair hearing in the open marketplace of ideas.

II. Carey McWilliams, Jr., in an article on student politics in the Daily Californian, September 28, 1958

. . . within the student community there is the implied premise that student government offers truth, beauty, love and
honor. In reality one finds insanity, impotence, irrelevance and
inside-ism. Cal students can't reform the school in the next year,
but Slate can help make the world a little more sane and just
than it has been in the last forty years.

III. The Daily Californian, May 4, 1960 on the HUAC hearings

The *Daily Californian* considers these hearings, the way they
will be conducted and their very existence as an affront to American concepts of due process and political freedom. . . . We
urge the abolishment of the entire Un-American Activities Committee as it is now constituted and as it now operates. . . . We
urge students to participate in the various protests. . . . It will
be an education for as many students who can be present to sit

in on the hearings, which are open, and to observe the tenor of what we feel to be in the truest sense "un-American activities."

4. *"On the Ideology of the Campus Revolution"* *

Dale L. Johnson was a graduate student in sociology at Stanford University, active in the student movement since the HUAC demonstrations in San Francisco. He was executive secretary of the Palo Alto Fair Play for Cuba Committee and an executive of the Bay Area Students Committee Against American Intervention in Cuba. He now teaches at the University of California in Riverside.

It used to be that the wise and benevolent elder generation bemoaned the apathy and lack of direction of their offspring. They wondered at the lack of response in the college atmosphere of ideas, they were amused at the prevalence of spring water fights and panty raids, and raised their eyebrows at those who withdrew to North Beach. In recent months it seems to many that a revolution has taken place on campus. Disturbed by recent student political activities, California legislators have questioned the wisdom of granting salary increases to a Berkeley faculty and administration which allowed its students to flaunt, unpunished, the "law and order" represented by the HUAC. Furthermore, U. of C. faculty members have been attacked as willing agents of the conspiracy to corrupt the pliable minds of youth.

Although many campuses are experiencing this upheaval, the center of activities seems to reside in the San Francisco Bay Area, particularly at the University of California. Space does not permit a complete analysis of the campus revolution's development but it is possible to note briefly something of the nature of the movement.

* *Studies on the Left,* Vol. II, No. 1, 1961.

U. of C. students, by and large inactive since the 1930s, took the first step several years ago by organizing SLATE, a "liberal" campus political party. Since the inception of SLATE, which managed to stimulate, organize, and direct student protest toward the world of politics, a multitude of single-purpose groups, permanent and *ad hoc,* have sprung up. Last year the Chessman case brought on a tremendous student drive for an end to the death penalty; there have been dramatic protests against compulsory ROTC; students have worked to end discrimination in housing; Woolworth's has been picketed almost daily; demonstrations against missile bases have been conducted by students with strong pacifist convictions. By far the most effective in stirring protest, however, have been the sit-ins and the demonstrations against the HUAC in San Francisco. The effective use of direct action techniques in the sit-ins and the highly dramatic nature of the anti-HUAC campaign brought nationwide attention. As a result of these instances, several thousand students of this area and throughout the country have become aware that they can express their discontent effectively by joining others of like mind on the picket line.

Since the May anti-HUAC "riots," new organizations and spontaneous protest movements have grown up; the socialist groups of the area have reported a high degree of interest in their programs (the Young People's Socialist League and the Socialist Party–Social Democratic Federation of Berkeley, blessed with highly skilled leadership, have been particularly successful of late). The American Legion Convention in San Francisco last summer invited a demonstration by manhandling a few students who had the audacity to carry signs questioning the wisdom of Legion resolutions. Several hundred from this area called for civil rights and "freedom now" in front of the Democratic Convention in Los Angeles. The audience for Nixon's San Francisco speech was shocked to see students raise placards calling for "No More U-2s." There was some talk, but not much action, for a "Vote No For President" campaign. Finally, and I think this may prove to be the most important of all, there has been the impact of the Cuban Revolution.

To a remarkable degree there are ideological similarities between the Cuban and campus revolutions. Both Cuban and campus rebels are *strong* dissenters, firm in their convictions and willing to speak out and act militantly in spite of the mighty coercive powers of the American state. Both are pragmatic, always putting first things first, with rarely an eye to ultimate ends. In Cuba this takes the form of "the year of agrarian reform," the "year of education," the "year of industrialization." . . . Here at home the pragmatic outlook is manifested in the multitude of single-issue groups devoted simply to getting things done in the most effective manner possible. Organizations form almost overnight to work on specific questions—civil liberties, academic freedom, ROTC, the death penalty, civil rights. Both Cuban and campus revolutions are inexperienced, groping movements, sometimes stumbling, sometimes making mistakes of a tactical nature—with either too much anti-Americanism or too much fear of offending or alienating "public opinion." Most important, their motivating ideologies are neither socialism—Marxian or otherwise—nor liberalism, although they combine elements of both. Rather, the ideology of both the *Barbudos* of Cuba and the campus revolutionaries is a refreshing combination of humanism and rationalism. The Fidelista *knows* the meaning of misery and exploitation, of disease and illiteracy, of unemployment and squalor in the midst of plenty, of graft and corruption —he has lived it; the campus rebel, lacking the Cuban experience, nonetheless *feels* it—it violates his sense of values. The Fidelista understands the ailments of Cuba—and of Guatemala, Haiti, the Dominican Republic, and all the remaining "hungry nations"—and he intends to translate this knowledge into action. In at least one sense the Fidelista is very fortunate. He is confronted with the opportunity to steer Cuba's, and perhaps Latin America's, destiny upon the path which he chooses. So he sets about, rationally, to build a new society. Many students at U. of C., Stanford, San Francisco and San Jose State Colleges, at Wisconsin, and Chicago and NYU grasp and appreciate this attempt to direct human history, to take hold of one's environment and shape it, to institutionalize the better human values. These students also recognize the dangers involved, both for themselves and the Cubans. They would oppose both American intervention and totalitarianism in the name of Cuban nationalism or socialism, but they are not without understanding for revolutionary excesses.

There are also, of course, important differences between the Cuban and campus rebels. The former are united, sure of themselves and where they are going. The latter, though often united on specific issues, are divided over basic questions, hesitant, and with no permanent goals or direction.

No all-inclusive term adequately characterizes the range of ideologies which influence the campus rebels. While such a characterization might fairly represent the convictions of one subgroup, it would radically conflict with those of another. The link which binds the various tendencies within the student movement is a firm belief in the value and necessity of *active dissent*. In the course of its short existence, the campus revolution has forged an ideology of dissent which sustains its adherents during the thick of political action and in some sense represents a compromise between the opposing trends of individualism and mass action.

Most of us radicals of the 1960s would agree with Daniel Bell that the postwar years have witnessed the "end of ideology." This we lament rather than applaud. We take violent exception to his statement that the "tendency to convert concrete issues into ideological problems, to invest them with moral color . . . is to invite conflicts which can only damage a society." This is the voice of a disillusioned man whose ideology is anti-ideology. It is a conservative message and it is nonsense.

The old left is dead; and many of the reasons offered in Bell's book seem valid. Contemporary "liberalism" is impotent; and no longer even *is* liberalism in our sense. We are tired of the stereotyped responses of the Marxist, and disgusted with the liberal's rhetoric, agnosticism, and incapacity for political action. We are radical, but disregard the orthodoxy of Marxism. We are liberal, but not tied to the status quo. In a sense we are eclectic, willing to accept the best of both philosophies. The books of C. Wright Mills are well-thumbed by us, and it is his sort of radicalism with which many of us identify. Yet Mills is not our intellectual leader, nor are we blind to his faults. We criticize him for his elitism and a certain callousness toward fact. These criticisms reflect what we have learned from the writings of Lenin and others about mass movements and from the neo-positivists about science.

In a sense we are lost, for we do drift about in rough and uncharted seas. We are fearful that if we do establish a steady course it may take us somewhere we do not want to go. We also know that the huge waves tossed up from the depths of conservative tradition and state authority may weaken, or even destroy us.

Perhaps this is why we have only a dissenting ideology. We unhesitantly express what we are against, but are less sure of what we are for. Because of this, we are rather more reformist than revolutionary. We tend to believe in nonviolence not only because it is effective, but also because it is inherently good.

To be sure, most of us are uncommitted—except to humanism, rationality, and an action program. However, we do number among our supporters some who are, but even their commitment may be of a transient nature. Some are "Stevensonians," others are social democrats, a few fall in with the Socialist Workers Party. The techniques of nonviolent action are appealing, especially to those among us of pacifist inclination. There are even a few among us who sympathize with the goals and means of the Communist Party. Communism is, of course, an issue that splits us. It is a thing pushed upon us by old loyalties and politics of the past. Fortunately, the freedom and tolerance that we preach and the tendency to issue-orientation minimize the potential disruptive aspects of the situation.

In short, our humanism and acceptance of democratic principles sensitize us to problems, our rational faculty reveals solutions consistent with our values, and both propel us to action. The future is replete with issues. Let us unite in optimism and action.

Postscript: The American intervention in Cuba, undertaken after this communication was in print, has had a tremendous impact on both the size of the student movement and its ideology, at least in the Bay Area. Many student "hangers-on" and potential rebels have been activated by the gross nature of the irrationality in high places. Most important, however, is the fact that U.S. imperialistic ventures have served to *radicalize* the dissenters. For example: (a) the concept of demonstration has been altered to include "dramatic nonviolent acts of civil disobedience;" (b) new and truly radical students have gained leadership positions and the old activists have moved to the left along with their student base of support.

5. *"On the New Left"*

If any one person was the intellectual father of The Movement, it was C. Wright Mills. Mills, a controversial and prolific writer, was a sociologist who became a social critic and pamphleteering moralist. His books, White Collar, New Men of Power, *and* The Power Elite *had enormous impact upon a whole generation of students.*

Mills used the phrase "New Left" in "Letter to the New Left," published originally in the British New Left Review, *September–October 1960.* Studies on the Left *reprinted the article, retitled "On the New Left," in early 1961 (Vol. II, No. 1), and SDS later made it into a booklet. It has also appeared in several foreign periodicals.*

Mills' main emphasis in this and many other essays was on attacking liberalism and the old, "futilitarian," left. In this essay, as in so many others, Mills called for the young intellectuals to recognize themselves as the new agency of social change. His death in 1962 was a profound personal blow to many young radicals who had never known him except through his writings. The mark of their esteem for him can be found in the fact that several Movement babies have been named C. Wright.

It is no exaggeration to say that since the end of World War II, smug conservatives, tired liberals and disillusioned radicals in Britain and the United States have carried on a weary discourse in which issues are blurred and potential debate muted; the sickness of complacency has prevailed, the bipartisan banal-ity flourished. There is no need to explain again why all this has come about among "people in general" in the NATO countries;* but it may be worthwhile to examine one style of cultural work that is in effect an intellectual celebration of apathy.

Many intellectual fashions, of course, do just that; they stand in the way of a release of the imagination—about the Cold War, the Soviet bloc, the politics of peace, about any new beginnings at home and abroad. But the fashion I have in mind is the weariness of many NATO intellectuals with what they call "ideology," and their proclamation of "the end of ideology." So far as I know, this fashion began in the mid-fifties, mainly in intellectual circles more or less associated with the Congress for Cultural Freedom and the magazine *Encounter*. Reports on the Milan Conference of 1955 heralded it; since then, many cultural gossips have taken it up as a posture and an unexamined slogan. Does it amount to anything?

I

Its common denominator is not liberalism as a political philosophy, but the liberal rhetoric, become formal and sophisticated and used as an uncriticized weapon with which to attack Marxism. In the approved style, various elements of this rhetoric appear simply as snobbish assumptions. Its sophistication is one of tone rather than of ideas: in it, the *New Yorker* style of reportage has become politically triumphant. The disclosure of fact—set forth in a bright-faced or in a deadpan manner—is the rule. The facts are duly weighed, carefully balanced, always hedged. Their power to outrage, their power truly to enlighten in a political way, their power to aid decision, even their power to clarify some situation—all that is blunted or destroyed.

So reasoning collapses into reasonableness. By the more naïve and snobbish celebrants of complacency, arguments and facts of a displeasing kind are simply ignored; by the more knowing, they are duly recognized, but they are neither connected with one another nor related to any general view. Acknowledged in a scattered way, they are never put together: to do so is to risk being called, curiously enough, "one-sided."

* See, for example, E. P. Thompson, ed., *Out of Apathy* (London: Stevens and Son, 1960).

This refusal to relate isolated facts and fragmentary comment to the changing institutions of society makes it impossible to understand the structural realities which these facts might reveal or the longer-run trends of which they might be tokens. In brief, fact and idea are isolated, so the real questions are not even raised, analysis of the meanings of facts not even begun.

Practitioners of the no-more-ideology school do, of course, smuggle in general ideas under the guise of reportage, by intellectual gossip, and by their selection of the notions they handle. Ultimately, the-end-of-ideology is based upon a disillusionment with any real commitment to socialism in any recognizable form. *That* is the only "ideology" that has really ended for these writers. But with its ending, *all* ideology, they think, has ended. *That* ideology they talk about; their own ideological assumptions, they do not. Yet these assumptions, which they snobbishly take for granted, provide the terms of their rejection of "all ideology"; and upon these assumptions, they themselves stand.

Underneath this style of observation and comment there is the assumption that in the West there are no more real issues or even problems of great seriousness. The mixed economy plus the welfare state plus prosperity—that is the formula. U.S. capitalism will continue to be workable; the welfare state will continue along the road to ever greater justice. In the meantime, things everywhere are very complex; let us not be careless; there are great risks.

This posture—one of "false consciousness" if there ever was one—stands in the way, I think, of considering with any chances of success what may be happening in the world.

First and above all, this posture rests upon a simple provincialism. If the phrase "the end of ideology" has any meaning at all, it pertains to self-selected circles of intellectuals in the richer countries. It is in fact merely their own self-image. The total population of these countries is a fraction of mankind; the period during which such a posture has been assumed is very short indeed. To speak in such terms of much of Latin America, Africa, Asia, the Soviet bloc is merely ludicrous. Anyone who stands in front of audiences—intellectual or mass—in any of these places and talks in such terms will merely be shrugged off (if the audience is polite) or laughed at out loud (if the audi-

ence is more candid and knowledgeable). The end-of-ideology is
a slogan of complacency, circulating among the prematurely
middle-aged, centered in the present, and in the rich Western
societies. In the final analysis, it also rests upon a disbelief in the
shaping by men of their own futures—as history and as biogra-
phy. It is a consensus of a few provincials about their own immediate and provincial position.

Second, the end-of-ideology is of course itself an ideology—a
fragmentary one, to be sure, and perhaps more a mood. The end-
of-ideology is in reality the ideology of an ending: the ending of
political reflection itself as a public fact. It is a weary know-it-all
justification, by tone of voice rather than by explicit argument,
of the cultural and political default of the NATO intellectuals.

II

All this is just the sort of thing that I at least have always
objected to, and do object to, in the "socialist realism" of the
Soviet Union.

There too, criticisms of milieux are of course permitted, but
they are not to be connected with criticism of the structure itself: one may not question "the system." There are no "antagonistic contradictions."

There too, in novels and plays, criticisms of characters, even
of party members, are permitted, but they must be displayed as
"shocking exceptions"; they must be seen as survivals from the
old order, not as systematic products of the new.

There too, pessimism is permitted, but only episodically and
only within the context of the big optimism; the tendency is to
confuse any systematic or structural criticism with pessimism
itself. So they admit criticisms, first of this and then of that, but
engulf them all by the long-run historical optimism about the
system as a whole and the goals proclaimed by its leaders.

I neither want nor need to overstress the parallel, yet in a
recent series of interviews in the Soviet Union concerning socialist realism I was very much struck by it. In Uzbekistan and
Georgia, as well as in Russia, I kept writing notes to myself at
the end of recorded interviews: "This man talks in a style just
like Arthur Schlesinger, Jr." "Surely this fellow is the counter-
part of Daniel Bell, except not so—what shall I say?—so gos-

sipy; and certainly neither so petty nor so vulgar as the more envious status-climbers. Perhaps this is because here they are not thrown into such a competitive status-panic about the ancient and obfuscating British models of prestige." "The would-be enders of ideology," I kept thinking, "are they not the self-coordinated or, better, the fashion-coordinated, socialist realists of the NATO world?" And: "Check this carefully with the files of *Encounter* and *The Reporter*." I have now done so; it is the same kind of thing.

Certainly there are many differences: above all, the fact that socialist realism is part of an official line, while the end of ideology is self-managed. But the differences one knows. It is more useful to stress the parallels, and the generic fact that both of these postures stand opposed to radical criticisms of their respective societies.

In the Soviet Union, only political authorities at the top, or securely on their way up there, can seriously tamper with structural questions and ideological lines. These authorities, of course, are much more likely to be intellectuals (in one or another sense of the word—say a man who actually writes his own speeches) than are American politicians. Moreover, since the death of Stalin, such Soviet authorities *have* begun to tamper quite seriously with structural questions and basic ideology, although for reasons peculiar to the tight and official joining of culture and politics in their set-up, they must try to disguise this fact.

The end-of-ideology is very largely a mechanical reaction, not a creative response, to the ideology of Stalinism. As such it takes from its opponent something of its inner quality. What it all means is that these people have become aware of the uselessness of vulgar Marxism, but are not yet aware of the uselessness of the liberal rhetoric.

III

But the most immediately important thing about the "end of ideology" is that it *is* merely a fashion, and fashions change. Already this one is on its way out. Even a few diehard anti-Stalinists are showing signs of a reappraisal of their own past views; some are even beginning to recognize publicly that Stalin himself no longer runs the Soviet party and state. They begin to see the poverty of their comfortable ideas as they come to confront Khrushchev's Russia.

We who have been, in moral terms, consistently radical in our work throughout the postwar period are often amused nowadays that various writers, sensing another shift in fashion, are beginning to call upon intellectuals to work once more in ways that are politically explicit. But we should not be merely amused; we ought to try to make their shift more than a fashion change.

The end-of-ideology is on the decline because it stands for the refusal to work out an explicit political philosophy. And alert men everywhere today do feel the need for such a philosophy. What we should do is to continue directly to confront this need. In doing so, it may be useful to keep in mind that to have a working political philosophy means to have a philosophy that enables you to work, and that at least four kinds of work are needed, each of them at once intellectual and political.

In these terms, think for a moment longer of the end-of-ideology:

(1) It is a kindergarten fact that any political reflection that is of possible public significance is *ideological;* in its terms policies, institutions, and men of power are criticized or approved. In this respect, the end-of-ideology stands, negatively, for the attempt to withdraw oneself and one's work from political relevance; positively, it is an ideology of political complacency which seems the only way now open for many writers to acquiesce in or to justify the status quo.

(2) So far as orienting *theories* of society and of history are concerned, the end-of-ideology stands for, and presumably stands upon, a fetishism of empiricism: more academically, upon a pretentious methodology used to state trivialities about unimportant social areas; more essayistically, upon a naïve journalistic empiricism—which I have already characterized above —and upon a cultural gossip in which "answers" to the vital and pivotal issues are merely assumed. Thus political bias masquerades as epistomological excellence, and there are no orienting theories.

(3) So far as the *historic agency of change* is concerned, the end-of-ideology rests upon the identification of such agencies

with going institutions, perhaps upon their piecemeal reform, but never upon the search for agencies that might be used for, or that might themselves operate toward, a structural change of society. The problem of agency is never posed as a problem to solve, as "our problem." Instead there is endless talk of the need to be pragmatic, flexible, open. Surely all this has already been adequately dealt with: such a view makes sense politically only if the blind drift of human affairs is in general beneficent.

(4) So far as political and human *ideals* are concerned, the end-of-ideology stands for a denial of their relevance, except as abstract ikons. Merely to hold such ideals seriously is in this view "utopian."

IV

But enough. Where do *we* stand on each of these four aspects of political philosophy? Various of us are of course at work on each of them, and all of us are generally aware of our needs in regard to each. As for the articulation of ideals, there I think your magazines have done their best work so far.* That is *your* meaning—is it not?—of the emphasis upon cultural affairs. As for ideological analysis and the rhetoric with which to carry it out, I do not think any of us is nearly good enough. But that will come with further advance on the two fronts where we are weakest: theories of society, history, and human nature, and— the major problem—ideas about the historical agencies of structural change.

We have frequently been told by an assorted variety of dead-end people that the meanings of left and of right are now liquidated, by history and by reason. I think we should answer them in some such way as this:

The *Right,* among other things, means what you are doing: celebrating society as it is, a going concern. *Left* means, or ought to mean, just the opposite. It means structural criticism and reportage and theories of society, which at some point or another are focussed politically as demands and programs. These criticisms, demands, theories, programs are guided morally by the humanist and secular ideals of Western civilization—above all,

* This refers to *The New Left Review, The New Reasoner,* and *Universities & Left Review,* all of Great Britain.—Eds.

the ideals of reason, freedom and justice. To be "left" means to connect up cultural with political criticism, and both with demands and programs. And it means all this inside *every* country of the world.

Only one more point of definition: absence of public issues there may well be, but this is not due to any absence of problems or of contradictions, antagonistic and otherwise. Impersonal and structural changes have not eliminated problems or issues. Their absence from many discussions is an ideological condition, regulated in the first place by whether or not intellectuals detect and state problems as potential *issues* for probable publics, and as *troubles* for a variety of individuals. One indispensable means of such work on these central tasks is what can only be described as ideological analysis. To be actively left, among other things, is to carry on just such analysis.

To take seriously the problem of the need for a political orientation is not, of course, to seek for A Fanatical and Apocalyptic Vision, for An Infallible and Monolithic Lever of Change, for Dogmatic Ideology, for A Startling New Rhetoric, for Treacherous Abstractions, and all the other bogeymen of the dead-enders. These are, of course, "the extremes," the straw men, the red herrings used by our political enemies to characterize the polar opposite of where they think they stand.

They tell us, for example, that ordinary men cannot always be political "heroes." Who said they could? But keep looking around you; and why not search out the conditions of such heroism as men do and might display? They tell us that we are too "impatient," that our "pretentious" theories are not well enough grounded. That is true, but neither are our theories trivial. Why don't they get to work to refute or ground them? They tell us we "do not really understand" Russia and China today. That is true; we don't; neither do they. We at least are studying the question. They tell us we are "ominous" in our formulations. That is true: we do have enough imagination to be frightened, and we don't have to hide it. We are not afraid we'll panic. They tell us we are "grinding axes." Of course we are: we do have, among other points of view, morally grounded ones, and we are aware of them. They tell us, in their wisdom, that we do not understand that The Struggle is Without End. True: we want to change its form, its focus, its object.

We are frequently accused of being "utopian" in our criticisms and in our proposals and, along with this, of basing our hopes for a new left *politics* "merely on reason," or more concretely, upon the intelligentsia in its broadest sense.

There is truth in these charges. But must we not ask: What now is really meant by *utopian?* And is not our utopianism a major source of our strength? *Utopian* nowadays, I think, refers to any criticism or proposal that transcends the up-close milieux of a scatter of individuals, the milieux which men and women can understand directly and which they can reasonably hope directly to change. In this exact sense, our theoretical work is indeed utopian—in my own case, at least, deliberately so. What needs to be understood, and what needs to be changed, is not merely first this and then that detail of some institution or policy. If there is to be a politics of a new left, what needs to be analyzed is the *structure* of institutions, the *foundation* of policies. In this sense, both in its criticisms and in its proposals, our work is necesarily structural, and so—*for us,* just now—utopian.

This brings us face to face with the most important issue of political reflection and of political action in our time: the problem of the historical agency of change, of the social and institutional means of structural change. There are several points about this problem I would like to put to you.

v

First, the historic agencies of change for liberals of the capitalist societies have been an array of voluntary associations, coming to a political climax in a parliamentary or congressional system. For socialists of almost all varieties, the historic agency has been the working class—and later the peasantry, or parties and unions composed of members of the working class, or (to blur, for now, a great problem) of political parties acting in its name, "representing its interests."

I cannot avoid the view that both these forms of historic agency have either collapsed or become most ambiguous. So far as structural change is concerned, neither seems to be at once available and effective as *our* agency any more. I know this is a debatable point among us, and among many others as well; I am by no means certain about it. But surely, if it is true, it ought not to be taken as an excuse for moaning and withdrawal (as it is by some of those who have become involved with the end-of-ideology); and it ought not to be bypassed (as it is by many Soviet scholars and publicists, who in their reflections upon the course of advanced capitalist societies simply refuse to admit the political condition and attitudes of the working class).

Is anything more certain than that in 1970—indeed, at this time next year—our situation will be quite different, and—the chances are high—decisively so? But of course, that isn't saying much. The seeming collapse of our historic agencies of change ought to be taken as a problem, an issue, a trouble—in fact, as *the* political problem which *we* must turn into issue and trouble.

Second, it is obvious that when we talk about the collapse of agencies of change, we cannot seriously mean that such agencies do not exist. On the contrary, the means of history-making—of decision and of the enforcement of decision—have never in world history been so enlarged and so available to such small circles of men on both sides of The Curtains as they now are. My own conception of the shape of power, the theory of the power elite, I feel no need to argue here. This theory has been fortunate in its critics, from the most diverse political viewpoints, and I have learned from several of these critics. But I have not seen, as of this date, an analysis of the idea that causes me to modify any of its essential features.

The point that is immediately relevant does seem obvious: what is utopian for us, is not at all utopian for the presidium of the Central Committee in Moscow, or the higher circles of the Presidency in Washington, or, recent events make evident, for the men of SAC and CIA. The historic agencies of change that have collapsed are those which were at least thought to be open to *the left* inside the advanced Western nations, to those who have wished for structural changes of these societies. Many things follow from this obvious fact; of many of them, I am sure, we are not yet adequately aware.

Third, what I do not quite understand about some new-left

writers is why they cling so mightily to "the working class" of
the advanced capitalist societies as *the* historic agency, or even
as the most important agency, in the face of the really impressive historical evidence that now stands against this expectation.

Such a labor metaphysic, I think, is a legacy from Victorian
Marxism that is now quite unrealistic.

It is an historically specific idea that has been turned into an
historical and unspecific hope.

The social and historical conditions under which industrial
workers tend to become a-class-for-themselves, and a decisive
political force, must be fully and precisely elaborated. There
have been, there are, there will be such conditions. These conditions vary according to national social structure and the exact
phase of their economic and political development. Of course
we cannot "write off the working class." But we must *study* all
that, and freshly. Where labor exists as an agency, of course we
must work with it, but we must not treat it as The Necessary
Lever, as nice old Labour Gentlemen in Britain and elsewhere
tend to do.

Although I have not yet completed my own comparative
studies of working classes, generally it would seem that only at
certain (earlier) stages of industrialization, and in a political
context of autocracy, *etc.,* do wage-workers tend to become a-
class-for-themselves, *etc.* The *etceteras* mean that I can here
merely raise the question.

VI

It is with this problem of agency in mind that I have been
studying, for several years now, the cultural apparatus, the intellectuals, as a possible, immediate, radical agency of change. For
a long time, I was not much happier with this idea than were
many of you; but it turns out now, at the beginning of the 1960s,
that it may be a very relevant idea indeed.

In the first place, is it not clear that if we try to be realistic in
our utopianism—and that is no fruitless contradiction—a writer
in our countries on the left today *must* begin with the intellectuals? For that is what we are, that is where we stand.

In the second place, the problem of the intelligentsia is an
extremely complicated set of problems on which rather little fac-

tual work has been done. In doing this work, we must, above all, not confuse the problems of the intellectuals of West Europe and North America with those of the Soviet bloc or with those of the underdeveloped worlds. In each of the three major components of the world's social structure today, the character and the role of the intelligentsia is distinct and historically specific. Only by detailed comparative studies of them in all their human variety can we hope to understand any one of them.

In the third place, who is it that is getting fed up? Who is it that is getting disgusted with what Marx called "all the old crap?" Who is it that is thinking and acting in radical ways? All over the world—in the bloc, outside the bloc and in between— the answer is the same: it is the young intelligentsia.

I cannot resist copying out for you, with a few changes, some materials I recently prepared for a 1960 paperback edition of a book of mine on war:

"In the spring and early summer of 1960, more of the returns from the American decision and default are coming in. In Turkey, after student riots, a military junta takes over the state, of late run by Communist Container Menderes. In South Korea, too, students and others knock over the corrupt American-puppet regime of Syngman Rhee. In Cuba, a genuinely left-wing revolution begins full-scale economic reorganization, without the domination of U.S. corporations. Average age of its leaders: about 30—and certainly a revolution without Labor As Agency. On Taiwan, the eight million Taiwanese under the American-imposed dictatorship of Chiang Kai-shek, with his two million Chinese, grow increasingly restive. On Okinawa, a U.S. military base, the people get their first chance since World War II ended to demonstrate against U.S. seizure of their island; and some students take that chance, snake-dancing and chanting angrily to the visiting President: 'Go home, go home—take away your missiles.' (Don't worry, 12,000 U.S. troops easily handle the generally grateful crowds; also the President is 'spirited out the rear end of the United States compound'—and so by helicopter to the airport.) In Japan, weeks of student rioting succeed in rejecting the President's visit, jeopardizing a new treaty with the U.S.A., and displacing the big-business, pro-American Prime Minister, Kishi. And even in our own pleasant Southland, Negro and white students are—but let us keep that quiet: it really *is* disgraceful.

"That is by no means the complete list; that was yesterday; see today's newspaper. Tomorrow, in varying degree, the returns will be more evident. Will they be evident enough? They will have to be very obvious to attract real American attention: sweet complaints and the voice of reason—these are not enough. In the slum countries of the world today, what are they saying? The rich Americans, they pay attention only to violence —and to money. You don't care what they say, American? Good for you. Still, they may insist; things are no longer under the old control; you're not getting it straight, American: your country—it would seem—may well become the target of a world hatred the like of which the easy-going Americans have never dreamed. Neutralists and Pacifists and Unilateralists and that confusing variety of Leftists around the world—all those tens of millions of people, of course they are misguided, absolutely controlled by small conspiratorial groups of trouble-makers, under direct orders from Moscow and Peking. Diabolically omnipotent, it is *they* who create all this messy unrest. It is *they* who have given the tens of millions the absurd idea that they shouldn't want to remain, or to become, the seat of American nuclear bases—those gay little outposts of American civilization. So now they don't want U-2's on their territory; so now they want to contract out of the American military machine; they want to be neutral among the crazy big antagonists. And they don't want their own societies to be militarized.

"But take heart, American: you won't have time to get really bored with your friends abroad: they won't be your friends much longer. You don't need *them;* it will all go away; don't let them confuse you."

Add to that: In the Soviet bloc, who is it that has been breaking out of apathy? It has been students and young professors and writers; it has been the young intelligentsia of Poland and Hungary, and of Russia, too. Never mind that they have not won; never mind that there are other social and moral types among them. First of all, it has been these types. But the point is clear, isn't it?

That is why we have got to study these new generations of

intellectuals around the world as real live agencies of historic change. Forget Victorian Marxism, except when you need it; and read Lenin again (be careful)—Rosa Luxemburg, too.

"But it is just some kind of moral upsurge, isn't it?" Correct. But under it: no apathy. Much of it is direct non-violent action, and it seems to be working, here and there. Now we must learn from the practice of these young intellectuals and with them work out new forms of action.

"But it's all so ambiguous—Cuba, for instance." Of course it is; history-making is always ambiguous. Wait a bit; in the meantime, help them to focus their moral upsurge in less ambiguous political ways. Work out with them the ideologies, the strategies, the theories that will help them consolidate their efforts: new theories of structural changes of and by human societies in our epoch.

"But it is utopian, after all, isn't it?" No, not in the sense you mean. Whatever else it may be, it's not that. Tell it to the students of Japan. Tell it to the Negro sit-ins. Tell it to the Cuban Revolutionaries. Tell it to the people of the hungry-nation bloc.

SNCC—One Man, One Vote

1. Poems

Jane Stembridge is a white Southerner in her twenties who has been with SNCC from its founding convention in Raleigh, North Carolina, in 1960 through the present. She is SNCC's poet, one of the poets in the South whose talent might have remained hidden if not for SNCC.

There is nothing "beat" or "hip" about Miss Stembridge's poems, nor about most of the other SNCC poems. Walt Whitman's tradition, rather than William Carlos Williams', is the American grain of SNCC poetry.

I

The world is coming to a head
when dread of holding hands
puts rubber bands in peoples brains
and smoky rains in babies milk
and fuschia silk in contour sheets
when screaming streets
are swallowing

the nameless shapes
the country rapes
while tickertapes
are telling
widows

when to jump
and all our bridges
are becoming known as

diving
boards

The faceless hoards are dropping dead
beneath the tread of talking tanks
whose silent banks can stay at home
beneath the dome of self defense
where sense is smashed
and bodies mashed
against

cathedral doors
where gangrene pours
from bursting sores
and floods the floors
and roars in torrents

on the land
whose hateful brand
is heated hot
to rot

the human
flesh

America
is murdering the world

II

Socrates saw Jesus twice,
but not to talk to him.

The brothers of
the bottoms up, they memorize

the bloody cup
and take it down alone

as men decide
to kill themselves
for something big they saw

which spun
and smiled

at
them.

Worlds start over then.

Buddhist monks
are keeping on
the clothes they set to fire

the streets, their pyre
they kneel to pray

God give
a gentler world

while soldiers pass
Christian soldiers pass.

III. About towns like Van Cleve which isnt on a Standard Oil Filling Station Map

Van Cleve isnt on a Standard Oil Filling Station Map
because nobody goes to Van Cleve

and the reason that nobody goes to Van Cleve
is because there's no money there

just houses and trees and gardens
and fields and children and
puppies and rivers and
a great deal of
silence

for singing and
birds

and rabbits and
rabbits and

squirrels and pigs
and redbirds and
bluebirds
all in
one

house
and a
mouse

and a
Indian chief

who is hiding
from beads

but no
doctor

no
lawyer
no judge and no thief

just a Indian chief
who is just like the rest of the people there and they say

nobody asked them
whether they wanted

to go to Vietnam
and kill people

with
poison gas

The people in Van Cleve are crazy.
It isnt even on the map.
(please dont tell)

IV

There's not a high green hill
where lovers lay

belongs to them
they think it does

climbing up planting flags
of flowers

saying
here

but
in the shadows

of the bloody
flag

flowers cannot breathe
as deep and die and I

the sole
ambassador

to hills

bring heavy messages
to tell them that
America

is
mean

2. SNCC Documents

   SNCC's internal communication system consists of conversations between staffers, some of them often traveling across the country to talk to others, and letters, field reports, memos, and impression pieces. We reproduce a few of these to give some

*idea of how The Movement works, and how and in what style it
communicates to its members.*

James Forman, John Lewis, Stokely Carmichael, Julian
Bond, and many others have been in the SNCC leadership because they were able to win the respect of the other organizers
and, more important, of the Negro people. But Robert (Moses)
Parris was, more than any other SNCC leader, the inspiration
for thousands of students and poor people now in The Movement. He resigned from SNCC in 1965, partly because he was
afraid that a cult was developing around him, and this was
against his principles. He even changed his name from Moses to
Parris to put an end to this adoration. Although the division is
somewhat artificial, it might be useful to think of Moses-Parris
as the poet-visionary, which does not mean he lacks tactical or
common sense; rather, he is a utopian thinker who touches deep
nerves and emotions in other people.

The first of the following two documents is a speech about
fear given by Bob Moses at SNCC's fifth anniversary; the second
is some remarks about nonviolence by Moses and SNCC worker
Dennis Sweeney in January 1965.

I. "Questions Raised by Moses" *

(TRANSCRIPT OF THE TALK GIVEN BY BOB MOSES
AT THE 5TH ANNIVERSARY OF SNCC)

What you should suppose about SNCC people is that they are
not fearless. You'd have a better idea about them if you would
suppose that they were very afraid and suppose that they were
very afraid of the people in the South that they have to fight and
struggle against. And suppose also that they are very afraid of
this country. But suppose, then, that they had no choice, that is
they can, through many different ways, see that their backs, so
to speak, were against the wall and they had to move within that
fear. And then suppose that what they are trying to do is explore
how to move within the boundaries of fear and that what they've

* *Movement* [the SNCC California newspaper], April 1965.

got to learn about fear is that it paralyzes you so that you don't
move—you don't do what you think you should, be it ask a
question or take a person down to register. And suppose also
about the Mississippi people that they're not heroes and that
we're not heroes, that we're trying very hard to be people and
that is very hard. If anything, what we're trying to do, or have to
do, is to see how you can move even though you are afraid.

I have just one thing that I would like to share with you. It's a
question, it's a problem, that our country faces tangled up with
thousands of other problems. We suppose that the people who
murdered Mickey and Andrew and James were not like us, not
like most people in the country. And I think that that's a deep
mistake, that we don't understand the implication of that.
People keep asking me, "Do you think that they will get convicted?" and I keep saying, "No." But I also wonder why they
keep asking because if you think about that, it seems that our
experience will tell us that they cannot be convicted, that they
will not be convicted, that the chance of their being convicted is
almost zero. For them to be convicted would be for society to
condemn itself and that's very hard for society to do, any society. Condemnation seems to have to come from outside or from
the ranks within that are not a part of it.

So the jury that votes together to decide whether or not the
people, the eighteen or twenty-one people who evidently got together and sat down and then planned and then got up and then
murdered, that jury is like them. That's a hard thing to understand in this country.

The only place where they can be tried for murder is by a
jury, a local jury, called together in Neshoba County. They're
being tried now, not for murder, but for depriving people of
their civil rights in the act of murdering them. That's the actual
charge. People don't understand that.

That jury, that local jury, if you called it together, would presumably be the murderers' jury because the juries in the counties
in the South are called together under the auspices of the sheriffs
and the sheriff is presumably one of the persons indicted for the
conspiracy to murder. I am fascinated with that. It's a very, very
clear kind of thing. Suppose the sheriff killed somebody; then to
have his trial, he calls the jury together. So you have the mur-

derer's jury. And the problem seems to me to be, how can a society condemn itself?

I think that that question is a question for the country in this sense. The country refuses to look at Mississippi, and at the white people down there, as like them. So, therefore, they miss the main point, it seems to me, about the Deep South and about the people there and, also, about ourselves.

Life magazine had a picture of the people who did the murder and they pictured them eating and laughing and joking and talking as though they were morally idiots. And I think most people in the country reading that got that impression. But you don't put yourself in that classification so they're other people— they're not like you or like us. The *Saturday Evening Post* had a picture of a Ku Klux Klan on the front page just recently and at the end of the article talked about them as outcasts, as people who are in no way like most Americans, as rejects from the society. I think that's a false interpretation which people are getting and, therefore, they analyze the problem wrongly and, therefore, they look for wrong solutions.

The problem is so deep, all you can do is raise these questions. We feel that if we're going to get to the bottom, if we're going to go down there and try and create anything new, then we have to do this because it seems that right within our country you have that problem where everybody can focus on it and say what are the conditions which create a society in which people sit down and plan and kill and then pat themselves on the back as patriots. Because they're defending their liberties and what they hold most dear and their civilization?

That, it seems to me, is the point about us as a country where we are with the bomb and what we do in terms of Vietnam. We are not over there killing people primarily but defending liberty and defending our concept of what is democracy, civilization and so forth. There's no forum to raise those questions.

I raise them because I don't think we're going to escape that easily, because they're going on killing in Mississippi. At the same time that everyone knows about the three who were killed and the people who are on trial for that, no one asks about the two Negro boys whose bodies were severed in half, who were found while they were looking for the other three, because nobody knows about them. And nobody asks why did that grand jury let those people off who were indicted for that crime, on the same day that they indicted the people who were supposed to have killed the other three. And nobody asks because, again, nobody knows about it.

I have one other thing that I'd like to share. What we have begun to learn and are trying to explore about people is how they can come together in groups, small groups and large groups, and talk to each other and make decisions about basic things, about their lives. I think that that has application everywhere in the country. Whatever we currently mean by democracy, we don't mean that people should come together, discuss their main problems that they all know about and be able to do something about themselves. That was what the Free Speech Movement meant, as I understand it, as it unfolded in part.

One problem with people who might want to try to do this, say in S. F. or anyplace, is that they would first think that in order to go to people and get them together, they would have to have something for them to talk about. So they would have to have a program to carry to them or they would have to have something to organize them around. But it doesn't turn out to be true, from our experience. You could in the North, in the ghettos, get together ten or twenty people and out of their getting together and giving them a chance to talk about their main problems would come some programs, that they themselves decided on, that they thought about. If that happened and began to happen around the country, that would be the key to spreading some of the things that have happened in the South to the rest of the country. That not only goes for poor people but for the professional people as well. The last meeting where I was, where I was partially hooted down, was at a doctors' Medicare. The concept that doctors should discuss Medicare, pro and con, in their meetings seems to be alien to democracy.

II. "Nonviolence in the Ghetto" †

IN JANUARY OF THIS YEAR, CIVIL RIGHTS WORKERS BOB PARRIS AND DENNIS SWEENEY WERE ASKED SOME QUESTIONS ABOUT

† *Movement,* September 1965.

NONVIOLENCE AND THE GHETTO. THEIR ANSWERS, REPRINTED
HERE, DIRECTLY BEAR ON THE POSSIBILITY OF VIOLENCE IN
MANY NORTHERN CITIES.

What are the chances of violence by Negroes in the South?

BOB PARRIS   Where you will get organized terror will be in the
North in the big cities, because when you look at it those
are our jungles. It's in the ghettos in the North where the Negroes have room to hide so one can run out and bomb and
run back. It's very hard for them to do that in the South.
They're more exposed.

In Talahatchee County last winter a Negro shot a policeman. The policeman was messing with him and he shot him.
Now he went home, and immediately they organized a vigilante group, maybe a hundred people or more. They had machine guns, rifles, automatics. . . . They went to this guy's
house and they shot it up plank by plank and they dismem-
bered him. They started at the bottom plank and they went all
the way up. You have to ask yourself, "What happens to Negroes who know what would happen to a Negro who considers
arming himself to do violence against whites?"

We've come close to rioting in the South, but we don't have
as yet the same conditions that exist in Northern cities that
would lead to that kind of violence.

I think here you get into the basic question of nonviolence:
Is it possible to build some sense of community that moves in
such a way as to attack the people who are oppressing them
so that they don't have to resort to rioting, which is despair to
them. Nonviolence is the building of community. You try to
get together groups of people who can move with some sense
of meaning and do something about their lives.

I was talking to people last night about some gangs in San
Francisco. What's the approach to them? Do they form a kind
of community? It's a community organized around more or
less senseless violence; it ends in, I think, their own destruction. What's going to happen to them? It seems to me that the
program which society has for them is really a program of violence, because that's where it leads. In the end, the program of
the social worker, where he takes two or three of them and

tries to put them in jobs is meaningless; they can't all get jobs, and they're back in the streets soon.

In the end, say four, five years from now the harvest of that is violence; riots and everything, because they don't have anything and they don't get anything from that program.

The nonviolent program, it seems to me, for that group would be not to break them up, but to find some way to keep them together, to find some way to get them to attack the institutions that have them in that box.

What do you think about organizations for self-defense?

Organizing self-defense societies is a negative way of organizing community. What you want is to organize the community around things they can do to change their lives.

DENNIS SWEENEY   You have to look at the kinds of people who organize for self-defense. Take for instance the people in McComb who came to us this summer when we first got there and said "One shot in the air and you'll have fifty guns at your house immediately."

They were organized to protect themselves and after the bombs started going off they became even better organized. But these people who stand watch at night (not the ones who stand watch in their homes; just about everybody in McComb this summer and fall was staying up all night watching out the window), I'm talking about the organized people—these are not the people who would come to FDP Precinct meetings. They're not the people who send their children to Freedom Schools. They're not the people who come to meetings where we organize community centers. They're not the people who will go down to the courthouse. It's much easier for some of these people, and this is a very difficult thing to understand, to carry a gun and say they'll shoot a white man; but it's very difficult for them to overcome the fear of going down to the courthouse and trying to register.

BOB PARRIS   There's a distinction to be made between a city situation, like Dennis is describing, and a rural area. In the rural areas the people who are in the struggle are also the people who organize for self-defense.

III

MEMO: TO ALL DRIVERS!!! . . . AND THE
              NON-DRIVERS TOO.
FROM: THE FINANCE COMMITTEE
RE: CARS & $$$$

By January 25th, we have to pay the balance on our insurance premium—over $15,000 (enough to pay salaries for a two-week period). The total cost of insurance at this point is $30,000 (one month's payroll) and the figure moves up an additional $440 each time a car is added—plus $50 for each additional driver.

You might wonder why we pay such a "ridiculously high rate for insurance." The answer is simple and factual. Most of our drivers are: under age, careless, reckless, irresponsible, or indifferent. During an eight-week period from the middle of November until early January we spent over $5,000 out of the Atlanta office for car repairs (enough money to purchase two new cars). I specify the Atlanta office since I know that some projects have spent funds on car repairs that have not been reimbursed; thus, $5,000 is not an accurate figure for all money spent on car repairs for that period. However, using that figure as an example of our waste, let's evaluate exactly what the money was used for.

About ten of the 1964 Plymouths were driven in to Bill Speros in need of over $100 of work. In all cases, it is interesting to note that most of the repair bill was for labor rather than parts. (Oh well!). . . .

Brothers and Sisters . . . THAT DAY HAS ENDED. Houston Howard is now handling transportation in Mississippi. He is based in Jackson. Presently he is engaged in contacting specific body shops and garages through the state (also authorized Plymouth dealers) for Sojourner cars. These dealers will be the only authorized dealers for Sojourner Motor Fleet—dig! In addition, there will be two mechanics working in Jackson and one at this point, in the 5th District, as soon as we buy them some tools, who will be available to survey damages and make recommendation as to what course should be followed to repair them. This will mean a considerable savings in reference to the old cars at least since much too much money is spent on labor for those "heaps of junk." Those that can be reasonably repaired—so be it. Those that cannot be REASONABLY REPAIRED ($100 or less for good running condition) will be sold or junked. . . .

A NOTE ABOUT WHEN TO DRIVE: The last two near-fatal accidents in which we were involved happened as a result of weak, tired drivers who really should have been sleeping (or resting) and not driving. We can't change the past but we can be sensitive and sensible in the future. The chance of loosing a life is not worth taking. . . .

IV. Why People Become Corrupt

March 28, 1965

First of all, you have to figure out what you are working for. It's not enough to know what you're against—like I'm fighting segregation, or the system, or the power structure. In order to get the kind of world you want—a world without segregation and violence and misery—you have to know what you are for. What I think we are all working toward is people having enough to eat and wear, and enough room to live in comfortably, and being able to do the things that they enjoy and not being afraid of getting punished for expressing themselves. I think that's what The Movement is all about when you come down to it. Things like seeing that people have money or jobs or economic or political power are not basically what we're working for. If it were possible for people to get enough to eat and wear and for them to do what they enjoyed, *without* their getting money or economic or political power, that would be fine. Because money and economic and political power are only one means to an end, and the end is what really counts.

It seems to most people who are trying to bring about change (like civil rights workers) that the only way you can get a better life for people is by getting them more jobs and more money. And the only way to obtain money and jobs is by getting political power. Since the power in this country is held by a power structure consisting of President Johnson and the Democratic Party, and behind them the big corporations, it seems like the only way to get what people need is to get control of the power structure, so as to put some of the control over economic and political matters into your own hands.

So some people who are trying to change things end up working very hard at doing what will make them accepted by the power structure. They talk about dressing respectably and worry about Red-baiting; they try to get into the Democratic Party; they decide on courses of action, like demonstrating (or not demonstrating) on the basis of whether that action is "politically necessary"; and they urge compromise with the power structure, like accepting the two seats at Atlantic City. Of course, such a person has become corrupted. In trying to become part of the power structure, he is forced to lose his militancy; he forgets the people he should be fighting for. He has been taken over by the system.

Other people who are trying to bring about change talk as though they are completely opposed to the system. They prove to you how corrupt and brutal it really is ("Life with Lyndon" is a great example of this); they say that since the power structure is so immoral, what we should do to get power is to be sneaky and underhanded ourselves; they say that since the power structure works like an efficient and ruthless machine, we must be efficient and disciplined and ruthless ourselves in order to get power; they, too, base their actions on what is "politically necessary."

This second person probably sounds quite different from the first, because the first seeks to gain power by being accepted into the power structure, the other by fighting the power structure and taking its power away. However, both have a number of very important things in common. They both want to take over the power structure. This means that they are both forced to base their actions, not on what the people they represent want, but on the nature of the power structure itself. And they both end up becoming like the system they oppose, although in different ways.

It is easy to see that the first person is wrong. It is harder to understand how the second person is wrong, but I will try to explain why I think he has fallen into the same trap the first has.

Back at the beginning, I asked what we were working for, and I suggested that economic and political power were only means to an end. They are not necessarily the only way you can bring about a world in which people are free to enjoy themselves. In fact, the present system is based on money and power, and we know all about the misery and cruelty which is a result of that system. But the fact is, the second person is trying to take over a system he knows is bad, using the very means which make it so awful.

Where he has gone wrong is that in his own thinking and acting he has not gone beyond the way things are now. The system says that money and power are important and that you have to be ruthless and efficient to get them; so he is ruthless and efficient to get hold of money and power. Just like the compromiser, he has forgotten the *people* he is working for, and their basic desires. Instead, he lets the values and structure of the *system* determine what he does. He cannot bring about any changes in the way things are, because instead of working to build something new, he is all caught up in *reacting* to the system. He, too, has been taken over by the system.

I am going to write another paper later, explaining what I think we should be doing—how we have to act in terms of *what we want,* which is free people building their own lives, instead of being forced to react to the system we are stuck with now.

—*Barbara Brandt*

V. Letter from an Americus Jail

ABOUT ORGANIZING

I have found that it's better to go into a community if you are planning on staying for a while, and first getting to know people and letting people get to know you. Now you can become known and get to know people in many ways. You can first start by going to the churches, cafés, school dances, community club meetings, if there are such. And at all of these, whatever you go to, you should talk to people, and try to get them to either let you come around to their homes or you ask them to yours.

If you are young, like most of us are, then you must be careful about how you go about talking to older people. The best way to get to the older people is to have something to offer. If you have ever been in the field, often it is found that older people like to talk about jobs, bad streets, no street lights, bad housing, and how the white school is so much better than their own. People talk about these because most of the time they don't know enough about any of the other things that affect them to talk about them. So the thing for you to do is to kind of ask questions and answer them at the same time. To do this will, or would, give people other things to think about.

After you have made yourself known you are then able to ask things of the people. You can ask them why they are living in such a bad house and get an answer without offending the person whom you are talking to. But without being known you just can't talk truthfully with a man or woman who only makes $10 a week in Miss Ann's kitchen, or who toms for Mr. Charles for $25 or $30 a week, and look for an answer. I have found that now they will tell why they don't do anything or go along with the things The Movement does. I find mostly people will say that M. L. King won't give me a job when I lose the one I have, nor will he give me any food for my hungry children. So I am going to keep away from them Movement people like my boss told me, because she is the one who is going to help me.

What I will say is that the first thing you do when you go into a community is to get to know as many people as you can, not as a leader or anything of that kind, but as a person tired of living in bad houses on bad streets without lights, no place for your child to go after school, and not a very good school.

I don't think you should worry about making contact when you go into a community, because if you do the things I have stated heretofore then you have made your contacts. Also, by this time you should know who the key people are, whatever that means. Maybe I should ask what kind of people are considered as key people. Then maybe I could speak to that. I don't know how to get people into a leadership position. But there are ways, I know. Sometimes you just kind of force them one way or another by asking them to do little things, whatever may be the situation where you are or maybe where he's working. All people are not the same; it takes more to get some people going than others.

But to me there is something in your letter of which I have read, that has some real meaning to me. And that is how do you overcome fear, apathy, and suspicion—not only in the hard-core areas, but everywhere there is a movement under way. I don't believe anyone knows how to overcome these. One can only say what he or she feels is the best way to overcome fear, apathy, suspicion.

Before I say what I feel, I would like to go back to what Sherrod would say when he asked people to go down in a march or sit-in. He would look at you a while, then slowly he would say, "If you can free a person's mind, then he or she is able to think." In so many words he would say if you can give a blind man 20-20 vision, then he will be able to see when he comes to a corner. How do you free one mind? In my own mind I would say somewhat in the same way you overcome apathy, fear, and suspicion.

But there is just one thing that I worry about most; and that is fear; for I believe if you can overcome fear then all of the others you can easily overcome. There are many ways to overcome fear, and for some people a few or one of the ways will help them to overcome fear. And for others it may take all of them. The way to overcome fear could be for some people registering to vote, or going downtown in a march or sit-in, or going to the police station to go someone's bond.

—Randy Battle

VI. Notes About a Class Held by Stokely Carmichael

WAVELAND, MISSISSIPPI, WORK-STUDY INSTITUTE,
FEBRUARY–MARCH 1965

The most important class was "Stokely's speech class." He put eight sentences on the blackboard, with a line between, like this:

I digs wine	I enjoy drinking cocktails
The peoples wants freedom	The people want freedom

Whereinsoever the police-mens goes they causes troubles	Anywhere the officers of the law go, they cause trouble
I wants to reddish to vote	I want to register to vote

STOKELY   What do you think about these sentences? Such as— The peoples wants freedom?

ZELMA   It doesn't sound right.

STOKELY   What do you mean?

ZELMA   "Peoples" isn't right.

STOKELY   Does it mean anything?

MILTON   People means everybody. Peoples means everybody in the world.

ALMA   Both sentences are right as long as you understand them.

HENRY   They're both okay, but in a speech class you have to use correct English.

(*Stokely writes "correct English" in corner of blackboard*)

ZELMA   I was taught at least to use the sentences on the rights side.

STOKELY   Does anybody you know use the sentences on the left?

CLASS   Yes.

STOKELY   Are they wrong?

ZELMA   In terms of English, they are wrong.

STOKELY   Who decides what is correct English and what is incorrect English?

MILTON   People made rules. People in England, I guess.

STOKELY   You all say some people speak like on the left side of the board. Could they go anywhere and speak that way? Could they go to Harvard?

CLASS   Yes . . . No. Disagreement.

STOKELY   Does Mr. Turnbow speak like on the left side?

CLASS   Yes.

STOKELY   Could Mr. Turnbow go to Harvard and speak like that? "I wants to reddish to vote."

CLASS   Yes.

STOKELY   Would he be embarrassed?

CLASS   Yes . . . No!

ZELMA   He wouldn't be, but I would. It doesn't sound right.

STOKELY   Suppose someone from Harvard came to Holmes County and said, "I want to register to vote?" Would they be embarrassed?

ZELMA   No.

STOKELY   Is it embarrassing at Harvard but not in Holmes County? The way you speak?

MILTON   It's inherited. It's depending on where you come from. The people at Harvard would understand.

STOKELY   Do you think the people at Harvard should forgive you?

MILTON   The people at Harvard should help teach us correct English.

ALMA   Why should we change if we understand what we mean?

SHIRLEY   It is embarrassing.

STOKELY   Which way do most people talk?

CLASS   Like on the left.

(*He asks each student. All but two say "left." One says that Southerners speak like on the left, Northerners on the right. Another says that Southerners speak on the left, but the majority of people speak like on the right*)

STOKELY   Which way do television and radio people speak?

CLASS   Left.

(*There was a distinction made by the class between Northern commentators and local programs. Most programs were local and spoke like on the left, they said*)

STOKELY   Which way do teachers speak?

CLASS   On the left, except in class.

STOKELY   If most people speak on the left, why are they trying to change these people?

GLADYS   If you don't talk right, society rejects you. It embarrasses other people if you don't talk right.

HANK   But Mississippi society, ours, isn't embarrassed by it.

SHIRLEY   But the middle class wouldn't class us with them.

HANK   They won't accept "reddish." What is reddish? It's Negro dialect and it's something you eat.

STOKELY   Will society reject you if you don't speak like on the right side of the board? Gladys said society would reject you.

GLADYS   You might as well face it, man! What we gotta do is go out and become middle class. If you can't speak good English, you don't have a car, a job, or anything.

STOKELY   If society rejects you because you don't speak good English, should you learn to speak good English?

CLASS   No!

ALMA   I'm tired of doing what society say. Let society say "reddish" for a while. People ought to just accept each other.

ZELMA   I think we should be speaking just like we always have.

ALMA   If I change for society, I wouldn't be free anyway.

ERNESTINE   I'd like to learn correct English for my own sake.

SHIRLEY   I would too.

ALMA   If the majority speaks on the left, then a minority must

rule society? Why do we have to change to be accepted by the
minority group?
(*Lunchtime*)

STOKELY   Let's think about two questions for next time: What
is society? Who makes the rules for society?

The class lasted a little more than an hour. It moved very
quickly. It was very good. That is, people learned. I think they
learned because:
—people learn from someone they trust, who trusts them. This
   trust included Stokely's self-trust and trust, or seriousness,
   about the subject matter;
—people learn more, and more quickly, from induction rather
   than deduction;
—people learn when they themselves can make the connection
   between ideas; can move from here to here to here to there;
—people learn when learning situations emphasize and develop
   one single idea, which is very important to them personally;
—people learn when they can see what they are talking about.
   Stokely used the board.
   Among other things . . . they themselves concluded:
—there is something called "correct English" and something
   called "incorrect English";
—most people in the country use some form of incorrect or
   broken English;
—it is not embarrassing to these people themselves;
—it is made embarrassing by other people
   because it is embarrassing to them;
—they are a minority, the people who use correct English;
—they decide what is correct English;
—they make that important and use it to shame people and keep
   them out of society;
—they make that a requirement for jobs and acceptance;
—they decide who is acceptable to society
   by shame
   but not everybody can be shamed
   not Mr. Turnbow, for example;

—the main thing is to understand what people mean when they
talk;
—that is not the main thing to society;

I recorded the whole class because it is a whole thing—one
thing. That is why people learned. At least, that is why I learned.

I think the best way to write about Waveland is to tell about
that class, because that was what the Waveland Institute was
about. Some other classes were good and some were bad. Vicki
Levy and Phyllis Cunningham came and we all talked about sex.
That was good because what we talked about was important and
Vicki was free to talk about it freely, as was most of the class.
No one seemed to assume that sex was anything but great!
Hurray! Jeanette's class was good when the kids got to talk
freely about the Atlanta staff meeting and they had plenty that
needed to get out . . . and needs to be heard. My class was
good because I talked about myself and my hang-ups, which
made them able to do that—or begin to. About shame. About
fear of shame. About guilt. Morty's class in math was good, I
hear, because he is very dynamic and because the kids were tired
of words by that time. Carole Merritt was good when she talked,
but she had to handle administration and, in the case of guest
speakers, retreat. She should teach.

Audio-visual was good because it is better to see things. The
kids didn't like to see films about poverty and hunger. They
liked story movies. They liked Casey and Mary and Emmie's
filmstrip on F.P. I liked *Viva Zapata*. So did they.

The opposite of Stokely's class was Zinn's. He started with
three words on the board: Freedom, Education, Power. It took
a long time to kind of start over with specifics. He also had way
too much material and lectured too much. He had a lot to give
and he wanted to, but he wasted himself. I did that, too. We
didn't know. I think we learned a lot.

I don't want to make conclusions or proposals. I think
Stokely's class can stand on its own. Not only that, I think it is
better than anything I could say. Just two things: he spoke to
where they were at, and they were at different places, and the
places changed during the movement of the discussion. Sec-

ondly, he trusted them and he trusted himself . . . and they trusted him.

I think the primary hang-up was not the staff's lack of knowledge or concern, but the lack of freedom to put it across. Self-trust. Self-love or something like that. I think we have to be pretty damn free to teach anyway. Or to learn?

—Jane Stembridge

VII. Notes on Organizing

Since I am under the impression that SNCC workers are organizers, I think that this is what they should do.

A SNCC worker should never take a leadership role in the community unless he is in his own community. A SNCC worker should give the responsibility of leadership to the community person or persons whom he has or is building. The SNCC worker should give form and guidance to the people's organization, and/or their programs.

I think that in each area one faces different kinds of problems. I've attempted to state some of the problems found in small communities such as Ruleville and Indianola, Miss.

The larger, more middle-class communities will be somewhat different.

I think you at first meet the people on their own terms, or you lose.

ENTERING THE COMMUNITY

There are two ways to enter a community: the *invited* and the *uninvited* way.

The *invited* is the easiest, because you know that somebody wants you. Somebody will put you up for a while, and through this person or persons, you will meet others.

An invited person goes to live with X person in Y community, Mr. X carries the person to church on Sunday. He introduces him to his friends and neighbors. You are there to do a job which at this time is undefined; so you act friendly, smiling and greeting the ladies as they approach you. Then, with your warm, friendly face you say to the people: "I want to do something for this community." That afternoon you are asked out to someone's home for dinner. Go, because this is one time you will be able to talk with a family, or maybe several families. Remember, try to answer all questions asked of you at this point, because you are on trial. You must impress, as well as express.

An *uninvited* worker faces many difficulties; first, he is unexpected and in many cases unwanted by the do-nothing leaders of the community. He is a stranger to the people, and therefore, he is alone in a strange place. If he is to be successful, he must become a part of the community.

HOW ONE BECOMES PART OF THE COMMUNITY

First, get a place to stay. It is best to get a place in the community, with a well-known family. Once you have a place to stay, you have made the first contact in the community; however, in many cases it will not be as easy as writing words on paper.

It may just happen that you are not able to find a place for weeks; but do not give up. You may have to get a room in a rooming house; but try to stay as close to the community as possible. This will enable you to spend long hours in the community without worrying about a way home afterwards.

MAKING CONTACT

Since you have found a place to stay, say with a family, then the work starts, and it starts just as do most things, in the home.

You should spend as much time as the family has talking to them, because they have information about the people—both white and black. They have been there all of their lives; they know the community; they know the people who will help. Take time and talk to them; ask questions, for it is here that you get real *community education.*

Now you know the key people in the community, from this talk with the family. But some of them work out; do not get discouraged. Keep on pushing.

Canvass the whole community one afternoon. Talk with the people, laugh with them, joke with them; do most anything that gets some attention on you, or on some kind of conversation. It is very important to learn what bugs them. It may happen that they are thinking about trying to get the vote. You'll know when they talk.

The most important thing is to move the community by action; the community will move when the people move. The people will move when they are *motivated*.

SOME WAYS OF MOTIVATING PEOPLE

Canvass two or three days the first week. Do not worry too much about what you hear from the people. If you just talk and ask questions, some of them may talk about Chicago or Welfare checks; this is good, this is what is on their minds presently.

During canvassing, be sure to take down the names and addresses of the people who talked, who seemed to you that there is hope in them. This could be only two people; or it could be ten. No matter what the number is, these are contacts. You have a small group of people. Now you need a *place to meet* with them. Try to get a church or an empty building; if you cannot get either, use one of the person's homes for a meeting place. Again, start with the people where you live; ask to hold the meeting there.

Building Leaders

The reason for using this home is that you have now found that dependable leadership does not exist. You must, from this little group, find and build a leader or leaders. How?

In this meeting, plan some kind of action. You put suggestions before the group. Let them talk over the suggestions, about paved streets, stop signs, street lights, or recreational facilities, and how the vote can get these and more.

You may need to hold ten or more of these kinds of meetings; at the same time, trying to get a church, getting the word out about the house meeting by leafletting or word of mouth. But let it get out! Elect a chairman to chair the meetings; you should not do this after the first meeting. Each meeting, give more and more of the responsibilities to this group, and as the group grows, form committees so as to involve more of the people.

To overcome the fear, many of the things above mentioned

will apply. By getting the people together, they will see that they are not alone. By stopping by each one's home as much as possible, you will let them know you are sincere, in what you say and do—that you not only care about the meetings but you are interested in continued progress in their community and family life. The feeling of being close together will help overcome the fear.

Apathy will disappear when you give the people some responsibility. When you subject them to association with each other, through the conversations of personal and community problems, the apathy will disappear. At first the family educated you; now together they are educating each other.

Suspicion comes from mistrust. So many have led us wrong, that it is hard to trust people we don't know. You must be friendly, reliable, and most of all trustworthy. With this, suspicion will disappear. When the people trust you and trust your judgment, suspicion will be a thing of the past.

—*Charles McLaurin*

VIII. Two Statements from Jackson

The following statements were taken verbatim in the Atlanta SNCC office:

My name is Mrs. Annie Mae King and I live in Sunflower County, Mississippi.

We were arrested about twelve noon Monday, and they put us in a paddy wagon. It was so hot in there—there were twenty of us in there and we couldn't get no air. When they carried us out to the barn, they let us stay in the paddy wagon about thirty minutes before they let us out. When they taken us out they pushed us into the barn.

When we got inside the barn there were about a hundred or more cops and patrolmen and they began to push us from one side to the other. They yelled, "Get back, nigger, get back." They pushed us all into each other. One of them pushed me across the back with one of the blackjacks and said, "Get on up there in the line." And they just beat up children, pushing them and hitting them in the head. (The children were twelve years and older.)

After they registered us in on Monday night, they carried us in another stock barn. They made us sit down on the concrete floor about five in a row. They wouldn't let us sit against the wall, and we had to sit on the floor the whole time. About ten that night they gave us some little, old, thin mattress.

At five in the morning they made us stand up and give up the mattress. Everytime some white girls would come in they would be dragged out if they would not walk. They knocked one white girl in the head.

It's a long story, but the saddest of all—it was a lady that weighed about three hundred pounds (Mrs. Maggie Gordon), and we didn't have no kind of privacy because about twenty-five or thirty cops would be in there all through the night. And this lady had rinsed out her panties, and she was lying on a pallet. And they asked her to get up. And they snatched the tick out from under. And as she lied on the floor two cops taken her by her feet, and they drug her about twenty-five feet across the hall, and they kicked her all in her privates and beat her terrible.

And it was two young ladies there pregnant, and they beat one of them so she had a miscarriage.

I got out Thursday noon. It's a long story. I can't explain it all; I just say what I saw. During this time when they separated us and taken our name and separated the ladies from the men, they were very, very cruel. The food was very, very poor. We didn't get a shower until Wednesday night.

There's lots more. . . .

My name is Mrs. Maggie Gordon. I'm from Holmes County, Mississippi. I was arrested on Tuesday and taken to the Fairgrounds. About 6:30 Wednesday morning the officer came over and said, "Get up and get over there." I said "Okay." So when I attempted to move, he said, "Let's drag her."

So I said, "Please don't. I don't have my underpants on." So it was four of them. They grabbed me, and just pulled my legs apart and they kicked me in the privates. And they pulled me from that side to the other side. And they were steadily kicking me with their feet in the privates. And I caught one of the policemen by the leg, and they had those things called billy clubs, and they were hitting me on my arms and hands and to get me loose from him. He fell over and I reached to get the billy club and it was kicked away from me.

When I did manage to get up they had pulled and stretched me and tore my clothes off me. So when I managed to get up the one that had kicked me, I caught him on his shoulder and I hit him with my fist. And about twenty-five or more ganged up and pulled out their clubs and were standing around me. So excuse this expression—I said to all of them, I said, "I am not afraid of none of you motherfuckers." So then they ganged me and taken me out to the police car, and on the way out there one of these patrolmen hit me on the back end, juked me with the stick as we went to the car.

After we got to the car they handcuffed me and leaned me over and beat me all across the back end and back. So from there to the City Hall the one that had already kicked me in the privates, he asked me my name, and I refused to tell him my name. So he said, "We assume you don't have no name." Then he says to me, "Do you know what you are?" I say what he said: "You are a stupid, nasty, stinking bitch." So I said to him, "You are a stupid, stinking, motherfucking bitch." So I hit him and he hit me back. Then the three of them ganged me then, twisting my wrist and my arm behind me. They said, "Let's put her in solitary."

That's in a dark, small room, and on the way up to the room, they throwed me down, stomped me all in my body and still were kicking me. They dragged me in this dark cell and I was in there for twelve hours without water or food or a place to go to the bathroom. Some of the people at the Fairground told my lawyer where I was and he called up to see about me and he came up, and that's why they got me out of this dark place.

And they also had other police to come in and said, "Maggie, we come to take you to have X-rays so we're not the ones that hurt you. We're not going to hurt you." So they did. They were nice.

I talked to the FBI and gave them a statement on Thursday morning in jail. The FBI men didn't say too much. They took pictures of my head bruises and I was already naked from tearing my clothes off and they took pictures of my back end where I had been beaten. I signed a statement and then I got out. The FBI didn't say anything to me about what they would do. There were just two FBI men.

3. Lowndes County Freedom Organization Voting Pamphlet

In the summer of 1965 SNCC helped organize the Lowndes County Freedom Organization in the Black Belt voting district in Alabama. Although Negroes greatly outnumber whites in Lowndes County, they have been prevented from voting. After the passage of the 1965 Voting Rights Bill, SNCC workers began registering rural Negroes in the hope they might establish a political organization and vote for their own local candidates in 1966. The Black Panther party, as it became known because of its symbol, explains the most rudimentary political and electoral information to its constituency.

Politics

WHAT IS POLITICS?

Politics is the coming together of people to make decisions about their lives. For example, who is going to be sheriff, who will be elected to the school board, who will be the mayor of your city. However, in the past, Negroes have not been permitted to practice politics. A few people, most of them white, have worked in politics to benefit themselves.

HOW HAVE WE BEEN KEPT OUT OF POLITICS?

1. Certain laws and practices have kept Negroes from voting.

2. Negroes have been kept out of political parties.

3. Negroes have been beaten when they tried to register to vote, and told time and time again that politics and voting were "white folks' business."

4. They have told us that we are not "qualified" to practice politics, that we are not "qualified" to run our own lives! Every-

one knows if he will think about it that each and every grown man and woman is just as "qualified" as anyone else to decide what he wants his life to be like. There may be some information that some of us need in order to decide how to go about making our lives what we want them to be, but we can get that information and we can learn it just as well as anyone else can.

5. They have told us that Negroes "just can't stick together."

WHY COME TOGETHER?

When you come together you can determine who from your own community can do the thing you want done. If you don't come together, the people who have been running the show will put their own candidates up and vote for programs that will benefit them only and you will have no say at all.

WHAT CAN YOU DO WHEN YOU COME TOGETHER?

If you are a qualified elector (voter), that is, if you have registered to vote and paid the poll tax for two years, you can form your own political organization. . . .

NOW IS THE TIME!

If ever there was a time for Negroes to leave the white supremacy Democratic Party of Alabama alone—now is the time!

If ever there was a time for Negroes to leave the white supremacy Democratic Party of Alabama alone—now is the time!

If ever we had a chance to do something about the years of low pay, beatings, burnings of homes, denial of the right to vote, bad education and washed-out roads—now is the time!

4. Interviews with SNCC Staffers

The following excerpts are from interviews conducted in August 1965 in Mississippi. Neither the woman nor the man is typical of SNCC; they are examples of the kinds of thinking, the levels of awareness and education, current among SNCC staff in Mississipi.

A twenty-year-old, unmarried Negro girl from Hattiesburg, Mississippi. Her parents are separated, and her grandmother supports the family as a domestic servant. They are practicing Catholics. She graduated from a segregated high school.

I joined SNCC in November 1963. My friends convinced me that more black people had to join The Movement. I could help change the system in Mississippi and help other kids to grow up different.

The system is segregation and police brutality. That's what I know 'cause it's what I saw. I didn't need much convincing. I began doing door-to-door canvassing, getting people registered. I went to Washington, D.C., and worked on the freedom election, day and night. But I don't feel tired. There's more hope now than ten years ago. Look at all the students that got involved. In Hattiesburg we organized a school boycott through the Mississippi Student Union.

I want to feel free to go where I want, or go to college if I want.

The Movement is in worse shape now than a year ago. There's conflict between black and white on the staff. Negroes are not prepared for whites coming down. It takes on a sex thing. Most of the Negro men never have been close to a white girl before.

What I want? I want the bread-and-butter demands and freedom and dignity and free choice. All of them.

I read James Baldwin's *Go Tell It on the Mountain, Another Country* (I liked that one best), and *The Fire Next Time.* I read *Nigger* by Dick Gregory. He said, "Not poor, but just broke." That meant something.

Sex is one thing; The Movement is another. And the two shouldn't mix. There's an unhealthy attitude in The Movement toward sex. The Negro girls feel neglected because the white girls get the attention. The white girls are misused. There are some hot discussions at staff meetings.

I don't smoke pot. Some people do, but I just can't dig it. I have no principle against it. I mean, I don't know why you ask. It's not important.

I've changed a lot since I joined The Movement. I used to be involved with a gang. Now that sounds stupid. The Movement is part of me. I thought of quitting, but as long as you're black you can't get The Movement out of you if you stay in Mississippi. I guess I'll stay with The Movement full time for the next few years.

A twenty-seven-year-old, unmarried Negro man, a SNCC staff member, who was born in the East but grew up in Los Angeles. He has a BA in economics from a large California university.

I became active in college with a Marxist-humanist group that put out a newsletter, and we used to sell them at the gates of aircraft plants. I wrote some letters for this publication. In 1960 I picketed Woolworth's because it discriminated at its lunch counters in the South, but this humanist group didn't respond to this so I left. After I graduated I went to Florida and worked with local civil rights groups in Jacksonville. I floated around Florida for a while and then went to Mississippi, where I worked for Aaron Henry, who was running for Governor. I've been in Mississippi since then; with the SNCC staff since the fall of 1963, in Yazoo City, Greenwood, Jackson. Most of the time I got $20 a week, working on voter registration and getting people ready for freedom votes.

Since I've been in The Movement most of my reading has been Movement literature, from SNCC and SDS. I guess SDS is trying to do the same thing in the North that SNCC is doing in the South. When I was in college I read a lot of George Bernard Shaw, not only plays but his essays. He had a real effect on me.

The SNCC ideal is different for different people. Some want a society where people really decide for themselves; others are more interested in seeing people's basic needs taken care of, making them free from want. I think you could say that the people who've been in SNCC longer want the people to really decide. Those who came in recently are more interested in basic needs, bread-and-butter issues. But that's too simple. Everything written on SNCC is too simple, like the Rabinowitz-Fruchter debate in *Studies on the Left*. SNCC is so many different people with shades of differences in their ideas.

It's hard to talk about my political philosophy. I'm not certain any more about the agency of change. I used to believe that the masses would get social change through organized protest. But now I feel that small numbers of people are the only units that would be equipped to start revolutionary activity. I say revolution because that's what is needed if freedom is going to mean anything in this country. It means people would be informed about things that affected them. There would be meaningful participation in the decision-making process. With those things accomplished I think a lot of the rest would fall into place.

I don't have any illusions about the poor. They haven't had the opportunity to become corrupted. I believe in role as the determinant as to the degree of corruption or corruptness. If you could do away with corporation leaders, there would be no need to organize the poor. Seriously, if you had different kinds of roles in different kinds of institutions, you would have different values.

I didn't come to the South with any illusions about winning a quick revolution. The tools we have aren't the tools we need. We can win minor reforms like the Voting Rights Bill. Many people come down with illusions about being revolutionaries. In truth, we have an unfavorable effect on what might be true agents of social change. They can't find a social base because of SNCC and SDS. In one sense, SNCC and SDS are larger threats to a truly radical group than the NAACP or the unions. Young people hook up with SNCC and feel they are doing something revolutionary.

Really the newsletter and reports of SNCC and SDS are largely lies. For example, they give the impression that SDS is really organizing the poor, and SNCC is the only group that can organize the rural poor. Actually others might do it better, but are fearful of hurting SNCC and SDS. If Malcolm X was to organize the poor, he would have to use SNCC contacts, and this would mean cutting into SNCC. Don't misunderstand me. There are true radicals in SDS and SNCC that can't break away.

The next question involved the opinion of a Delta ministry organizer in Greenville who believed that an unfortunate separation existed between the state and the local Freedom Democratic Parties

I agree. The FDP is not organized. Its chief concern is the Challenge in Washington, and for that it needs a numerical base, not an active base. It must say and prove that it has a large constituency. This base is a political leverage until the party gets a program. Until it does that it won't be able to do much with local groups. You see, the people don't decide on the Challenge because the local groups have nothing to decide. The Challenge was decided on a year ago. It's unfortunate, but there's no need for local participation.

We're going to poke along the way we are. Things will stay pretty much the same. The effect of organizing the poor is to keep things from getting worse. You see if the radical organizers left The Movement it would really be unfortunate, for the constituency that they have built up hope and expectations too.

In a recent interview Stokely Carmichael was asked to define Black Power

. . . the projection of black power has been given by the white press. They're the ones who have maliciously distorted it. Black power seems to me to mean nothing more than black people coming together as a political, economic, and social force and forcing their representatives or electing their representatives to speak to their needs, and that if that doesn't work, they then decide what tactics they use to get the things they need in this country.

Students for a
Democratic Society

1. "The Port Huron Statement"

*S*tudents for a Democratic Society (SDS) was founded in June
1960 at a New York convention sponsored by the League for
Industrial Democracy. But at the 1962 SDS convention at Port
Huron, Michigan, SDS's differences with the League became
manifest. "The Port Huron Statement" established the basic
guidelines for SDS, in ideology and action.

In "The Port Huron Statement," which bears the stamp of a
single author (Tom Hayden), there is criticism of both the path-
ological anti-Communism which characterizes American politics
and Communism itself. "The Port Huron Statement" has a special relevance for middle-class intellectuals and college students;
it is not a "Communist Manifesto," outlining programs for revolution, but rather a general, broad critique, suggesting guidelines
for a radical politics. It is not aimed at a working-class constituency, nor does it depend upon a program for the working class,
or for any class. A similar paper today would emphasize building an "independent power base" among the poor.

The 1962 SDS statement relies on working with and through
"liberal" institutions, the ADA, the labor movement, political
parties. A great deal of time is spent on Congressional reform,
for example. It shows a faith in the student civil rights move-

*ment as the engine of change to build a coalition of liberal-labor-
civil rights forces.*

INTRODUCTION: AGENDA FOR A GENERATION

We are people of this generation, bred in at least modest comfort, housed now in universities, looking uncomfortably to the world we inherit.

When we were kids the United States was the wealthiest and strongest country in the world; the only one with the atom bomb, the least scarred by modern war, an initiator of the United Nations that we thought would distribute Western influence throughout the world. Freedom and equality for each individual, government of, by, and for the people—these American values we found good, principles by which we could live as men. Many of us began maturing in complacency.

As we grew, however, our comfort was penetrated by events too troubling to dismiss. First, the permeating and victimizing fact of human degradation, symbolized by the Southern struggle against racial bigotry, compelled most of us from silence to activism. Second, the enclosing fact of the Cold War, symbolized by the presence of the Bomb, brought awareness that we ourselves, and our friends, and millions of abstract "others" we knew more directly because of our common peril, might die at any time. We might deliberately ignore, or avoid, or fail to feel all other human problems, but not these two, for these were too immediate and crushing in their impact, too challenging in the demand that we as individuals take the responsibility for encounter and resolution.

While these and other problems either directly oppressed us or rankled our consciences and became our own subjective concerns, we began to see complicated and disturbing paradoxes in our surrounding America. The declaration "all men are created equal . . ." rang hollow before the facts of Negro life in the South and the big cities of the North. The proclaimed peaceful intentions of the United States contradicted its economic and military investments in the Cold War status quo.

We witnessed, and continue to witness, other paradoxes. With nuclear energy whole cities can easily be powered, yet the dominant nation-states seem more likely to unleash destruction greater than that incurred in all wars of human history. Although our own technology is destroying old and creating new forms of social organization, men still tolerate meaningless work and idleness. While two-thirds of mankind suffers undernourishment, our own upper classes revel amidst superfluous abundance. Although world population is expected to double in forty years, the nations still tolerate anarchy as a major principle of international conduct and uncontrolled exploitation governs the sapping of the earth's physical resources. Although mankind desperately needs revolutionary leadership, America rests in national stalemate, its goals ambiguous and tradition-bound instead of informed and clear, its democratic system apathetic and manipulated rather than "of, by, and for the people."

Not only did tarnish appear on our image of American virtue, not only did disillusion occur when the hypocrisy of American ideals was discovered, but we began to sense that what we had originally seen as the American Golden Age was actually the decline of an era. The worldwide outbreak of revolution against colonialism and imperialism, the entrenchment of totalitarian states, the menace of war, overpopulation, international disorder, supertechnology—these trends were testing the tenacity of our own commitment to democracy and freedom and our abilities to visualize their application to a world in upheaval.

Our work is guided by the sense that we may be the last generation in the experiment with living. But we are a minority—the vast majority of our people regard the temporary equilibriums of our society and world as eternally functional parts. In this is perhaps the outstanding paradox: we ourselves are imbued with urgency, yet the message of our society is that there is no viable alternative to the present. Beneath the reassuring tones of the politicians, beneath the common opinion that America will "muddle through," beneath the stagnation of those who have closed their minds to the future, is the pervading feeling that there simply are no alternatives, that our times have witnessed the exhaustion not only of Utopias, but of any new departures as well. Feeling the press of complexity upon the emptiness of life, people are fearful of the thought that at any moment things might be thrust out of control. They fear change itself, since change might smash whatever invisible framework seems to hold back chaos for them now. For most Americans, all crusades are suspect, threatening. The fact that each individual sees apathy in his fellows perpetuates the common reluctance to organize for change. The dominant institutions are complex enough to blunt the minds of their potential critics, and entrenched enough to swiftly dissipate or entirely repel the energies of protest and reform, thus limiting human expectancies. Then, too, we are a materially improved society, and by our own improvements we seem to have weakened the case for further change.

Some would have us believe that Americans feel contentment amidst prosperity—but might it not better be called a glaze above deeply felt anxieties about their role in the new world? And if these anxieties produce a developed indifference to human affairs, do they not as well produce a yearning to believe there *is* an alternative to the present, that something *can* be done to change circumstances in the school, the workplaces, the bureaucracies, the government? It is to this latter yearning, at once the spark and engine of change, that we direct our present appeal. The search for truly democratic alternatives to the present, and a commitment to social experimentation with them, is a worthy and fulfilling human enterprise, one which moves us and, we hope, others today. On such a basis do we offer this document of our convictions and analysis: as an effort in understanding and changing the conditions of humanity in the late twentieth century, an effort rooted in the ancient, still unfulfilled conception of man attaining determining influence over his circumstances of life.

VALUES

Making values explicit—an initial task in establishing alternatives—is an activity that has been devalued and corrupted. The conventional moral terms of the age, the politician moralities—"free world," "people's democracies"—reflect realities poorly, if at all, and seem to function more as ruling myths than as descriptive principles. But neither has our experience in the universities brought us moral enlightenment. Our professors and administrators sacrifice controversy to public relations; their curriculums change more slowly than the living events of the world; their skills and silence are purchased by investors in the arms race; passion is called unscholastic. The questions we might want raised—what is really important? can we live in a different and better way? if we wanted to change society, how would we do it?—are not thought to be questions of a "fruitful, empirical nature," and thus are brushed aside.

Unlike youth in other countries we are used to moral leadership being exercised and moral dimensions being clarified by our elders. But today, for us, not even the liberal and socialist preachments of the past seem adequate to the forms of the present. Consider the old slogans: Capitalism Cannot Reform Itself, United Front Against Fascism, General Strike, All Out on May Day. Or, more recently, No Cooperation with Commies and Fellow Travelers, Ideologies are Exhausted, Bipartisanship, No Utopias. These are incomplete, and there are few new prophets. It has been said that our liberal and socialist predecessors were plagued by vision without program, while our own generation is plagued by program without vision. All around us there is astute grasp of method, technique—the committee, the *ad hoc* group, the lobbyist, the hard and soft sell, the make, the projected image—but, if pressed critically, such expertise is incompetent to explain its implicit ideals. It is highly fashionable to identify oneself by old categories, or by naming a respected political figure, or by explaining "how we would vote" on various issues.

Theoretic chaos has replaced the idealistic thinking of old— and, unable to reconstitute theoretic order, men have condemned idealism itself. Doubt has replaced hopefulness—and men act out a defeatism that is labeled realistic. The decline of utopia and hope is in fact one of the defining features of social life today. The reasons are various: the dreams of the older left were perverted by Stalinism and never recreated; the congressional stalemate makes men narrow their view of the possible; the specialization of human activity leaves little room for sweeping thought; the horrors of the twentieth century, symbolized in the gas ovens and concentration camps and atom bombs, have blasted hopefulness. To be idealistic is to be considered apocalyptic, deluded. To have no serious aspirations, on the contrary, is to be "tough-minded."

In suggesting social goals and values, therefore, we are aware of entering a sphere of some disrepute. Perhaps matured by the past, we have no sure formulas, no closed theories—but that does not mean values are beyond discussion and tentative determination. A first task of any social movement is to convince people that the search for orienting theories and the creation of human values is complex but worthwhile. We are aware that to avoid platitudes we must analyze the concrete conditions of social order. But to direct such an analysis we must use the guideposts of basic principles. Our own social values involve conceptions of human beings, human relationships, and social systems.

We regard *men* as infinitely precious and possessed of unfulfilled capacities for reason, freedom, and love. In affirming these principles we are aware of countering perhaps the dominant conceptions of man in the twentieth century: that he is a thing to be manipulated, and that he is inherently incapable of directing his own affairs. We oppose the depersonalization that reduces human beings to the status of things—if anything, the brutalities of the twentieth century teach that means and ends are intimately related, that vague appeals to "posterity' cannot justify the mutilations of the present. We oppose, too, the doctrine of human incompetence because it rests essentially on the modern fact that men have been "competently" manipulated into incompetence—we see little reason why men cannot meet with increasing skill the complexities and responsibilities of their situation, if society is organized not for minority, but for majority, participation in decision-making.

Men have unrealized potential for self-cultivation, self-direction, self-understanding, and creativity. It is this potential that we regard as crucial and to which we appeal, not to the human potentiality for violence, unreason, and submission to authority. The goal of man and society should be human independence: a concern not with image of popularity but with finding a meaning in life that is personally authentic; a quality of mind not compulsively driven by a sense of powerlessness, nor one which unthinkingly adopts status values, nor one which represses all threats to its habits, but one which has full, spontaneous access to present and past experiences, one which easily unites the fragmented parts of personal history, one which openly faces problems which are troubling and unresolved; one with an intuitive awareness of possibilities, an active sense of curiosity, an ability and willingness to learn.

This kind of independence does not mean egotistic individualism—the object is not to have one's way so much as it is to have a way that is one's own. Nor do we deify man—we merely have faith in his potential.

Human relationships should involve fraternity and honesty. Human interdependence is contemporary fact; human brotherhood must be willed, however, as a condition of future survival and as the most appropriate form of social relations. Personal links between man and man are needed, especially to go beyond the partial and fragmentary bonds of function that bind men only as worker to worker, employer to employee, teacher to student, American to Russian.

Loneliness, estrangement, isolation describe the vast distance between man and man today. These dominant tendencies cannot be overcome by better personnel management, nor by improved gadgets, but only when a love of man overcomes the idolatrous worship of things by man. As the individualism we affirm is not egoism, the selflessness we affirm is not self-elimination. On the contrary, we believe in generosity of a kind that imprints one's unique individual qualities in the relation to other men, and to all human activity. Further, to dislike isolation is not to favor the abolition of privacy; the latter differs from isolation in that it occurs or is abolished according to individual will.

We would replace power rooted in possession, privilege, or circumstance by power and uniqueness rooted in love, reflectiveness, reason, and creativity. As a *social system* we seek the establishment of a democracy of individual participation, governed by two central aims: that the individual share in those social decisions determining the quality and direction of his life; that society be organized to encourage independence in men and provide the media for their common participation.

In a participatory democracy, the political life would be based in several root principles:

> that decision-making of basic social consequence be carried on by public groupings;

that politics be seen positively, as the art of collectively creating an acceptable pattern of social relations;

that politics has the function of bringing people out of isolation and into community, thus being a necessary, though not sufficient, means of finding meaning in personal life;

that the political order should serve to clarify problems in a way instrumental to their solution; it should provide outlets for the expression of personal grievance and aspiration; opposing views should be organized so as to illuminate choices and facilitate the attainment of goals; channels should be commonly available to relate men to knowledge and to power so that private problems—from bad recreation facilities to personal alienation—are formulated as general issues.

The economic sphere would have as its basis the principles:

that work should involve incentives worthier than money or survival. It should be educative, not stultifying; creative, not mechanical; self-directed, not manipulated, encouraging independence, a respect for others, a sense of dignity and a willingness to accept social responsibility, since it is this experience that has crucial influence on habits, perceptions and individual ethics;

that the economic experience is so personally decisive that the individual must share in its full determination;

that the economy itself is of such social importance that its major resources and means of production should be open to democratic participation and subject to democratic social regulation.

Like the political and economic ones, major social institutions —cultural, educational, rehabilitative, and others—should be generally organized with the well-being and dignity of man as the essential measure of success.

In social change or interchange, we find violence to be abhorrent because it requires generally the transformation of the target, be it a human being or a community of people, into a depersonalized object of hate. It is imperative that the means of violence be abolished and the institutions—local, national, international—that encourage nonviolence as a condition of conflict be developed.

These are our central values, in skeletal form. It remains vital
to understand their denial or attainment in the context of the
modern world.

THE STUDENTS

In the last few years, thousands of American students demonstrated that they at least felt the urgency of the times. They
moved actively and directly against racial injustices, the threat
of war, violations of individual rights of conscience and, less
frequently, against economic manipulation. They succeeded in
restoring a small measure of controversy to the campuses after
the stillness of the McCarthy period. They succeeded, too, in
gaining some concessions from the people and institutions they
opposed, especially in the fight against racial bigotry.

The significance of these scattered movements lies not in their
success or failure in gaining objectives—at least not yet. Nor
does the significance lie in the intellectual "competence" or "ma-
turity" of the students involved—as some pedantic elders allege.
The significance is in the fact the students are breaking the crust
of apathy and overcoming the inner alienation that remain the
defining characteristics of American college life.

If student movements for change are still rareties on the campus scene, what is commonplace there? The real campus, the
familiar campus, is a place of private people, engaged in their
notorious "inner emigration." It is a place of commitment to
business-as-usual, getting ahead, playing it cool. It is a place of
mass affirmation of the Twist, but mass reluctance toward the
controversial public stance. Rules are accepted as "inevitable,"
bureaucracy as "just circumstances," irrelevance as "scholarship," selflessness as "martyrdom," politics as "just another way
to make people, and an unprofitable one, too."

Almost no students value activity as citizens. Passive in public, they are hardly more idealistic in arranging their private
lives: Gallup concludes they will settle for "low success, and
won't risk high failure." There is not much willingness to take
risks (not even in business), no setting of dangerous goals, no
real conception of personal identity except one manufactured in
the image of others, no real urge for personal fulfillment except
to be almost as successful as the very successful people. Atten-

tion is being paid to social status (the quality of shirt collars, meeting people, getting wives or husbands, making solid contacts for later on); much, too, is paid to academic status (grades, honors, the med school rat race). But neglected generally is real intellectual status, the personal cultivation of the mind.

"Students don't even give a damn about the apathy," one has said. Apathy toward apathy begets a privately constructed universe, a place of systematic study schedules, two nights each week for beer, a girl or two, and early marriage; a framework infused with personality, warmth, and under control, no matter how unsatisfying otherwise.

Under these conditions university life loses all relevance to some. Four hundred thousand of our classmates leave college every year.

But apathy is not simply an attitude; it is a product of social institutions, and of the structure and organization of higher education itself. The extracurricular life is ordered according to *in loco parentis* theory, which ratifies the administration as the moral guardian of the young.

The accompanying "let's pretend" theory of student extracurricular affairs validates student government as a training center for those who want to spend their lives in political pretense, and discourages initiative from the more articulate, honest, and sensitive students. The bounds and style of controversy are delimited before controversy begins. The university "prepares" the student for "citizenship" through perpetual rehearsals and, usually, through emasculation of what creative spirit there is in the individual.

The academic life contains reinforcing counterparts to the way in which extracurricular life is organized. The academic world is founded on a teacher-student relation analogous to the parent-child relation which characterizes *in loco parentis*. Further, academia includes a radical separation of the student from the material of study. That which is studied, the social reality, is "objectified" to sterility, dividing the student from life—just as he is restrained in active involvement by the deans controlling student government. The specialization of function and knowledge, admittedly necessary to our complex technological and so-

cial structure, has produced an exaggerated compartmentaliza-
tion of study and understanding. This has contributed to an
overly parochial view, by faculty, of the role of its research and
scholarship, to a discontinuous and truncated understanding, by
students, of the surrounding social order; and to a loss of personal attachment, by nearly all, to the worth of study as a hu-
manistic enterprise.

There is, finally, the cumbersome academic bureaucracy extending throughout the academic as well as the extracurricular
structures, contributing to the sense of outer complexity and
inner powerlessness that transforms the honest searching of many
students to a ratification of convention and, worse, to a numb-
ness to present and future catastrophes. The size and financing
systems of the university enhance the permanent trusteeship of
the administrative bureaucracy, their power leading to a shift
within the university toward the value standards of business and
the administrative mentality. Huge foundations and other private financial interests shape the under-financed colleges and
universities, not only making them more commercial, but less
disposed to diagnose society critically, less open to dissent.
Many social and physical scientists, neglecting the liberating heritage of higher learning, develop "human relations" or "morale-
producing" techniques for the corporate economy, while others
exercise their intellectual skills to accelerate the arms race. . . .

There are no convincing apologies for the contemporary malaise. While the world tumbles toward the final war, while men
in other nations are trying desperately to alter events, while the
very future qua future is uncertain—America is without community, impulse, without the inner momentum necessary for an
age when societies cannot successfully perpetuate themselves by
their military weapons, when democracy must be viable because
of the quality of life, not its quantity of rockets.

The apathy here is, first, *subjective*—the felt powerlessness of
ordinary people, the resignation before the enormity of events.
But subjective apathy is encouraged by the *objective* American
situation—the actual structural separation of people from power,
from relevant knowledge, from pinnacles of decision-making.
Just as the university influences the student way of life, so do
major social institutions create the circumstances in which the

isolated citizen will try hopelessly to understand his world and himself.

The very isolation of the individual—from power and community and ability to aspire—means the rise of a democracy without publics. With the great mass of people structurally remote and psychologically hesitant with respect to democratic institutions, those institutions themselves attenuate and become, in the fashion of the vicious circle, progressively less accessible to those few who aspire to serious participation in social affairs. The vital democratic connection between community and leadership, between the mass and the several elites, has been so wrenched and perverted that disastrous policies go unchallenged time and again.

POLITICS WITHOUT PUBLICS

The American political system is not the democratic model of which its glorifiers speak. In actuality it frustrates democracy by confusing the individual citizen, paralyzing policy discussion, and consolidating the irresponsible power of military and business interests.

A crucial feature of the political apparatus in America is that greater differences are harbored within each major party than the differences existing between them. Instead of two parties presenting distinctive and significant differences of approach, what dominates the system is a natural interlocking of Democrats from Southern states with the more conservative elements of the Republican Party. This arrangement of forces is blessed by the seniority system of Congress which guarantees Congressional committee domination by conservatives—ten of seventeen committees in the Senate and thirteen of twenty-one in the House of Representatives are chaired currently by Dixiecrats.

The party overlap, however, is not the only structural antagonist of democracy in politics. First, the localized nature of the party system does not encourage discussion of national and international issues: thus problems are not raised by and for people, and political representatives usually are unfettered from any responsibilities to the general public except those regarding parochial matters. Second, whole constituencies are divested of the full political power they might have: many Negroes in the South are prevented from voting, migrant workers are disenfranchised by various residence requirements, some urban and suburban dwellers are victimized by gerrymandering, and poor people are too often without the power to obtain political representation. Third, the focus of political attention is significantly distorted by the enormous lobby force, composed predominantly of business interests, spending hundreds of millions each year in an attempt to conform facts about productivity, agriculture, defense, and social services, to the wants of private economic groupings.

What emerges from the party contradiction and insulation of privately held power is the organized political stalemate: calcification dominates flexibility as the principle of parliamentary organization, frustration is the expectancy of legislators intending liberal reform, and Congress becomes less and less central to national decision-making, especially in the area of foreign policy. In this context, confusion and blurring is built into the formulation of issues, long-range priorities are not discussed in the rational manner needed for policy-making, the politics of personality and "image" become a more important mechanism than the construction of issues in a way that affords each voter a challenging and real option. The American voter is buffeted from all directions by pseudo-problems, by the structurally initiated sense that nothing political is subject to human mastery. Worried by his mundane problems which never get solved, but constrained by the common belief that politics is an agonizingly slow accommodation of views, he quits all pretense of bothering.

A most alarming fact is that few, if any, politicians are calling for changes in these conditions. Only a handful even are calling on the President to "live up to" platform pledges; no one is demanding structural changes, such as the shuttling of Southern Democrats out of the Democratic Party. Rather than protesting the state of politics, most politicians are reinforcing and aggravating that state. While in practice they rig public opinion to suit their own interests, in word and ritual they enshrine "the sovereign public" and call for more and more letters. Their speeches and campaign actions are banal, based on a degrading conception of what people want to hear. They respond not to dialogue, but to pressure: and knowing this, the ordinary citizen sees even greater inclination to shun the political sphere. The politician is usually a trumpeter to "citizenship" and "service to the nation," but since he is unwilling to seriously rearrange power relationships, his trumpetings only increase apathy by creating no outlets. Much of the time the call to "service" is justified not in idealistic terms, but in the crasser terms of "defending the free world from Communism"—thus making future idealistic impulses harder to justify in anything but Cold War terms.

In such a setting of status quo politics, where most if not all government activity is rationalized in Cold War anti-Communist terms, it is somewhat natural that discontented, super-patriotic groups would emerge through political channels and explain their ultra-conservatism as the best means of Victory over Communism. They have become a politically influential force within the Republican Party, at a national level through Senator Goldwater, and at a local level through their important social and economic roles. Their political views are defined generally as the opposite of the supposed views of Communists: complete individual freedom in the economic sphere, non-participation by the government in the machinery of production. But actually "anti-Communism" becomes an umbrella by which to protest liberalism, internationalism, welfareism, the active civil rights and labor movements. It is to the disgrace of the United States that such a movement should become a prominent kind of public participation in the modern world—but, ironically, it is somewhat to the interests of the United States that such a movement should be a public constituency pointed toward realignment of the political parties, demanding a conservative Republican Party in the South and an exclusion of the "leftist" elements of the national GOP. . . .

2. *"Some Problems, Issues, Proposals"*

Dick Flacks is an instructor in sociology at the University of Chicago. The following excerpts are from a working paper written for the June 1965 SDS convention in Kewadin, Michigan.

Flacks links personal with political goals, a concern that characterizes both SDS and SNCC.

If I understand what we are trying to work on when we say we are building a "movement," I think it has to do with two types of goals. One, which we might call "existential humanism," is expressed by the desire to change the way we, as individuals actually live and deal with other people. We speak of the attempt to achieve "community" to reach levels of intimacy and directness with others unencumbered by the conventional barriers of race, status, class, etc. We strive at every occasion to enhance the ability of people to affect their environment, to be centers of initiative, to be self-expressive, to be free. And the achievement of some of this, on any occasion, we take to be intrinsically worthwhile.

Second, we say that we seek a radical transformation of the social order. In short, that we act politically because our values cannot be realized in any durable sense without a reconstruction of the political and social system. Thus we say that we want a redistribution of wealth and power in the society; that we want to develop new centers of power as a basis for such a redistribution; that we look toward the emergence of new political and social institutions which can authentically provide the conditions for freedom.

It must be stressed that the latter goals are *political* in meaning—they cannot be approached without a profoundly serious commitment to *political* involvement. That is not necessarily true for what I have called "existential humanism"—it seems to me entirely possible for each of us to guide our own way of living according to such standards and consequently strive to approach an ethical existence. And the achievement of some approximation of community for ourselves and those immediately near us seems plausibly independent of political change.

I think it is inescapable that our movement must encompass both sets of orientation. It is clear that a politics apart from an existential ethic becomes increasingly manipulative, power-oriented, sacrificial of human lives and souls—it is corrupted.

The danger involved in a social movement that is apolitical is, perhaps, less obvious and therefore needs to be stated and argued. The danger here it seems to me is that of irresponsibility: of a search for personally satisfying modes of life while abandoning the possibility of helping others to change theirs; of placing tremendous hope in The Movement of the immediate community for achieving personal salvation and gratification—then realizing that these possibilities are, after all, limited and, consequently suffering disillusionment. Involving too is an over-personalization of The Movement, a situation in which one's personal needs and hang-ups are increasingly acted out in the large arena, and attempts at solution of these take precedence over more collective concerns. The necessary distinction between the public and the private self breaks down, with the likely result that either the community is undermined, or personal freedom is sacrificed in order to preserve the community. It seems to me that a clear consciousness and commitment to *political* goals at least has the virtue of limiting the interpretation of the public and private.

The obvious difficulty with trying to encompass both existential humanism and radical politics is that they are not only plausibly independent, but sometimes incompatible. Thus the effort to be politically effective can involve one in efforts at manipulation and compromise. The effort to be morally consistent can radically separate one from effective communication with others.

The virtue of Students for a Democratic Society and SNCC, it seems to me, is that they have so far done a pretty good job of maintaining the necessary tension between these two orientations. It seems to me that the fact that such tension exists within these organizations is an important way that they are different from others on the "left." The tension is maintained first of all because it is *in* most of the participants. Second, because people tend to emphasize one orientation more than another, the tension is maintained by fostering the active participation of both types of people within the organizations. So when I say that SDS must encompass both orientations I think I mean something like this: we must keep centrally in view that we are a *political* movement (and the implications of this will be spelled out later); at the same time, we must remain receptive and responsible to the standards of "existential humanism," as guides for the way we treat each other and those in our immediate environment, as criticisms of everything we try to do as political actors. We must embrace the poet and the saint—but we must keep a necessary distance from them.

FOR A POLITICAL STRATEGY

One implication of stressing the political thrust of The Movement is that this restores the necessity for strategic analysis. By urging renewed attention to the problem of strategy, I am not calling for the imposition of abstract and impersonal criteria, nor for a disciplined restraint on action. I think many of us have assumed that the outlines of strategy emerge from our work, that, therefore, explicit and systematic preoccupation with strategy imposes artificial constraints, restricts spontaneity, and makes us unresponsive to what people really want. Furthermore, strategy tends to be the property of a few; acting in terms of strategy is elitist.

Nevertheless, it does seem to me that one of the key problems at the moment is that people lack a sense of priorities, that there is a great deal of inarticulateness; and almost random behavior among students who want to do effective social action, or—the other side of the coin—some few people do have formulated strategies which in the absence of systematic discussion, get imposed on the rest all unnoticed, all unexamined. . . .

3. *"Summer Report, Newark Community Union"*

SDS began its Economic Research and Action Project, (ERAP) in August 1963 under a grant from the United Auto Workers. Originally the program, under Al Haber's guidance, emphasized research, but in December 1963 SDS decided to begin community action projects. Led by Rennie Davis, with strong support from Tom Hayden, SDS members became full-time community workers in Northern cities from coast to coast.

Hayden and others had studied SNCC's working model first-hand in the South, and the ERAP projects were based on SNCC's experience. Tom Hayden and Carl Wittman prepared a report on the first four months of activity in the Newark project.

The Newark Project came into Clinton Hill, Newark, on the inaccurate assumption that both poor Negroes and whites lived there. As it turned out, only the eastern, or lower, half of the area could in any sense be called poor—the rest was working- and middle-class, mostly Negro also. In a city where over half the population is Negro or Puerto Rican, there are only three areas where white unemployment is significant, only one of them of any size.

Despite the racial imbalance of the SDS group (all but one were white, and all three of the present staff are white) there was practically no overt opposition within the project area to the staff. Instead, both old members of the Neighborhood Council (our host group) and the newly organized block members accepted us with remarkable alacrity and warmth. And by the time the projects came under major attack, from a group whose spokesmen included Negro liberals, neighborhood people defended the white staff instead of capitulating to the race-baiting of our antagonists. It would be highly desirable to have Negro organizers on the staff, but at this point that is not mandatory. . . .

One important fact is the substantial integration of big business with the city government and the Urban League, NAACP and CORE. City officials themselves testify to this fact as a reason for the absence of summer riots, and they depend on it for continued social peace, urban renewal and the local war on poverty.

This unity is not unbreakable—CORE, for instance, has picketed both City Hall and certain business establishments; and the Essex County Democrats contain a faction opposed to the city administration. But there is a widely held consensus on "acceptable" program, and a high degree of coordination among elite groups compared to other cities. The consensus on program is that society should adjust to the Negro only in terms of racial attitudes, not in terms of national economic change; that the Negro should adjust to society through greater basic education and improvement of skills. This outlook characterizes the leading civil rights groups, the business leaders committed to civil rights, and the Newark war on poverty planners. This is not just an individually held consensus, but one that is generated in common because of the high rate of overlap and intermingling among groups.

This is the overt civil rights program of a sophisticated corporate-liberal establishment. The covert program is urban renewal, which removes Negroes from choice business sites and relocates them, at "best," in hideous high-rise ghettos. Newark is one of America's "pilot cities" in this field, having spent as many urban renewal dollars in the postwar period as any other city of comparable size. Built into the dynamics of "successful" urban renewal are the preconditions of an urban ruling elite: durable organization, comprehensive program, immunity from democratic review. The local Housing Authority elite, with a virtual empire of faithful staff and patronage, has lasted relatively intact through the last three city administrations. Besides its durability, the Housing Authority is comprehensive in the scope of operation—at this point all of Newark has succeeded in falling under the "blight" category in the federal housing codes. The Housing Authority becomes the institutional channel through which the city's economic and racial development proceeds. This process is simplified for the authorities by the undemocratic nature of the program. All research and decision-making is done privately among businessmen, federal agents, and the Housing Authority, then presented as fiat to the City Council. Urban renewal, then, is the basic response by this Northern liberal city to the problems of Negro poverty. Urban renewal has been nicknamed by its integrationist critics, "Negro removal." This is true only in part, for the real motivation would seem to be as much economic as racial. It is a major domestic means of government subsidy to private commercial growth; as such, it runs against the interests of all the poor, Negro as well as white.

Given this sophisticated elite operation, it is surprising that the project has been the object of so much alarm and hostility from "downtown" elements. Part of this can be explained by the temporary but profound fear of a summer race riot. The civil rights-city-business "coalition" had concurred in the so-called moratorium on demonstrations, so there was a somewhat undue amount of fear of the SDS "outsiders" when we scheduled the first of five demonstrations. But this fear of a riot does not explain the repeated attacks by our local councilman, comments from neighborhood people of city-owned reports and pictures of us participating in nearby riots and other subversive activity, scurrilous anti-project leaflets in the area, reliable rumors that one or more FBI personnel are assigned to the project, vehement attacks on block organizations by the local urban renewal representative, and threats from the councilman's local strongman. The causes of this tension seem to be: first, the general fear that the existing Negro majority will express itself militantly in city affairs; second, the specific fear of any new groups "outside" of the existing civil rights consensus; third, the fear that stable elite control of urban renewal will be upset by insurgent demands, leaving the city in a weakened competitive position in relation to other Northern areas. Whatever the reasons, the fact is that we can expect major attention from the city as our activity progresses, especially since our leaflets identify it with the slumlords and other moneymakers.

More surprising than the negative response from the city is the unwillingness of the small liberal circle in the city to accept the project and its implications. Since they had invited us to Newark, one would expect that the liberal community (the ADA, CORE, the activist wing of the NAACP, some labor unions, community improvement groups) would be a major ally. But major reconsideration of this assumption has been forced by the course of events. It has turned out that practically every one of the groups has come to see the project as a problem if not a danger, and the only significant support for the project is within the project area. This phenomenon should be dealt with on both the organizational and programatic plane.

Much of the difficulty and friction between the project and the liberal groupings is related to problems in the structure of the project. Originally it was to be directed by a group called the Newark Committee on Full Employment, which consisted of representatives from the various liberal groups. The organization through which policy would be implemented was also a leading force within the Committee: the Clinton Hill Neighborhood Council. The Council is a nine-year-old neighborhood improvement association, formed as the neighborhood began to turn from Jewish middle class to Negro middle and lower class. Its major accomplishment has been the litigation holding up the urban renewal in the lower or eastern half of the Hill (where we work). It consisted of several hundred members, once active and now mostly on paper. Its leadership was mostly white, its constituency mostly colored. It once was an all-homeowner group; it never contained many tenants.

The obvious problem is whether and how to build coalition with other "liberal forces" in the area. Our initial experience has been with extremely self-serving people who have wide community contact but no active and radical membership base. Their aspirations are for political self-aggrandizement and orthodox liberal reforms. The problem in any coalition with them is they they will work with nearly anyone to upset the city administration and send in a new set of officials; or, in general, their program would do very little to change the real lives of the poor. This means we are viewed by them as cogs and not as people whose need for democratic participation and basic change must be served. We cannot enter into this kind of political bartering without violating the basic trust we have with the neighborhood people. Our place is at the bottom. . . .

The problem of leadership was only in part identified by neighborhood people as racial: "this is 1964 and things is changin' all over" is the way one put it. However, the SDS staff was white also, a fact which neighborhood people defended when the local Negro CORE chairman used race-baiting arguments against SDS. The deeper way in which the problem was identified was, very simply, *democratic control*. The sharpest attacks were against domination of the people by a manipulative clique, and against anyone displaying marks of snobbishness or privilege. The neighborhood people readily identified themselves as "the little people," and they regarded SDS staff as "ordinary people" who were with them.

The positive manifestation of this democratic feeling was the form of the new organization which emerged: the program committee. This was a committee which was formed of representatives from all blocks, the staff, and *anyone who could attend the meetings*—one man, one vote. The committee would meet weekly and make all policy decisions, decide its own organizational form, and be chaired by an elected president rotating once a month. Although many of these suggestions were made by us, they were readily agreed upon and defended when questioned.

One of the larger questions throughout the summer was how a mostly white staff would relate to a Negro constituency. The subject is often discussed, and especially when broached by us, in a frank manner. For obvious reasons, there is no consciousness of poor whites being their allies, as none have come to them as allies. But partly because of the economic orientation of our program, partly because of our occasionally pushing the idea, and partly out of a flexibility in their outlook as to who allies are, the possibility of hooking up with white groups does not seem at all difficult.

In contrast to an apparent informality in race consciousness, the attitudes toward class are somewhat tighter. There is a strong strain of being of a deprived class, resenting and ridiculing privilege; picketing a slumlord at his suburban residence inspired glee as well as fear; the "lower" hill consciousness is strong, as is "the little people" concept. The corresponding attitude toward "the other America" is to lump all those with power and privilege into one group; little which the mass media, or the statements of the liberal protest groups say has any effect on our constituency.

However, there is a strange mix of attitudes toward those immediately above and below them on the economic ladder. Probably a minority of the group has no antagonistic or snobbish feelings about anyone in the neighborhood: they are either the very "nitty" tenants in the worse slums, or people in leadership who are comfortably situated. But in contrast to this, there is a strong feeling among many that much of the problem is the people's fault, and that they must be educated to be responsible; the reason things are so bad is that people are lazy, stupid, and apathetic. This is not only a homeowner attitude: anyone who is already in the movement has certain initiative, and they often resent or scorn those who do not have this initiative or ability to stay above water.

One function of this attitude is a belief in individualism rather than group action, and further, that change comes about through argument and instruction rather than through power. On the other hand, the rent strikes function completely on a collective basis, premised on the concept of power and conflict. . . .

On the other hand, the world of local politics seems quite real. They comprehend how local politics works, and realize they are of interest to local politicos. It is perfectly possible for the movement to turn to politics as an arena, and even now our telephone squads invite politicians to demonstrations, in order to line them up with or against us.

4. "Newark: Community Union"

The Newark project successfully organized the neighborhoods against a "Negro removal" plan of urban renewal. Several hundred people worked actively with the project, and several neighborhood people joined the staff. After initial successes the project became bogged down, partly because most of the leaders were uncertain about where to go. Debates then took place over the problem of leadership. This was resolved, and the project is now well-organized and actively promoting radical political organization in addition to community services. Jesse Allen, a staff member of the Newark project, was a union organizer who worked on the rent strike in Newark. This article appeared in the Winter 1965 Studies on the Left.

1. RENT STRIKE

Some of the people from the neighborhood council came around to visit me and they saw the condition of the building I was living in, such as peeling paint, broken plaster, bad plumbing, bad wiring, broken stair steps, rats and roaches, and they began to visit more houses on the blocks and found most of the

houses in the same condition. We complained to City Hall. We
got no cooperation from the Board of Health. We did not get
any cooperation from our mayor, and the landlords just
wouldn't fix up. So some of us got together and started talking
and we decided to set up a block committee and talk to people.
Once you start talking to people and bring them together you
can start moving to do something for your neighborhood. We
organized eight blocks in our neighborhood in about six weeks.
We called a meeting with the people and discussed our problems. We found that most all of us had the same problems. We
decided to go on a rent strike. We were not going to pay the
landlord any more money until he did something. When the
landlords came around for the rent we told them we're not paying any more rent to them. We had their money, but we were
putting it into the bank until they fixed the houses. Some of the
landlords started to repair right away, such as Lee Bernstein,
our South Ward City Councilman. Others did not do anything.

We started picketing the houses we were renting in our neighborhood. First we picketed at Ray Shustak's building, one that
the Mayor himself had come down and looked at and found 125
violations (after a delegation of people had complained to him
about it). The Mayor made us all sorts of promises but failed to
carry out any of them. Our City Councilman Lee Bernstein told
us we should have come to him before and he would have done
something about it. At the time he had apartment houses in the
neighborhood with lots of violations and he wasn't doing anything about fixing them up. But he was collecting one hundred
and ten dollars a month rent from each of his apartments. He
tried to get us not to picket, but we picketed anyway. Bernstein
called it a disgrace.

The landlords took us into court and the judge took the
money into the court and told Robert Inlander, a landlord, that
he would take the money every time our rent was due. The landlord and the city called us troublemakers. About two months
later the landlord took us back into court again. This time he did
not want any rent money. He wanted us out of his buildings. We
told the judge that we were still paying our money to the court.
The judge said to us that the landlord didn't want the money,
that we had to move out of the buildings. Our lawyer, Felix

Neals, argued the case, but the judge would not give out any justice. He was all the way on the landlords' side.

We found out that Inlander lived in the richest part of Maple-wood, his house valued at $90,000. So we decided to put a picket line around it. Three days later he asked us if we were going to continue to picket if we moved. We told him yes. He said why would you keep on picketing when the judge says that you must move anyway. We told him that we wanted a decent place to live for the next tenants that moved in. So he said that if we wanted to stay on in the building, we could. He had stated in the newspaper after we picketed his home that he was not the owner of the property in question, but merely the overseer. By doing research, we found that he did own the property, so we told him that if he didn't own the property how could he tell us that we could stay on after all. He said don't worry about that, I can fix it up. We told him that we were sorry that we had spent his money, and he said some of you are good people so we told him that when we were willing to pay the money to the court that he wouldn't accept the money and after the judge had given us a week to move out, we told the judge and the landlord that if we found decent apartments to live in within a week we would move out. But if we didn't we would stay on and be thrown out. Some of us found apartments, but did not move into them at the time. We wanted to see if the city would continue to let absentee landlords have their way when they knew the conditions of the buildings we were living in. So we stayed on a couple of weeks longer, but no one ever came to throw us out. . . .

4. THE BEATING AT KLEIN'S

Clyde Wright, another member of NCUP, was chained and beaten bloody in Klein's Department Store by their security guards. After being beaten he was charged with shoplifting and assault and battery. Klein's says the beating never happened. Some employees say it did. They testified that they were called in to clean up the blood in the basement before the police were called in. Klein's still says it never happened.

Since the NCUP has started its protest in this matter, we learned that this was not the first time that people have been beaten in the basement of Klein's. Maybe Clyde Wright is not guilty of shoplifting or maybe he is. As far as we have learned the only packages he carried he had paid for.

We are now protesting at Klein's against such brutality. It is time that Klein's and City Hall learn that brutality must go. It never will, and neither will slumlords, unless the people in the community come forward together and stand up to City Hall. Right now NCUP is fighting alone but before the year is over we think that other wards of Newark will be standing and fighting with us.

The Newark Community Union is an organization that is built by the people and for the people in the South Ward. We organize ourselves by block groups. We don't believe in leadership. We believe in one man, one vote. We have a program committee meeting once a week. All our blocks that we have organized come together at the program committee meeting. We discuss each problem that occurs on our blocks and let the people decide what kind of action they want to take to solve the problem. Therefore, we carry through a vote where all the people in the community will have a voice in what kind of decision is to be made, and what kind of action we must take, to solve the problems that our poor people face today. We have rotating chairmen who serve four weeks and then are replaced by the program committee. We in NCUP do not believe in leadership because so many organizations have been sold out by leaders. That is why we demand one man, one vote.

5. *Interviews with SDS Staffers*

These excerpts are from two interviews conducted in June 1965 at Kewadin, Michigan. Both people have been with SDS since their late teens, and both are important in the organization. The interviews are printed to offer an idea of SDS thinking, how it developed, and what the "kids" are like as whole people, rather than only as "protestors." These interviews were not "typical," in the sense that they reflect a fixed SDS "type"; there is no such single type. But the people are typical in the sense that they are in their early twenties, are college graduates, come from middle-class homes, and see their futures in The Movement.

A twenty-two-year-old man, now working in the SDS National Office. He graduated from a high-ranking Eastern college in 1964, is unmarried. He comes from a middle-class Jewish background; both of his parents were members of the Socialist Party in the 1930s.

I did some political work for ADA types when I was in high school; it wasn't until I got to college that I became deeply involved. After I saw the HUAC movie *Operation Abolition* I became really angry. It's hard to describe the strong identification I had with the students in that movie. It also showed me that the student movement was important, and I became active in the anti-HUAC campaign.

I had accepted the Communist threat idea, more in terms of the Soviet Union than American Communists. I was influenced by the Cold War stuff. Communist speakers on campus helped me to overcome the idea that they were dangerous. They were so innocuous.

I guess there was a gradual radicalization that took place from reading, talking, getting involved later in the peace movement and anti-HUAC. I went to the SDS convention and I remember being very impressed by Tom Hayden, Al Haber, and Robb Burlage.

The Power Elite and the books and magazines of the English New Left made big impressions on me; and so did *Communitas.* But when I heard Goodman speak, I was turned off. I read the *Correspondent* and I guess it made me a peacenik. I was moved by Edgar Snow's *Red Star Over China.* I read a little Marx, but only through courses, from Lewis Feuer's anthology; and a little Fromm, Camus, Sartre, after graduating. I spent most of my time at college in meetings. I guess some of the liberal faculty members influenced us. I had an emotional reaction to *Grapes of Wrath* and *Man's Fate.* More recently, *Catch-22* and *One Flew Over the Cuckoo's Nest* have really moved me. And movies—I mentioned *Operation Abolition*—like *He Who Must Die* and *Come Back, Africa* affect me deeply.

It's funny you ask about sex. In SDS, fucking is a statement of community, and there's a lot of inter-fucking, but it's not casual. Sex comes out of a relationship and is used to build a relationship stronger. I'm not thinking of marriage, but I'm not promiscuous. There isn't much promiscuity, and from the people I know in SDS sex is usually linked to love. . . .

Again, pot isn't important except in a few chapters. There isn't any pot at SDS parties, and only in one or two chapters do SDS people turn on and call the rest of us square.

SDS has a serious role: to make a New Left movement with a radical politics and analysis—to build a new society.

We don't have many working-class contacts. We're trying to develop projects among the poor and unemployed to build community movements that challenge the power structure. You know, we fought the urban renewal program in Newark, and we're trying to organize unemployed in Chicago.

There are possibilities for organizing professionals around a movement of the poor. That's not so crazy. Like, look at all the lawyers who went to Mississippi and bolstered SNCC and MFDP.

I see my own role as a political organizer. I like it. I worked in the Chester, Pennsylvania, project and I'm going to Oakland to help set up the project there. I feel comfortable in the role of a student organizer, and I think SDS can out-organize the other groups because it is more in tune with the mood of students. The mood? It's searching, honesty, democracy, like we have inside SDS. We can out-organize the DuBois Clubs.

I was arrested at the Chase Manhattan Bank picket. Did you know that the ILGWU has $500 million deposited there? That's 4 percent of the total deposit. SDS people all saw what happens when you cooperate with liberals. It's not only the ILGWU. On the Washington teach-in this last spring, we were outvoted by the academic liberals on every issue. They made sure that it would be nice and safe.

I read some of The Movement magazines. I read *Studies on the Left* once in a while, but not as often as I should, because I think it is the closest to The Movement. I look at *Liberation* quite often, and occasionally at *Dissent.*

Right now I admire Wayne Morse and Isaac Deutscher. Eugene Debs is my hero.

(HOW DO YOU FEEL ABOUT THE CUBAN REVOLUTION AND THE UPRISING IN HUNGARY?)

I identify with the Cuban Revolution. Hungary, I remember vaguely when it happened. It was awful what the Russians did.

I forgot to mention the influence of anarchism on SDS. Dave Dellinger is very important to a lot of us, and so is Paul Goodman. Also, many SDS kids write masters' theses on C. Wright Mills.

Our most important experiment now, I think, is ERAP [Economic Research and Action Program]. I think we have made some breakthroughs. You know that in the projects that are organized the poor whites accept integration as a political objective. They see the need for alliance with poor Negroes. . . .

A twenty-two-year-old woman, now active in an SDS Community Organizing Project. She received her B.A. in political science in 1964; was married (no children) in 1963 and recently separated. Her husband was also in The Movement. Her parents are "good liberal Jewish Democrats."

In high school I had strong feelings about civil rights. I wanted to date Negroes, and I helped organize a group which went to the 1958 civil rights March. I was with a group of snotty intellectuals in high school. We talked about existentialism, values, and visions.

As a college freshman I met the founders of SDS and was elected officer of a campus club that became SDS. (*She laughed.*) You know, they needed a young girl as a kind of front.

I was active in various political projects around campus and NSA. We brought speakers, were involved in direct action on civil rights, peace, and HUAC, and we participated in student elections. I worked on a food-and-clothing drive for people in Fayette County who were being starved out. I felt an obligation to help them. I took a romantic trip South and I talked a lot about my experience in Fayette when I came back. The trip had both a responsibility filling and a fun-filled element to it.

I was active in discussions about university reform. This was part of SDS campus activities. We had many demonstrations, mostly in response to events.

In my sophomore year, I became more involved with my personal life, with the guy whom I was to marry. I had known him before because he was in The Movement, too. I was also intimidated because some of the older SDS leaders expected more from me than I felt I could deliver. This was a kind of dilemma because I wanted fiercely to participate and yet was afraid I couldn't live up to the expectations.

In my junior year I questioned the relevance of the particular academic work and quit college to work in a peace institute in Washington, D.C. The emphasis was on quitting college because it lacked meaning, on the one hand, and a desire to do work with meaning, on the other. My idea was that doing some other relevant work, for example, in the peace movement, might help me figure out a better idea of what I wanted to get out of college. I also worked for SDS and was arrested three times, all at civil rights demonstrations.

I think my radicalizing process came more through personal contact, action, and from my liberal family, than through books or great men. In high school I was deeply moved by Russian novels. Sartre and Camus had some impact on me, but a history teacher introduced me to the *New Republic* and the *Nation*.

In college I read very little Marx—for courses only—and I didn't understand the economics. The alienation parts seemed more relevant and exciting.

(THE INTERVIEWER ASKED: DID YOU CONSIDER YOURSELF A MARXIST? HER ANSWER: I REJECT LABELS.

I read C. Wright Mills's *White Collar, Power Elite,* and *Causes of World War III,* some of them for courses, others independently. I was very impressed but I questioned Mills's role in writing *White Collar*. Was he a victim of the same thing he was describing? But Mills and Floyd Hunter [*Community*

Power Structure] helped me understand how the U.S. was run.

I always read a lot. I read *I. F. Stone's Weekly* religiously, and usually the *New Republic, Nation, Studies on the Left, Liberation, Progressive,* and *Dissent.*

The importance to me of the sex questions stemmed from expectations about girls and sex in The Movement. I wasn't hung up over, but was aware of, those problems, and derived part of my own outlook in response to then current notions (e.g., radicals in politics should be radical in sex; therefore, girls should sleep around a lot. That's an inane example, but the kind of thing that made me develop an "outlook"). My first sex experience was in college, and I had thought and talked about it for a long time. When I first made love I felt I knew what I was doing and I knew I was in love. I would describe my attitude toward sex as liberal, never let it be a hang-up, but sex is always linked to love in my mind. I am repulsed by the idea of sex for the sake of sex; I dislike physical contact that is insincere.

We talk a lot about the woman's role. SDS, like almost everything else in this country, has strong male supremacy. Look at the leadership and how many women do you find?

I never smoked pot. I have no desire and have no close friends who smoke it. I feel indifferent towards it.

My taste in music is classical and Baroque. I more or less like rock 'n' roll. I loved Pete Seeger for his content in high school. I like the New Lost City Ramblers and Joan Baez; I dislike the Kingston Trio and Chad Mitchell—they're commercial and slick.

I've worked for a year at the community project because I believe in the vision that SDS is trying to make a reality. My role was to organize poor whites to build organizations that would help the poor to control their own lives, to make decisions, to have power over their own lives. After a year of this I'm not convinced that organizing the poor will bring a revolution, but it is still vital and necessary and I can play a role at it.

I went into the project because I shared the SDS analysis of corporate liberalism, the faceless bureaucracy, etc. That matters less now than my concern for people being able to develop their potential and be good with each other. I work in one place trying to do that, and it doesn't matter, let's say, if the job situation improves. People are still impotent, squashed by society. As an individual I might not be able to change their material lives, but I can share with them my vision and try to convince them to get together and change things.

The Leftovers

1. The Progressive Labor Party

In 1962 the Maoists, the Progressive Labor Movement (PLM), split from the Communist Party. In 1964 they formed the Progressive Labor Party (PL). The documents and journals of PL read as if they were written in the late twenties and early thirties by officials of the Communist International. In those years, known as the Third Period, the Party line was based on a conviction that the collapse of capitalism was imminent and that the working class was becoming radicalized enough to establish a proletarian revolution with the Party as its vanguard. That same spirit emanates from the publications of the Progressive Labor Party today. It is an organization in deadly earnest about its role, and it is convinced that its version of socialism, based on the Chinese rather than the Soviet model, will triumph.

I. Perspectives for the Left *

When we talk about the political perspectives of the American left, we are really talking about new demands and the new movements that will come into existence to fight for these demands.

* *Progressive Labor,* January 1965.

From the viewpoint of the Progressive Labor Movement, a key characteristic of these new demands is their revolutionary content. Broadly speaking, demands fall into two categories: (1) Demands which the ruling, capitalist class can meet without seriously threatening their own supremacy, their own power; and (2) Demands which the ruling class cannot meet because such demands if carried out would transfer effective political power from the capitalist class to the working class.

The ultimate revolutionary demand is the demand for a government controlled by working people—in the classical terminology (which is today somewhat out of favor), a revolutionary dictatorship of armed workers. This is easy enough to see, and most "leftists" bend over backwards to repudiate this goal in theory and practice. After all, this demand is the ultimate in sedition, in subversion. In a word, it is revolutionary.

It is not so easy to classify other demands. Depending on the historical circumstances, almost any demand can be revolutionary on the local or national scene. To the local aristocracy of Mississippi and Alabama, the bourgeois demand of "one man, one vote" is revolutionary. But universal suffrage is deep within the context of bourgeois liberalism. Even in Mississippi, the right to vote will become operative within the next decade. The national ruling class will endeavor (with initial success) to channel these millions of new black voters into a slightly liberalized Democratic Party. There are only a few hundred counties in the South which have a black majority. These counties will have black local governments just as Harlem has a black Congressman (and even a black police captain). A few local bigots will suffer, but the capitalist class will reign supreme and unchallenged as before.

Trade union organization, while detested by the ruling class as a cause of decreased profits, is not inherently revolutionary. But the CIO sit-down strikes of the late 1930s certainly had revolutionary overtones. By taking possession of industrial plants (even on a temporary basis), those militant workers threatened the economic foundation of capitalist political power, the ownership and management of the productive facilities of the country. If workers start taking over plants, this doesn't mean merely reduced profits . . . it means no profits at all (and hence no political power). The ruling class quickly (in most cases) moved to recognize the new unions because their power was being directly threatened. In those cases where concessions were not forthcoming, the strikes were suppressed by police and national guard violence.

Economic demands tend to be more revolutionary then political demands, up to but not including the ultimate demand for a government controlled by working people. When universal suffrage exists, where do you go from there?

The advocates of a new "Liberal-Labor-Negro" coalition around a program of welfare-state demands are obviously no challenge to the ruling class; indeed the Johnson regime has greatly benefited from the present existence of such a coalition.

Let us suppose for a moment that the advocates of new coalitions to the left of the Johnson regime were so successful that they succeeded in building a mass movement (within the Democratic Party, of course) that demanded nationalization of certain basic industries (steel, railroads, etc.). How is a nationalized enterprise managed by governmental representatives of the capitalist class any genuine improvement over the present situation? Witness, for example, the recent strikes by British railroad workers against the government-owned railroads at a time when a Labor Party government was in power. Moreover, government employees in the U.S. do not have the right to strike.

The same argument applies to the proponents of the Clark Bill (which provides for national economic planning in the "public sector"). National economic planning by a capitalist government in a capitalist economic context is not socialism and is not a step toward socialism.

New coalition advocates are left with a strategy of infiltration. The liberal wing of the Democratic Party seeks to infiltrate and take over the entire Democratic Party. The left-liberals (Henry Wallace progressives) try to infiltrate and take over the liberal wing of the Democratic Party. The Socialist Party seeks to infiltrate and take over the left-liberal wing of the Democratic Party. The Communist Party seeks to infiltrate and take over the whole spectrum from Norman Thomas to Jacob Javits and beyond. I won't venture to predict the successes and failures of these comic endeavors, but it is a pretty safe bet that everyone will be thoroughly confused by the whole thing except the ruling class; they will be amused.

The only other significant political development in recent years has been the rise and fall of "the peace movement." In nearly all cases, this movement has put forward demands to which the ruling class can pay effective lip service (test-ban, partial disarmament, etc.). It seems that Red-baiting has effectively disarmed the disarmers. Within the peace movement, the only radical challenge has come from such groups as the Committee for Non-Violent Action, the May 2nd Movement, etc. These groups, particularly the latter, have demanded an end to imperialist wars habitually conducted by the American ruling class against the emerging socialist countries of Africa, Asia, and Latin America. This demand strikes at the heart of one of the main supports for the capitalist tyranny in this country—the exploitation of the labor and resources of foreign countries. The ruling class cannot afford to give up the profits of such exploitation and it is obviously willing to go to war to protect such profits. Any group which tries to mobilize public opinion against those wars can expect nothing from the ruling class except persecution . . . and that has been the historical record (May 2nd Movement, CNVA, Women's Strike for Peace, etc.). The demand for an end to the war in Vietnam (i.e., unconditional withdrawal) is a revolutionary demand, especially when linked to a continuing campaign against U.S. intervention anywhere at any time.

The emphasis in the next few years seems more likely to be economic; new demands and new tactics will be forthcoming to deal with the rising crisis of automated unemployment and resulting poverty.

Already emerging is the demand for a "guaranteed income" regardless of employment (a variation of the "jobs or income" approach with the emphasis on the income). This demand certainly goes against the grain of bourgeois ideology, and there is little reason to think that the ruling class would agree to meet it. But can this demand be said to be more than abstractly "revolutionary"? Proponents of this scheme have not yet put forward a political and economic strategy for achieving this demand. Will it be done through unions of the unemployed, community syndi-

calism, the Democratic Party or a new party or what? This demand (like the demand for "Peace, Land, Bread!") could be a
useful slogan for radicalizing people and educating them to the
necessity of workers' power; and it could also turn out to be just
another utopian slogan (like Henry George's "Single Tax" or
Upton Sinclair's "End Poverty in California!"). The demand for
a guaranteed income is abstractly revolutionary—more than
that cannot be said at this time.

The demand for "Freedom Now!"—i.e., the total and absolute abolition of all forms of discrimination and deprivation
within the next few years—is closer to the mark. The super-
exploitation of foreign countries is one of the main supports of
capitalist tyranny in this country. Moreover that support is becoming more important as U.S. imperialism is driven out of
other parts of the world. Thus, the extra profits arising from the
super-exploitation of black people will not be given up without
a severe struggle. Overt racism does not sit well on the face of
bourgeois liberalism; therefore, the ruling class can be expected
to make partial and token concessions to the Black Freedom
Movement in the next few years. But if the demand for "Freedom Now!" is constantly reiterated and disciplined organizing
(possibly through community syndicalism) takes place around
this demand, a revolutionary situation will be in the making.
Millions of black people will be demanding something the ruling
class cannot deliver! . . .

There is today what I think to be a very significant controversy in the American Left. I refer to the dispute between those
who advocate reliance on the traditional "agent of social
change"—the existing trade unions—and those who propose
unions of employed and unemployed workers on a residential
basis (community unions or what is known as "community syndicalism"). The significance of this controversy lies in the fact
that those who rely on the trade unions must perforce modify
their demands so as not to offend conservative union leadership; while those who propose community unions bypass the
trade union leadership and are free to make their demands as
revolutionary as the situation and their courage permit.

Roughly 75 percent of the American working class is unorganized. There is little reason to believe any of the existing trade

unions are prepared to undertake massive organizing drives. The situation is certainly ripening toward a new federation of labor; it remains to be seen whether an insurgent movement within one of the existing (maverick) unions will take the lead or whether the initiative will come from a successful and expanding community union movement . . . quite possibly both may happen. Either way, this new wave of organizing will have revolutionary overtones. Will the overtones become explicit or will they flourish briefly and die away as in the case of the old CIO?

Perhaps the answer to this question may be found in both the parent and the child of the CIO . . . the New Deal. The New Deal and those groups gathered around it demanded everything but revolution. To paraphrase an old saying: "Our rulers giveth and our rulers taketh away." All the victories won by the New Deal have been eroded away or abruptly withdrawn. Compulsory arbitration (as in the threatened railroad strike over job security) has rendered the "Magna Carta of Labor" (the Wagner Act) meaningless. Social security and welfare benefits have been eroded by the rising cost of living to a point where it is barely possible to survive on them. The same is true of unemployment compensation while the Federal Minimum Wage is below the Government's own figures on what constitutes a poverty-level income. Unemployment is chronic and beginning to rise. We have virtually lost all that once we gained.

The same thing is true concerning single-issue and less massive multi-issue groups. People unite and pursue some limited goal. They are bought off with token concessions that are later, after the movement dies down, gradually withdrawn. We need in America a group that has a basic understanding of the meaning of capitalist political power and the determination to overthrow this power and set up a government controlled by working people. We need a group that understands the mechanism of class struggle, a group that will not let movements die down but will stimulate and lead mass movements towards the achievement of their political destiny . . . the seizure of power. In short, we need a Marxist-Leninist party. And we shall have it.

The next few years will see the emergence of a Marxist-Leninist party in the United States. The growth of this party will

be slow at first, for no political party has put forward the demand for revolutionary socialism as a meaningful and attainable
goal to the American working class for more than three decades.
The party's base will be the most oppressed elements of the
working class; Black ghettos, the automated unemployed, and
working-class youth who will never have a job under capitalism.
Additional sources of strength will be found in insurgent movements in the trade unions, in the freedom movement of the
South, and in the student movement. Campaigns will be waged
for immediate gains and reforms while, at the same time, agitation and recruitment will be conducted around the ultimate revolutionary demand with which this pamphlet began . . . the
abolition of the capitalist tyranny which oppresses our land and
the establishment of a revolutionary government controlled by
working people.

Such, in my view, are the perspectives of the Progressive
Labor Movement, and to these ends I am committed. It shall be
for others (and there will be many others) to settle for a brief
modification of tyranny. Our cry is the cry for liberty and our
numbers shall be millions! And should our deeds be worthy of
our words, our victory is all but certain.

II. Constitution*

PREAMBLE

The great American dream of "life, liberty and the pursuit of
happiness" has been turned by a ruthless regime into a nightmare of death, destruction and the pursuit of dollars. On behalf
of the tens of millions of our fellow citizens who have seen their
dream betrayed, we convene today.

In the midst of the corruption and terror of the past—and the
present—we have come together to plant the flag of the future.

Even as we meet, the rulers of our nation are sending off more
planes, bombs, guns and gases in a desperate effort to paralyze
the progress of history, to terrorize and destroy those around the

* Reprinted from *Progressive Labor,* May-June 1965.

world who hold freedom more dear even than life when life means slavery. At home, these same rulers enforce a society of fear with police dogs, cattle prods and prisons.

The most hated government in the world today is the government of our country. In the remotest corner of the earth, the initials U.S.A., which once stood for hope, have replaced the crooked cross of Nazi Germany as the symbol of tyranny and death.

Yet there is another U.S.A.: the U.S.A. which once declared to the world "that whenever any form of government becomes destructive . . . it is the right of the people to alter or to abolish it, and to institute a new government laying its foundations on such principles, and organizing its powers in such forms, as to them shall seem most likely to effect their safety and happiness" (Declaration of Independence); the U.S.A. of the men and women who sweat in factories to produce goods, of the housewives who struggle to keep the homes and raise the children, of the students, artists and honest intellectuals who want desperately to create new beauty for life and not bombs and billboards for death.

It is for this U.S.A., often fooled, sometimes silenced, but still seeking a better life, that we meet today. This U.S.A., in the ghetto streets and tenements, will not go along with the gas chamber plans of this country's ruling class. This U.S.A., beaten, down time and again, deceived and denied, is still ready to organize and to resist. And it is to build that organization and that resistance that we launch our Party today.

"But you will get into trouble," some of our more cautious friends advise us. And, indeed, even as a loosely-organized movement, we have met that "trouble." Several of our comrades are in jail today and many more face the same because of our revolutionary activities. Our newborn Party has already had its baptism of fire.

Yet, we were in trouble before we began to organize; our whole people was in trouble. Are we not in trouble when black men and women and children are beaten, bitten and shot down in the streets for wanting equality? Are we not in trouble when ten million workers can find no work and tens of millions more

face layoffs because progress is measured in profits? Are we not
in trouble when working people forced to hold two or three jobs
can barely earn enough to keep their families going or when
there are more gray rats living in our apartments than there are
tenants? When our children, learning nothing but slogans, ex-
cuses and techniques of war, go through school on an assembly
line—are we not in trouble? And if we see all this and do nothing, are we not in the greatest trouble of all?

"But aren't you afraid?" respond the hesitant friends. And,
indeed, we have come to learn new fears—fears of pre-dawn
gestapo-style raids on our homes, fears of being jailed or seeing
our loved ones dragged to jail and denied bail, fears of frame-
ups, fears of physical assault and even assassination organized
by the ruling class and its police force.

Yet we know a greater fear: the fear of seeing our country's
government dropping death-bombs on innocent families around
the world and seeing ourselves sitting with our hands in our
pockets and doing nothing; the fear of raising our children in a
land that teaches hate and laughs at love and seeing ourselves
unable to show our children a way to a new life; the fear of
turning on the TV set and watching the diseased and dying of
our own nation paraded across the screen in cynical appeals for
charity while Congress spends billions for bombs, and seeing
ourselves every night sinking into sleep alone with our night-
mares.

With the birth of our new Party, we dedicate ourselves to end
those fears and those troubles. We resolve to build a revolutionary movement with the participation and support of millions of
working men and women as well as those students, artists and
intellectuals who will join with the working class to end the
profit system which breeds those fears and those troubles. With
such a movement, we will build a socialist U.S.A., with all
power in the hands of the working people and their allies.

We recognize that the fight will be long and hard. The kings,
queens and bishops of modern finance capital and their political
pawns have made it clear they will use every form of force and
violence in their desperation to hold onto their stolen billions.
We will be prepared to continue the struggle on whatever level

and with whatever forms are necessary. Surrender is a word we will not know.

To win, we will have to work closely together, disciplined by the urgency of the goal before us; we will have to study and learn to utilize our communist principles and the science of Marxism-Leninism to evaluate honestly our own strengths and weaknesses and those of the enemy at each new stage of the campaign.

Regardless of personal sacrifice, we resolve to demonstrate through constant organized action that the struggle can be carried—and won—to defeat the present system of war and oppression; that the working class can—and will—control its own destiny.

We know full well that with this resolve we fix our fates in a future of fire.

Yet we know, too, that from the very flames of our fight—the fight of all honest working people, students, housewives and intellectuals of our country and the world—a new society shall be built—in which our children, our children's children, and the billion billion children to come will never be forced to hunger for food or shelter or love—a new society without exploitation of man by man, a society, a nation, a world of revolutionary socialism.

To this end, we here resolve to give our every energy, our resources, and our lives.

INTRODUCTION

In order to draw closer to the people, learn from the people, and serve the people as the vanguard of the working class and its allies, we adopt the scientific principles of democratic centralism.

Democratic centralism enables us to gather ideas from the masses, formulate them scientifically, and go back to the masses with our program and strategy.

Democratic centralism enables us to act together as a solid, unified body, increasing manyfold the effect of our efforts.

Democratic centralism unites leaders and members in bonds of mutual confidence and trust, while developing an iron discipline far stronger than military discipline, since it is based on voluntary association, not on fear; on understanding, not command.

There are certain habits which we all derive directly from the exploitative system which we have vowed to destroy. These habits put a strangle-hold on our full potential. As communists we cannot tolerate in ourselves or in our comrades any form of racism, or male supremacism. Male supremacist attitudes, which limit the full participation of women, and racism are among the most effective ideological weapons of the ruling class, and we must struggle constantly against divisions on the basis of race, national origin and sex.

For members of the entire party we adopt the method of consistent criticism and self-criticism.

2. DuBois Clubs

> "Like, it's their system, baby . . .
> And it's a bitch."

These two lines, the opening of an article on education in The Insurgent, *give something of the flavor found in the DuBois Clubs' publications. Written in a breezy, semi-hip style,* The Insurgent *is far less political than* Progressive Labor. *Indeed, in a letter to the editor, published in the May-June 1965 issue, the magazine is commended for being "the kind of magazine that will appeal to a variety of people; one that doesn't drip with political theory yet has great political orientation. . . ." In the summer of 1964 the DuBois Clubs cemented the local clubs into a national organization. In March 1966, Nicholas deB. Katzenbach called for their registration as a "Communist front" group. The Clubs denied the charge and have maintained that they were singled out for attack because of their opposition to the war in Vietnam.*

I. Introduction

The two statements reprinted here were written by the national executive committee of the W.E.B. DuBois Clubs of

America for presentation to the platform committee of the Democratic Party at its 1964 convention. As such, they do not represent the full position of the DuBois Clubs on the election issues of civil rights, poverty and foreign policy. They are intended, however as realistic proposals by which the Democratic Party might effectively deal with some of the crucial problems, domestic and international, faced by the American people.

As socialists, then, we advocate more radical changes in principles and policies than are suggested by the following papers. For example, while we petition the Democratic Party to withdraw American troops from South Vietnam and to reconvene the fourteen-nation Geneva Conference on Vietnam, the full position of the DuBois Clubs, as expressed in the resolutions of our founding convention, calls for support of the National Liberation Front of South Vietnam. However, in the context of an appeal to the Democratic Party, it is our intention to influence the reality of United States policy as effectively as possible. We must not isolate ourselves by making demands that are so out of touch with today's political realities that they can have little promise of moving people toward positive change. This is not to say that we must compromise our position, or ignore our socialist perspective. What we say is that we must always bear in mind our conception of how change occurs, and base our actions upon an understanding of how best to implement that change within the context of a given situation.

II. Statement of the W.E.B. DuBois Clubs of America on foreign policy written for presentation to the Platform Committee of the Democratic Party National Convention, August 1964

The W.E.B. DuBois Clubs of America is a youth organization committed to socialism as the best and only effective solution to the social problems of our time. These problems, we believe, have reached crisis proportions. At home, the Negro people have risen against the whole inhuman system of rascist oppression, and in so doing have laid bare the poverty, disease, and insecurity that haunt the lives of millions of Americans, white as well as black. Abroad, the policy of hostility to social revolution continues to generate small wars, and the threat of escalation to world thermonuclear war. . . .

To the war crisis in Southeast Asia and the danger of a flare-up in the Carribean has now been added another even more dangerous threat to world peace. An alliance of the most extreme racists, McCarthyites, and militarists has imposed its spokesman as the candidate of the Republican Party. This alliance is committed to a policy of nuclear brinksmanship and of dismantling of the limited structure of agreements and peaceful relations with the Soviet Union. The implementation of the Goldwater policy will mean certain thermonuclear war.

Goldwater must be defeated this November, but the electoral defeat of Goldwater, by itself, will not mean the political defeat of the extreme right in the United States. A close election will be seen by the right as a political victory, making theirs appear to be the accepted political alternative to the foreign policy of the administration for the next four years. The only way to end the threat of what Governor Brown of California called "the stench of fascism," is for the Administration to turn away from the policies of the Cold War. Those who support the Democratic Party must recognize that the war program of Goldwater is merely the logical extension of the policy that has guided U.S. foreign policy since 1947 under the leadership of both major parties.

THE BASIS OF UNITED STATES POLICY

In the name of anti-Communism the administrations of Truman, Eisenhower, Kennedy, and now Johnson have sought to stem the tide of national liberation and the social revolutions that accompany it, by alliance with and military aid to the most brutal of dictatorial regimes.

This commitment to reaction and military repression of social revolution has resulted in a continuing series of war crises which severely hinder efforts, like the partial test ban treaty, to relax tensions between the United States and the Soviet Union. And, of course, the policy of stemming the tide of social revolution is a failure. It is a failure because revolutions grow out of unbearable social conditions. Misery, starvation, war, and exploitation make revolutionaries out of poor workers, peasants, and the best

men and women in any society. Repression and foreign intervention only create further oppression, resentment, and revolutionaries. Some of these revolutionary movements are led by Communists. All are committed to some form of socialism. Most of
exploited mankind today already realizes that only through
public ownership and control of a people's economic resources
can progress be made toward a decent life for all. . . .

III. Editorial

DISRUPTERS!

Why do we demonstrate? Because we live in a corrupt society, one which seems to have grown insensitive to human suffering—whether in Southeast Asia or Southeast U.S.A.—and we
can't sit back and allow things to continue that way. It's about
as simple as that. We aim to change the world for the better, and
demonstrations are one way of attempting to do just that.

In a TV documentary on American youth produced last year
by a major network, the narrator commented: "Most of today's
youngsters feel a sense of powerlessness to change society." In
contrast, a *Holiday* magazine study recently characterized
today's young Americans as "more thoughtful, more aggressive,
more willing to take chances and learn from occasional mistakes, and more interested in ultimately improving the world
about them than earlier generations have been."

There is truth in both of these remarks. Feelings of hopelessness and alienation are prevalent among young people today
. . . but they have not infected all of us. Millions of words are
being written about our generation's "desperate search for
values." It is ironic, then, that when some of us are moved to act
according to our society's most cherished values, the mass media
and the Establishment gang up to put us down.

A generation intent upon "improving the world" sees the necessity for action; for deliberate steps taken with some assurance
that the action will indeed contribute to the changes demanded.
Thousands upon thousands have acted, and the ranks of activists grow each day in number and determination. With this
growth has come the avalanche of condemnation, the accusation

of "beatniks" and "militant hotheads," the Freudian interpretations about "generational conflict," and the unending sermons
about "law and order."

Why? Because the principal weapon seized upon by those
who are seeking changes has been the public demonstration.
Peace marches, sit-ins, picket lines—these are the order of the
day. And somebody up there doesn't like it. Boiled down, about
all we can say is: TOUGH! Down here in the streets, we see the
necessity for our actions.

But why demonstrations? Aren't demonstrations the wrong
way to go about it? Doesn't direct action disrupt society and
violate the tradition of orderly democratic progress? Why don't
we use the established institutions of government to secure redress of grievances?

Because all too often "order" and democratic institutions are
expressions and devices of the *status quo*. We are all for order—
for elections, courts, laws and police, when and if they are by,
for and of the people. Our whole dream is to create a truly democratic society. But it is wrong to speak of this country as a truly
democratic one. For us, democracy must be more than a promise; it must function. That means real people, equipped with
knowledge, making the real decisions that affect their lives.

Look at the South. When the whole structure of government
and the force of economic power is bent on denying people
(white and black) their rights, how can anyone insist that the
drive for redress of grievances be contained within the framework of law and order and established political institutions?
The law is built to defend the white power structure. "Order"
means keeping people "in their place." The government, courts,
and police are manipulated by white-owned big business and
the nation's most backward, ignorant politicians.

We have seen time and again in the "liberal" North how well
the courts, the police, the legislatures serve the interests of the
status quo. We have learned how little can be accomplished by
polite argument and rational discussion, and we have learned
the true meaning of "deliberate speed."

There is great power in the Establishment, and we have no
choice but to meet that power with power of our own if we wish

to have our voices heard and our demands met. Our most elementary power lies in our bodies and our numbers and our knowledge of what bodies and numbers can do together.

We wonder whether those "liberals" who are so quick to condemn militant demonstrations and yet so pleased with last year's civil rights act really think that act blossomed out of Congressional good will. Do they really believe the President gave his "We Shall Overcome" speech and rushed through his voting rights bill because he suddenly decided it would be a nice thing to do? Even Johnson himself credited the demonstrations with provoking his action. That speech and that legislation (which really does little more than reaffirm the long-standing power of the Federal Government to ensure the rights of citizens) are the direct result of tremendous pressure by a Movement grown strong enough to move Washington.

In the election of 1964, the overwhelming majority of Americans took a stand against the blindly aggressive policies of the extreme right, only to see those policies adopted by the elected government. Can we stand silently by and watch this happen?

No, we must publicly demonstrate our will, and attempt by force of numbers to make our voices heard, to wrest concessions from a power structure whose interests appear to be opposed to our own.

That's the way it has always been. In reality, we see no tradition of "orderly" progress in America. Instead, we see a history of militant struggle. This nation was founded on the rebellious uprising of a colonial people, beginning with that grandaddy of all our native civil disobedience, the Boston Tea Party. The Abolitionist movement before the Civil War was a nationwide conspiracy to break the hallowed laws of private property and destroy the established institution of chattel slavery.

Those American workingmen and women who today enjoy a pleasant standard of living owe their comfort to a century of bitter and militant direct action. The strike—called "disruptive" by its enemies—is the worker's right and his power. Without that weapon he would be at the mercy of his employer. And the history of labor organizing testifies that the lawlessness and violence came not from the side of those seeking redress, but from those who would deny it—the owners, their militia, their courts and vigilantes. So it is in the South today: violence injected by segregationists into a nonviolent movement of masses seeking their civil rights.

Would the timid friends of social justice have us hold our peace and stop, just because someone else is going to start trouble? Where is all the dignity, power and grandeur of our democratic institutions when people get shot in Mississippi? Oh, they are being embarrassed into action—slowly; they are being prodded by thousands in the streets with picket signs. But our government has yet to ensure the safety of those who go about doing the work of gaining full citizenship for all Americans—a job the government should have done long ago. It is our right to demonstrate; it is the duty of a democratic government to help us exercise that right.

We are quite aware, as are many others, that the current attacks on young activists are not motivated primarily out of concern over street demonstrations in Mississippi or Alabama cities. They are rather motivated by the knowledge that this current challenge to Southern power will also change the balance on Capitol Hill; that real democracy for people in the Deep South will have far reaching effects across the nation—effects that in time will extend to Vietnam, the Congo and other far-off lands. Indeed, for some sections of the power structure, the threat of that happening makes mere demonstrations preferable.

This is not to say that we consider demonstrations the only or even the most viable form of political activity. Until now, the focus for activists was the sporadic picket, sit-in, strike, march —The Movement growing from action to action, slumping, then gaining larger life in some new and unexpected spot. But behind these outbursts of ever-growing action, something new is coming. The time is ripe for political organization, incorporating all the experiences of recent years, but building on far stronger foundations; uniting activists, racial minorities and great numbers of working people—and those who can't find work—into a permanent political force.

We are not dreaming, or giving advice. We are describing what we see. We see the organization of the forgotten in the United States—the Negro people, Puerto Ricans, Mexican-

Americans, the ex-miners of Appalachia. In nearly every community in the land the work is going on: block committees, un-
ionization, tenants' councils, unemployed councils. The most
impressive aspect of this emergent political organization is the
drive to bring the political process to the grass roots, with such
developments as the Mississippi Freedom Democratic Party
which has begun to operate on a ward level across the state. Such
work will spread, and with it the possibility for the People to
assume the power and transform America into a real democracy
—a socialist democracy.

We received another one of those little white cards the other
day saying there was some "Communist propaganda" waiting
for us at the Post Office. We had heard a few days earlier that
the Supreme Court had ruled the Postmaster couldn't keep lists
of persons receiving publications from other countries, so we
called the local post office to find out what was going on. "Just a
minute," the answering voice said, "I'll connect you with our
propaganda unit." In a voice that sounded straight out of Franz
Kafka, the chief of the Propaganda Unit told us the matter was
still "under consideration" and in the meantime we would continue to get the little white cards.

We have since learned the real story of what had happened.
Under a U.S. censorship law, the Customs Bureau reads every
publication coming into the country and decides which is "Communist Propaganda." There apparently is no designation of
Fascist, monarchist or Peronist propaganda. Communist propaganda is defined as anything that seems to "prevail upon, indoc-
trinate, convert, induce or in any other way influence a recipient
or any section of the public within the United States with refer-
ences to the political or public interests, policies, or relations of
a government of a foreign country or a foreign political party or
with reference to the foreign policies of the United States or promote in the United States racial, religious or social dissensions."

Somehow or another, *Pravda, New Times, Soviet Sport* and
Bulgaria Today fall under this definition.

Then the Post Office sends out this little card saying: We've
got a piece of "Communist propaganda" here and strange as it

may seem your name and address appear on the cover. Do you want it?

So you check off "yes I want it," and in a few days you get it. If you don't return the card, or if you say you don't want it, they don't bother to send it back from whence it came; they conduct a ritual magazine burning.

Now, if you checked yes, then obviously you, as a willing recipient of "Communist propaganda," are suspect of something and your name should be turned over to the House Committee on Un-American Activities. Of course. Well, believe it or not, for the past fifteen years that's exactly what they've been doing. And when you went for that job as gym coach at East Elm High School, you were more than likely asked, "Why did you subscribe to *Soviet Sport?*"

Well, one man got tired of filling out the little white cards. It seems he wanted to receive copies of a Chinese magazine printed in Esperanto, and he was confronted with the little cardboard inquiries. (Which seems fishy, as it's hard to believe there is anyone working for Customs who reads Esperanto.) He went to the Supreme Court.

The court agreed to hear the case and a First Amendment decision on the whole matter was anticipated. But as soon as the court began considering it, the justices received a note from the Postmaster saying he was doing away with the lists.

The lists were done away with, or at least so the public has been told. And in their place, a new regulation has gone into effect. Now not only do you have to agree to accept each publication, you have to also agree to accept each edition of the publication, which in the case of *Pravda* (daily) can become somewhat of a bore.

This all seems to us to be a bit obscene, and quite un-American.

There have been numerous and increasing suggestions that we do away with the system of Grand Juries. Wisconsin has already done away with it. England, from whom we got the system in the first place, did away with it in 1933. We don't have a firm opinion at this moment, but it would make a good debate topic for the National Forensics League. We do, however, know one good reason for abolishing or changing the system. In practice it's a perversion of what it is intended to be. Grand Juries are supposed to be panels of our peers. But the chances are very, very small that if you ever get called before one you'll see anyone who seems even remotely like you.

A tragic and criminal example of this is the New York jury that has indicted sixteen people connected with the Negro demonstrations in Harlem last July. The twenty-three man jury is all white and composed of twelve corporation executives, two stockbrokers, two professionals, one secretary and two well-heeled housewives. Their average income is $20,000 a year.

3. The Young Socialist Alliance

The Young Socialist Alliance is the orthodox Trotskyist youth group associated with the Socialist Workers Party. Like its parent group, YSA remains unchanged in its views of society and the role of the working class as the agent of revolutionary change, and it still criticizes Stalinism, while upholding Trotsky's view of the permanent revolution. Its membership has remained small, and its influence on the new radicals is minimal. Perhaps the most interesting aspect of the YSA is that it was one of the first youth groups to identify itself with Malcolm X, the murdered Negro leader who broke from the Black Muslim movement and possessed the potential of becoming the most successful voice of the black ghettos.

"In Tribute to Malcolm X"*

. . . Fidel Castro's dedication to political independence and to economic development for Cuba led him eventually to opposition to capitalism. So also Malcolm's uncompromising stand against racism brought him to identify with the revolutions of the colonial people who were turning against capitalism, and

* *The Young Socialist, May–June 1965.*

finally to conclude that the elimination of capitalism in this country was necessary for freedom. Just as Fidel Castro discovered that there can be no political independence and economic development in a colonial country without breaking from capitalism, so Malcolm had come to the conclusion that capitalism and racism were so entangled in the United States that you had to uproot the system in order to eliminate racism.

Malcolm's black nationalism was aimed at preparing black people to struggle for their freedom. "The greatest mistake of the movement," he said in an interview in the February 25 *Village Voice,* "has been trying to organize sleeping people around specific goals. You have to wake the people up first, then you'll get action." "Wake them up to their exploitation?" the interviewer asked. "No, to their humanity, to their own worth, and to their heritage," he answered.

All he said to the black people was designed to raise their confidence, to organize them independently of those who oppressed them, to teach them who their enemies were, who was responsible for their condition; who were their allies. He explained that they were part of the great majority—the non-whites and the oppressed of the world. He taught that freedom could be won only by fighting for it; it has never been given to anyone. He explained that it could only be won by making a real revolution that uproots and changes the entire economic, social and political structure of this society.

Thus it is not surprising that many who considered themselves socialists, radicals and even Marxists could not recognize and identify with Malcolm's revolutionary character. They could not recognize the revolutionary content of this great leader clothed in the new forms, language, and dark colors of the American proletarian ghetto.

Even with all his uniqueness and greatness as an individual, he could not have reached this understanding unless the conditions in this country were such that it was possible. Even though no one can fill his shoes, the fact that he did what he did, developed as the revolutionary leader he was, is the proof of more Malcolms to come.

He was a proof like Fidel was a proof. Fidel stood up ninety

miles away from the most powerful imperialism in the world and
thumbed his nose and showed us, "See, it can be done. They
can't go on controlling the world forever."

Malcolm went even further than Fidel. Because Malcolm
challenged American capitalism from right inside. He was the
living proof for our generation of revolutionists that it can and
will happen here.

Our job, the job of the YSA, is to teach the revolutionary
youth of this country to tell the difference between the nationalism of the oppressed and the nationalism of the oppressor, to
teach them to differentiate the forces of liberation from the
forces of the exploiters; to teach them to hear the voices of the
revolution regardless of the forms they take; to teach them to
differentiate between the self-defense of the victim and the violence of the aggressor; to teach them to refuse to give an inch to
white liberalism and to reach out to Malcolm's heirs, the vanguard of the ghetto, as brothers and comrades.

4. *The Young People's Socialist League*

*The Young People's Socialist League is affiliated with the
youth and student sections of the Socialist Party. It is small and
its activities are rather limited. Politically, it identifies itself as
"committed to a program not of inevitable victory but of hope—
hope for a democratic and humanist solution to the problems
which press in upon the people of America and the world." In
"Open Letter to Liberal Students" and "A Democratic Left,"
the Norman Thomas Chapter of the YPSL spells out the role it
visualizes for itself among students and youth. The section reproduced here is characteristic of YPSL's political views.*

I. "Open Letter to Liberal Students"

WHY IS SOCIALISM SO WEAK IN THE U.S.?

Socialism in the United States is very weak. Few Americans
stop to think how peculiar this is. In every other democratic
country of the world, politically significant Social Democratic

parties are part of the life of the nation. Not only is America's chief ally—Britain—now ruled by a democratic Socialist government, but socialism is a powerful world movement. *The New York Times,* reporting on the most recent congress of the Socialist International, wrote:

> There was no mistaking the air of optimism that permeated the congress. . . . The Socialist parties in the 47 nations that sent delegates to the meeting have become a force to be reckoned with, and they know it.

But in the United States—while a moral symbol like Norman Thomas, writers like Michael Harrington, and Civil Rights and labor leaders like Bayard Rustin and A. Philip Randolph, show that democratic Socialists can win the respect of many Americans—the socialist movement itself remains very small. The reasons are many and are rooted in the social, economic, and political history of our country. The American economy has been the most dynamic and relatively prosperous capitalism in the world throughout most of its history. Our electoral system places severe disadvantages in the path of third parties. There is confusion in the minds of many people between democratic socialism and totalitarian Communism. But in one important respect socialists themselves have contributed to their own failures —through a narrow and unimaginative sectarianism. Too often we have treated liberals, who are our potential friends, with suspicion and hostility, more interested in preserving ideological "purity" than in trying to convince those closest to us of the value of our ideas. We have been afraid to "get our hands dirty" working for liberal candidates within the Democratic Party and for progressive principles within Democratic clubs.

When the pall of McCarthyism and apathy lifted toward the end of the '50's, the democratic socialist movement in this country saw that new and promising opportunities were opening for it. But before these opportunities could be taken advantage of, American socialists faced the task of formulating new programs and new approaches dealing with the problems of today, not of yesterday. Part and parcel of this task was the overcoming of the sectarian heritage to which we have just referred. This has taken several years. During that time, socialists, while playing an active and honorable role in movements for civil rights, social progress, and a sane foreign policy, often missed the opportunities for modest but meaningful gains that were opening up to us. We now stand at the threshhold of a new and exciting era. We face the challenge and the opportunity to start building a *democratic left* among American students.

II. A Democratic Left

What do we mean by a "democratic left"? It would seem that there are a great variety of organizations already existing on the campus. Why do we need another one? In the first place, we must emphasize that the YPSL does not seek to be a competitor of *any* group working for democratic social progress, whether in the field of civil rights, political campaigning, peace, or education. In fact, we encourage cooperation and even cross-membership with other democratic progressive student organizations. But we feel there *is* a role and a need for an organization which will *supplement* the activities of other groups in important ways. There is a need in campus politics which the YPSL seeks to fill. We are starting to build a current of student opinion that is on the Left, that is democratic, and that is political. The creation of such a current, we are convinced, would be a major contribution to the health and vitality of student politics.

We want to build a movement that is *on the Left,* that is radical in its critique of injustice, privilege and oppression wherever they are found.

We want to build a movement that is *democratic.* One of the tragedies of student politics is that some intelligent, articulate, and idealistic students, moved by a rejection to the injustices and hypocrisies of our society, feel compelled to become apologists for totalitarian movements and regimes. One of the important contributions of the democratic left is its insistence that true radicalism means commitment to human freedom *everywhere,* and criticism of police-state methods whether they are used in Mississippi, South Africa, the Soviet Union, or Cuba. The historical and social factors which gave rise to the "Communist" societies are, of course, highly complex. But one thing upon which democratic leftists must insist is that such societies deserve no more support from American liberals and socialists than do any other anti-democratic regimes. To some, the mere statement of such a principle is "Red baiting." But there is more than one kind of anti-Communism. There is the reactionary brand of Goldwater and HUAC, which seeks to struggle against Communism through anti-democracy and reaction; and there is a progressive kind which rejects Communism because it is anti-democratic and which counterposes effective democracy to Communism. Furthermore, the great majority of American students—for many bad reasons, but for many good ones also—are anti-Communist. A movement which insisted on harboring illusions about the Communist world would find itself under severe handicaps in appealing to the awakening campus community.

Finally, we want to build a movement that is *political*. As we pointed out above, the struggle for political realignment and the destruction of the power of the conservative coalition in Congress and of the Dixiecrat clique within the Democratic Party is a central one for all those interested in political progress. A democratic left will strive to bring a political perspective to student politics—a perspective aimed at influencing the centers of political power. This does not mean that precinct work and activity in political party clubs is a substitute for picket lines, demonstrations, and general educational work, but if "direct-action" is to be truly effective it must become *part* of an orientation toward *politics*.

We do not imagine that the YPSL can become a mass movement in the foreseeable future. But a democratic left on the campus—even as a small minority—could have an important effect on student politics; as a gadfly, as a center for new ideas and programs, as an educational force dedicated to the ideals of social democracy.

We are sure that today there are thousands of students across the country who are looking for a movement that is social democratic in its values, nonsectarian in its approach, and has a clear commitment to democracy around the world—a movement that would be a *democratic left wing within the liberal community*.

The FSM—Revolt
Against Liberal
Bureaucracy

1. "FSM's Joy to U.C.—Free
Speech Carols"

In the spirit of farce and of Christmas, these songs were written and sung. We of the FSM are serious, but we hope we are still able to laugh at ourselves, as well as those who would restrict our Constitutional freedoms."

Those lines from the liner notes of the record Joy to U.C.— Free Speech Carols *describe part of the Free Speech Movement which received very little attention: its humor. The lyrics to the carols were written by members of the FSM and recorded by The Free Speech Five Plus Four.*

I

Oski dolls, Pompom girls, U.C. all the
   way.
Oh, what fun it is to have your mind
   reduced to clay.

Civil rights, politics, just get in the way.
Questioning authority when you should
    obey.

Sleeping on the lawn
In a double sleeping bag
Doesn't get things done—
Freedom is a drag.

Junk your principles
Don't stand up and fight
You won't get democracy
If you yell all night

II

U. C. Administration
Your clumsy punchcard mind
Has put your back against the wall
And tied you in a bind.

Yet in the darkness shineth
An Oakland Cop's flashlight
To strengthen all your arguments
And prove your cause is right.

III. It belongs to the University

On the first of semester
The dean said to me:
    It belongs to the University
On the second of semester
The dean said to me:
    No bumper stickers, it belongs . . .
3rd Don't ask for members
4th Don't collect money
5th NO civil rights
6th NO organizing
7th NO mounting action

8th NO demonstrations
9th You'll be suspended
10th We'll call out troopers
11th Maybe we'll bargain
12th Our word is law

2. Excerpts from I. "Barefoot in a Marshmallow World" * II. "Generational Revolt and the Free Speech Movement" †

Literally millions of words have been written about the Free Speech Movement at the University of California at Berkeley. The events have been described, analyzed, debated about, and polemicized by journalists, academics, commentators, students, and thousands of cocktail-party arguers. But in almost all of these discussions part of the essential element has always been missing: the poetic spirit of the happening, the élan of those who were so committed to their cause, the sense of brotherhood that was felt inside the patrol wagons taking the students to the jails.

Michael Rossman, one of the FSM leaders, writes of this spirit in a review of three books published about the events in Berkeley in "Barefoot in a Marshmallow World." The same spirit emanates from Gerald Rosenfield's description of the student sit-in in the lobby of the Sheraton Palace Hotel in San Francisco and Sproul Hall in Berkeley; the excerpt is from Rosenfield's two-part article "Generational Revolt and the Free Speech Movement."

I. Barefoot in a Marshmallow World

Berkeley: The New Student Revolt by Hal Draper; Introduction by Mario Savio. New York: Grove Press. 246 pp. 95c.

* *Ramparts,* January 1966.
† *Liberation,* December 1965–January 1966.

Revolution at Berkeley edited by Michael V. Miller and
Susan Gilmore; Introduction by Irving Howe. New York:
Dell. 384 pp. 95c.
The Berkeley Student Revolt edited by Seymour Martin
Lipset and Sheldon S. Wolin. New York: Doubleday
Anchor. 585 pp. $1.95.

"What do you feel about the FSM books?" I asked my
friend Steve Weissman, who was on the FSM Steering
Committee with me.
"The Academics are at the dungheap with their forceps
again."
"You can tell the bird by his droppings?" I suggested.
"Maybe. But you can't tell the way he flies."
Those who were FSM will understand this, will understand
how I struggle without poetry to say something about these
books, which is not in their image and dead names, missing the
point as they miss theirs; to articulate the indelible sense of unreality, of irrelevance they leave me with. The sense is familiar,
the conflict was cloaked in fog: were these writers talking to us,
hearing us, even seeing us? How ironic, how fitting, to find it
again, from the same sources and for the same reasons. I can
only say—with the same strange Chaplin humor that infused
every action of the FSM, yet finds no notice in these books—
that the Failed Seriousness Quotient is very high.
FSM happened at the locus of Modern Scholarship. The entire armament of analysis hung poised and desperately avoiding
contact with the Perfect Chance that shook a fist in its face;
while we sang "I write theses/about feces/and it greases/my
way up the line." Were we unfair? No sociologist finds it relevant that the novels Berkeley most quickened to in the past
decade were Kesey's *One Flew Over the Cuckoo's Nest* and
Heller's *Catch-22,* or that we lived that autumn semester in their
grim worlds. Heller says: "There were terrifying, sudden mo-
ments when objects, concepts and even people . . . inexplica-
bly took on an unfamiliar and irregular aspect never seen before
. . . which made them seem totally strange. . . ."
Why did we do it? Everyone who doesn't think we were all
Neurotic Dupes agrees: Civil Rights, Civil Liberties, Educa-

tional Alienation (the surveys tend to contradict these views, and are thus ignored). But in the Great University, 1965 Model, we're all alienated-civil-rightist-libertarians. Why now? Why us? Why this way? Why so intensely? Why, simply *why?* The explanations are so convenient, so glibly plausible, so circular (like a psychosomatic nostrum), that it's easy to escape the frightening fact that they explain nothing. . . .

For example, the Police Car Episode. . . . Understand it, and you understand FSM: for FSM was forged around that car, *not* at the later 'convention,' and those two days were a miniature of the entire conflict. They furnished the emotional impetus for our fight, they were our signature on a promissory note of the heart; given the nature of the participants, events thereafter unrolled with the Greek inexorability remarked by us all (and unmentioned, unexplained in these books). But *why* should up to three thousand students surround a cop-car for two days, and risk expulsion, arrest, violence (and as some students, faculty and administrators felt) death? . . .

We used four million sheets of paper to expand those barefoot thoughts (and *only* those) spoken atop the car in the first true dialogue I have heard in America. It was all there: the "nonnegotiable" issues; the unexpected intensity of our commitment and community; our strange honest humor; the absent estrangement of the faculty; the administration's refusal to speak to us save via 650 cops, or even to see us, encamped under its nose; our desperate spontaneous democracy; and the total loneliness . . . no single real element—psychological, tactical, dialectical, compositional—entered the controversy from then till its climax: all that we were, all that we faced, was there full-fledged around the car, in every sense.

Is this fact merely an aesthetic curio? Or does it lead to an idea: that around the car an irrevocable commitment to the creation of an Event was made, that the stalemate of Nothing New had to ensue until the Event dropped its other shoe or was made to? And if so, what was the nature of the Event, and why the commitment? No one asks these questions because they're truly terrifying. . . .

Let us go back to "given the nature of the participants . . .": what was our nature? I don't have an easy bag to put it in, but let me make notes on its strangeness by examining some details. of another key incident: the Abortive Sit-In. Two months later FSM sat, five thousand strong on a Friday lawn, to hear our representatives denied audience before the Regents, the Highest Authority. Instead, they rejected the central technical point (on advocacy) of our whole fight, by a policy formulated five weeks earlier (before the "negotiations" they calmed us with); and visited gratuitous punishment on "hostages" from before the Police Car Episode.

Our Monday response was remarkable. In part, we *sang:* not the tired, self-conscious protest songs of the '30s, but our own felt words to Beatles' tunes and Beethoven, serenading the IBM card from the steps of the Administration Building, the death of responsibility caked in liberal rhetoric that had stalked the campus like Heller's plaster-cased soldier come to life, our loneliness in a pluralist marshmallow world. Those songs are a gold mine (untapped, natch) for the anthropologist, folklorist, social psychologist. I'll excuse my impulse to examine just one—a tribute to our President—by saying that such impulses were part of FSM's style. . . .

As background—three sets of words that everyone knew, part of the fog we flew through: the "Property of the Regents . . ." plaque on the slim strip of brick from which activities had been removed, the quote in the metropolitan dailies, that "49% of the hard-core (demonstrators) are followers of the Castro-Mao line," (which Kerr claimed on campus months later was a misquote, but never bothered to retract before the public in whose name we were later arrested); and Kerr's description of the institution to which our lives were committed: "The university and segments of industry are becoming more alike. . . . The production, distribution, and consumption of 'knowledge' in all its forms is said to account for 29 percent of the gross national product . . . and 'knowledge production' is growing at about twice the rate of the rest of the economy."

And so we sang an early carol: "Joy to U.C., the word is come:/Clark Kerr has called us Red!/If you are 49%/you can't work for the government:/the knowledge factory/turns out more GNP/without your subversion/on its property." And sang it *joyously.* For what other sane response was possible, to a bankruptcy of the heart whose dimensions were inexpressible in analytic prose? Certainly, we were seriousness personified; we've jail sentences to show for this. But faced with the absurd, in every sense, there is a dimension of response without which seriousness is meaningless. We had it; it is hard to examine; but our ubiquitous "humor" is an essential testimony to our sanity. That "humor" was also an indelible stamp on our use of words like "democracy" and "moral commitment," which—for the first time in our American lives—had become alive and real. In a rhetoric fog of words without substance, we often treated ours lightly, as if leaning on them too seriously might again crush the life from them.

After the songs, we had a sit-in, which the commentators to a man dismiss as signaling FSM's death. (True, we were dispirited in the remarkable meeting that followed, in which almost a hundred people aired grievance and analysis, speaking in strict rotation from the doubled circle of face-to-face without which we could not meet. But the dispirit was, I think, the realization that the other shoe still hung, and would have to be forced.)

No one notes that the movement had been steadily gathering momentum, that a process was in progress which was fueled, not killed, by Friday; that we left the sit-in singing; and that the "formal apparatus" of FSM continued its activity unchecked. Everyone attributes FSM's "miraculous revival" to the "ill-timed" action of the Administration in calling up students for fresh punishments on stale charges. (Was what we laughingly called "the Inevitable Atrocity Theory of Administrative Activity" only a metaphor?) . . .

In these books taken together, FSM appears in reverse: the absent dimensions are revealing. There is no humor, no poetry, no community, no contact with the real, no collective sense of value, no sense of the strange. The atmosphere is one of analytical structures that refuse to become relevant, to function properly. Ironically, no one notes the most characteristic theme of FSM's dialogue on education, politics, scholarship, etc.: not that the structures should be changed, but that they should function properly and relevantly: we did not want new channels, new methods, but the proper functioning of those that were.

—*Michael Rossmann*

II. "Generational Revolt and the Free Speech Movement"

. . . I had walked on picket lines before, but picketing is cheap in a big city where you're anonymous and can return to your job the next day without anyone being much the wiser about who you are. While we were picketing outside the hotel, negotiations were going on inside for the hiring of more Negroes by the San Francisco Hotel Association. No progress was made, despite the presence of two thousand of us on the line, and the leadership finally asked us to go inside the hotel and sit in the lobby. This could mean being arrested, so one had to decide how much the cause meant to him: whether it was worth jail, a police record, maybe loss of a job and, perhaps most important, being recognized by the hostile majority of the city as being on the other side.

We went inside, most of us acting in civil disobedience for the first time; the boisterousness of the picket line quieted to a hush, most of us being a little nervous. Once inside, however, one could relax, for one was committed at last in some way to those things one had been told as a child were right and valuable—liberty, justice, equality. Each of us knew at last that he believed in those things. The lobby was filled, the lobby and the long corridors on either side, and we each realized, scanning the mass of a thousand faces, that *we were not alone.* One spent a lifetime, in America, hedging one's bets, keeping up one's guard, never letting anyone else look too deep for fear of being laughed at or looking foolish; but here we were, a thousand strong, and, each in our own way, we knew that we believed, that we all believed, that we had some core of our lives to share with one another. We spent that night together, some in jail, most of us sleeping-in in the hotel lobby, a small army encamped in the fortress of the enemy. Instead of returning to our private lives we stayed and lived together that night and through the next day, and when it was over we were no longer strangers to one another. For twenty-four hours we were a community.

It is only when the pull of involvement finally wrenches you in some way from the accustomed routine of privateness, from the doubts and ambiguities and compromises, day in day out, of life in America that it is possible to have sense of oneself, and to feel alive. A night in the Sheraton-Palace, a summer in Mississippi to know that there is a battle raging, to know that you are personally involved, and to know, finally, which side you are on.

So when the press pointed out the following day that 80 per cent of the demonstrators at the Palace were white students, and questioned what they were really there for, whether they were agitating for jobs for Negroes or only using that as a pretext for something else, they were essentially right. We were concerned about those jobs, but there was much more at stake that night.

What this experience gave us, and what their experience in the civil rights movement gave the students who committed themselves to it, was the knowledge that a community is possible, that the basis for a viable society is not the protection of each man from his neighbor, who without restraint would be his enemy and destroy him for his own ends, but rather a shared humanity and mutual need for each other. To the Beat insight of the basic rightness of the inner feelings of the individual, and therefore the basic worth of the individual, the civil rights movement added the assertion that *it is possible for the good society to exist.* (This is the underlying motif of SNCC's community organization in the South, as well as of student efforts at community organization of the Negro ghettos in the North.) . . .

Those who said they agreed with the ends of the Free Speech Movement but took offense at the means it used, claiming it should have sought judicial rulings through the courts or statutory changes by the legislature to achieve its ends, failed to understand what the ends of the movement were, for the means the students used *were* the ends of the movement. What the students were fighting for was the right to participate directly in the world they live in, for the right to confront other men and not catalogs and regulations, forms and procedures, an amplified voice and a televised face. To resort either to legal processes, in which other men, lawyers, argue the merits of the case while the protagonist sits and watches, or to electoral tactics, in which one chooses other men or brings pressure to bear on other men to act on one's behalf, would have been to surrender the life of the movement.

What enlivened the Free Speech Movement was the exhilaration of feeling that you were, for once, really acting, that you were dealing directly with the things that affect your life, and with each other. You were for once free of the whole sticky cobweb that kept you apart from each other and from the roots of your existence, and you knew you were alive and what your life was all about. "For a moment all the hypocrisy was swept away and we saw the world with a greater clarity than we had before" (Savio). It was the tactics of direct action, the sense of immediate personal involvement, that made this possible.

The value of direct action is that it reduces the issues to the magnitude of the individual man. As Rossman told *Look* magazine, "We're making changes in society with our own two hands; that's a new feeling for my generation." The trouble with trying to understand politics and society as they are taught in the university is that everything seems so complex, so subject to a multitude of seeming unrelated or contradictory constructions and interpretations. It is only when one can confront it himself, only when it is reduced to its ultimate terms of what it means to the lives of individual men, that "society" can really be known and understood.

The style of the Free Speech Movement made possible the vitality and spirit and the genuine feeling of camaraderie among its participants. There was something more in this style, too; there was a good-natured humor, an informality, a looseness—a relaxed acceptance of themselves that goes back, I think, to the Beat's rejection of the taboos of society and his attempt to attune himself to the needs of his own body. The frank acceptance of one's sexual nature, the openness to new experiences, the appreciation of the rhythms of jazz in the Beat, the Hip, the Negro elements of this generation's development have contributed to its character. The FSM was a swinging movement.

The FMS, with its open mass meetings, its guitars and songs, its beards, and its long-haired chicks, made the aloofness and reserve of the administrators, the turgid style of the pronouncements emanating from the University Information Office, the formality of the coat and tie world, seem lifeless and dull in comparison. And when the administration once managed to muster its dignity to produce the Extraordinary All-University Convocation at the Greek Theater, throwing every bit of gravity, every sacred symbol of classical education into the presentation, with President Kerr pronouncing the final solution worked out between himself and the Committee of Departmental Chairmen in the sonorous tones of the liberal rhetoric ("This community is divided not so much on ends as on means . . ."), the whole thing collapsed in confusion when Mario Savio walked up to the microphone with the intention of announcing an FSM rally.

Whatever beauty, grace, love, or joy was shown in the course of the struggle came from the students, and this was made possible by the sense of integrity they had gained; by the essential unity of their ideals with their actions, of their ends with their means, and, underlying this, the unity of their ideals with what it was necessary for them to do in order to be men.

—*Gerald Rosenfield*

3. *"A Letter to Undergraduates"*

Brad Cleaveland began his campaign against the University of California before the FSM. In the following excerpt from "Letter to Undergraduates," Cleaveland calls for a full-scale revolution by students that includes an educational revolution. The SLATE supplement, which publishes each semester a rating of classes and teachers, published Cleaveland's manifesto during the FSM crisis. His ideas gained a great deal of sympathy, as shown by one of the FSM symbols, an IBM card labeled: STU-DENT AT U.C.: DO NOT BEND, FOLD, OR MUTILATE.

THERE IS NO BLUEPRINT FOR AN EDUCATIONAL REVOLUTION!!!

It was like this: on the one hand there was substantial agreement that the University stamps out consciousness like a super-madison-avenue-machine; on the other, people saying, "So what?" or "Bring me a detailed and exhaustive plan." *But there*

*is no plan for kicking twenty thousand people IN THEIR
ASSES!* No plan will stop excessive greed, timidity, and selling
out. At best the University is a pathway to the club of "tough-
minded-liberal-realists" in America, who sit in comfortable
armchairs talking radical while clutching hysterically at respectability in a world explosive with revolution. At worst the University destroys your desires to see reality, and to suffer reality
with optimism, at the time when you most need to learn that
painful art. In between those two poles is mostly garbage: Bus
Ad; PhD candidates "on the make"; departmental enclaves of
"clever and brilliant" students who will become hack critics; and
thousands of trainees for high-class trades which will become
obsolete in ten years.

Dear undergraduate, let me make this crystal clear for you.
There is a contrast which exists on this campus between the
common (and sometimes beautiful) illusions which we have all
had, and what actually happens! . . . a gap which seems to be
reaching catastrophic proportions. I will offer two sets of utterly
obvious facts to show you that a violent contrast does exist; and
that the University is a grotesque perversion of the conditions
necessary for your freedom to learn reality and to suffer it with
optimism. The first set of facts is your Charter Day Ceremony,
the second is the essentials of your undergraduate routine—a
grotesque perversion of your freedom to learn.

YOUR UNDERGRADUATE ROUTINE

. . . your routine is comprised of a systematic psychological
and spiritual brutality inflicted by a faculty of "well-meaning
and nice" men who have decided that your situation is hopeless
when it comes to actually participating in serious learning. As an
undergraduate you receive a four-year-long series of sharp stac-
catos: eight semesters, forty courses, one hundred twenty or
more units, fifteen hundred to two thousand impersonal lectures,
and over three hundred oversized "discussion" meetings. Ap-
proaching what is normally associated with learning; reading,
writing, and exams, your situation becomes absurd. Over a period of four years you receive close to fifty bibliographies, ranging in length from one to eight pages, you are examined on more

than one hundred occasions, and you are expected to write forty to seventy-five papers. As you well know, reading means "getting into" hundreds of books, many of which are secondary sources, in a superficial manner. You must cheat to keep up. If you don't cheat you are forced to perform without time to think in depth, and consequently you must hand in papers and exams which are almost as shameful as the ones you've cheated on. You repeat to yourselves over and over as an undergraduate that "It doesn't make any difference . . . it's the grade that counts," . . . a threadbare and worn phrase (if you are lucky enough to make it to the third or fourth year); used as commonly as your word "regurgitation" in place of "exam." You know the measure of truth in those bits of slang: it *is* nauseous . . . you almost *do* "puke up your work" to professors. I personally have known students who have gotten physically sick by merely reflecting upon their routine. In the sciences and technical fields your courses are bluntly and destructively rigorous. . . . you become impatient with "that social sciences and humanities crap." How did you get to be such puppets? You perform. But when do you think? Dutifully and obediently you follow, as a herd of grade-worshiping sheep. If you are strong at all, you do this with some sense of shame, or if you are weak, you do it with a studied cynicism . . . as jaded youth with parched imaginations that go no further than oak-panelled rooms at the end of the line . . . BUT WHETHER YOU ARE STRONG OR WEAK YOU PERFORM LIKE TRAINED SEALS, AND LIKE SHEEP YOU FOLLOW . . . WITH THE THOROUGHBRED PHI BETA KAPPA SHEEP LEADING YOU!! up the golden stairway to the omnipotent A, to the Happy Consciousness, to success, and a very parochial mind. This is the core of your dutiful daily lives, and your homage to respectability. Reluctantly, or otherwise, you permit it to be applied by administrators who use computers on you as much because they are afraid of personal contact with you as for the reason that they wish to keep the assembly line moving efficiently. You permit professors to extract your performance by the coercion of grades. Why do you permit this apostasy of learning . . . a process which prevents you from extending your thought beyond a shallow dilettantism?

IF THE FACTS OF YOUR UNDERGRADUATE EXISTENCE WERE
SOLELY DETERMINED BY THE "COURSE/GRADE/UNIT SYS-
TEM," YOUR "INCIPIENT REVOLT," TO WHICH PRESIDENT
KERR HIMSELF IRRESPONSIBLY ALLUDED IN THE GODKIN
LECTURES, WOULD PROBABLY HAVE ALREADY OCCURRED.

The reason why you permit, dear undergraduate, your minds
to be abused, is because you are given a magnificent bread and
circus. What a pain reliever! . . . these "extracurricular" activities. Coming to you from your ASUC student "government,"
other special bureaucracies such as the Committee on Arts and
Lectures, and added to by more intellectual offerings from departmental and special grants lecture series, comes a semesterly
tidal wave of exciting and highly intense stimuli which dazzles
you away from the fact that you are obstructed from learning, or
even questioning whether you should be learning while you are
here. This bread and circus assures you that the world is really
not in the midst of anything so serious as *revolution,* much less
within your own sacred borders!! From the powerfully entertain-
ing to the scholastically intellectual you get films, debates, art
exhibits, athletics, drama, "spirit" groups, recreations, seduc-
tions of hundreds of social groups; this pyrotechnical explosion
of *Kultur* is something terribly "other directed"; happily away
from your puppet-like performance in the course/grade/unit
procedural core. Your attention is diverted away from your
treadmill to the candied goodness of the bread and circus. Hopefully, when you get your bachelor's degree, you will step up to
higher plateaus where many kinds of "success" await you. You
are blinded to the fact that you are really getting something of
terrible importance while you are here:

TRAINING IN THE CAPACITY FOR UNQUESTIONING OBEDI-
ENCE TO A COMPLEX FLOOD OF TRIVIAL BUREAUCRATIC
RULES. IN THE NAME OF HUMAN LEARNING YOU ACQUIRE
THE CAPACITY TO BE DOCILE IN THE FACE OF RULES. WHILE
YOU ARE TRAINING, THE RULES WHICH TELL YOU HOW TO
GO ABOUT YOUR TRAINING ARE DISPLACING YOUR FREEDOM
TO THINK. . . . SKILL AND OBEDIENCE ARE WHAT YOU AC-
QUIRE.

Aren't you the least bit aware that such a capacity is not only necessary for life in America's giant public and private corporations, but that it is also a first-class ticket to a traditional form of statehood under the designation of tyranny? No matter how well trimmed you keep your grassy lawns in suburbia after you get your bachelor's degree, your moral and spiritual servitude will not be reduced. If you have attended a Charter Day Ceremony, and can recall the feelings you had, you might feel the temptation to say that it is this indictment which is grotesque, and *not* the University . . . but *you* are the University . . . it is *your* life I have described in its essentials.

Has it ever occurred to you, dear undergraduate, that human learning is a painful and exhilarating process which comes from asking the kinds of questions which *YOU* would like to ask: "WHY AM I IN THE UNIVERSITY? WHAT IS KNOWLEDGE? WHAT IS EXTREMISM, AFTER ALL, AND HOW DOES POLITICAL EXTREMISM AFFECT ME? In your present situation, if you *insisted* on . . . now listen . . . if you *insisted* on the freedom to spend large amounts of time in a single-minded devotion to pursuing such questions, you would soon begin to feel rather out of it . . . you would be a kook. Any question of a fundamental, or a general character; or any question which hits you personally in a deep way, can only be considered naïve and stupid. Can you conceive of taking any such question and studying, talking, and reading about it for an entire semester—free of any other requirement—or for an entire year, or even more time? Without interference, but only earnest guidance from "teachers"? Or is it that you must always attend to that "other" paper, the "midterm next week," or the "reading in another course"? Or is it that you do this half the time and say to hell with it the rest of the time: go to an art film, or to Strawberry Canyon, or to an exciting lecture for a one-night stand on the topic of Western Civilization?

Dear undergraduate, you *know* what really happens to you. You almost don't have to be told. It is as though the BENEFACTORS OF THE FRUITS OF LEARNING said to you, "Here, take this beautiful piece of fruit . . . ," and you do, and you try to take a bite, when "STOP!!," you are being offered another piece of fruit, another, and then another. At the same time, before you really begin to taste and speculate about the taste of any one piece of fruit, your FRUIT BENEFACTORS, and FRUIT BENEFACTORS' ASSISTANTS, are demanding that you describe in detail the intricate beauty of each piece; they become impatient if you do not describe the fruit "properly," and they penalize you for thoughtful slowness by calling it stupidity, and by lowering your respectability rating. Most of you learn to hate the fruits of learning. But there are a few of you—the "clever and brilliant"—(preferably transfers from the Ivy League), who learn in a terrific quickness, to take quick little bites from the large and beautiful fruits and then furiously hurl them as far away as possible. You clever ones learn to devour the small fruits of skill and training; those fruits are your "security insurance" in life, or perhaps you think they will lead you later to an XK-E and sexy-intelligent-wife-in-silk-dress. You perform your tricks well: smiling up at your benefactors and saying "delicious. . . . excellent!" . . .

DEAR UNDERGRADUATES!!

I am no longer interested in cajoling you, arguing with you, or describing to you something you already know. What I am about to say to you at this point concerns you more directly. I will entreat you to furiously throw your comforting feelings of duty and responsibility for this institution to the winds and act on your situation. This institution, affectionately called "Cal" by many of you, or, as the *Daily Cal* might put it, "the Big U," does not deserve a response of loyalty and allegiance from you. There is only one proper response to Berkeley from undergraduates: that you *organize and split this campus wide open!*

> FROM THIS POINT ON, DO NOT MISUNDERSTAND ME. MY INTENTION IS TO CONVINCE YOU THAT YOU DO NOTHING LESS THAN BEGIN AN OPEN, FIERCE, AND THOROUGHGOING REBELLION ON THIS CAMPUS.

I would like to briefly explain to you now why such a course of action is necessary, and how, if such a revolt were conducted with unrelenting toughness and courage, it could spread to other campuses across the country and cause a fundamental change in your own futures.

I have used the phrase "world-in-revolution" several times to this point. I would like to say to you now that most of you are incompetent to deal with that phrase. It is a phrase which betrays a distinct view of reality . . . a view of reality out of which might grow an effective "opposition" in the present American scene where the only opposition seems to be crystallizing along reactionary lines. "World-in-revolution" is a phrase . . . a view of reality which contains a large measure of truth, one which is certainly debatable. BUT IT IS NOT DEBATED BY YOU. The catastrophic gap between the incubator world of your Multiversity, and the world of reality is represented by your ignorance of what "world-in-revolution" means. The University teaches you to bury your heads in the sand, trembling in ignorance of the American black revolution for Civil Rights, the impending revolution in Automation, and likewise in ignorance of political revolutions, which, like thunderclapping salvos, explode the world over. The Multiversity is the slickest appeal ever made for you to fortify your organization man mentalities, for you to lead privatized lives in which it is a virtue for you to go greedily "on the make." In urging you to rebellion, I have action in mind, not further understanding. What more is there to understand when you can so easily discover that a Peace Corpsman who left Cal is now living in Nigeria in a separate small house with the conveniences of suburban America, plus two houseboys, and that a young girl Civil Rights worker from the Bay Area who goes to Mississippi lives in abject poverty with a family of eleven black American citizens, in a shack with no running water, with lice, with rats, and in constant fear for her life?

In this Multiversity, you will not learn so much as a cursory meaning of what a world-in-revolution means to you. You will not learn the utterly profound fact of what a revolution is:

THAT A REVOLUTION COMES ABOUT WHEN ENORMOUS NUMBERS OF FELLOW HUMAN BEINGS ARE OPPRESSED TO POINTS FAR BEYOND WHAT WE BLANDLY LABEL AN "INTOLERABLE SET OF CONDITIONS."

Nor will you learn that to be a counter-revolutionary is to go about the business of slaughtering enormous numbers of hu-

man beings whose inflamed spirits and starved stomachs force
them to cry out for the freedoms which you spit upon in your
apathy.

> AND YOU WILL LEARN MOST OF ALL NOT TO ENTERTAIN SO
> MUCH AS THE POSSIBLY THAT AMERICAN FOREIGN POLICY
> IN KOREA AND SOUTH VIETNAM ARE PRECISELY COUNTER-
> REVOLUTIONARY . . . THAT THE AMERICAN NATION IS IN-
> VOLVED IN DESTROYING POPULAR NATIONAL REVOLUTIONS,
> AND APPEARS TO BE GETTING ITSELF LOCKED MORE AND
> MORE IN THAT SUICIDAL AND INHUMANE POLICY.

You will learn not to entertain such thoughts, even though
such statements have been made on the floor of the U.S. Senate
(by Wayne Morse, U.S. Senator from Oregon), where nobody seems to have taken these fantastic charges seriously. And
you will learn not to react when you hear other Americans say
"After all, God's on our side, we're savin' those illiterate sav-
ages from the Commies, even if we gotta mutilate 'em to do it,
Goddamit!!"

You will not learn that, at home, here in the good ole U.S.A.,
in the Civil Rights Revolution which is now going on, the
phrase "white backlash" is the simplest way to say "the bigotry
of the majority"; that "white backlash" is a counter-revolutionary
phrase, used by "scholars," so-called liberals, advocated by conservatives, or used by anyone else who adopts the hideous posture of "studying," or analyzing the "problem" of the black man
in America. Nor will you learn that the real meaning of "white
backlash" is "Don't bug me nigger . . . you're buggin' me with
that civil disobedience . . . now stop that or we'll show you
who has the tear gas, cattle prods, and shotguns!!" . . .

Regarding the radicals, those who are now going to jail in
the Civil Rights Revolution: they are beginning to learn what the
world-in-revolution means. I would make only one irreverent
comment to them. They shouldn't bitch because the whole campus doesn't go to jail with them: because they are the real leaders on the campus, and yet while *on the campus* they too
become sheep. They take the flunkings of professors, who penalize them for attending a San Francisco court rather than a
Berkeley class; the same professors who donate money to the

Civil Rights fight as long as it stays three thousand miles away in the South.

The only large group of students I personally respect, other than the Freedom Fighters, are the dropouts. Ignominious lot! What a fate . . . that one would be forced to give up that little registration card with respectability written all over it! This "Hidden Community" of unseemly hangers-on in Berkeley now numbers in the thousands. Those most bugged by this "element" are the ASUC types. They screech, "You can't even tell them from students sometimes (although some are very dirty) . . . and they're using *our* student union!" If they have flunked out (or dropped out) of the University how can they deserve respect? Well . . . if I thought it was a virtue to perform like sheep I wouldn't be urging revolt. The fact is that these students are the real ones. Many have had the guts to cut their social umbilical cords, become genuinely *free,* and to begin coughing up their own mistakes. They don't take the fatal step which the Cowell Psychiatric Clinic calls "regressive:" which means to go back to Mama, or, God forbid, to a Junior College. They face life in its own terms, and many do something rather shocking around Berkeley: they learn to read a book. And I might add that many of them are also Freedom Fighters. (Incidentally, do you know the latest figures? According to Cowell, close to 50 percent of those of you who are graced with the mantle of "Freshman at Cal" are eliminated by the end of the third year.)

Are you aware that the most salient characteristic of the "Multiversity" is massive production of specialized excellence? SPECIALIZED EXCELLENCE. It will be some time before machines will displace the super-trades; thus massive training centers are necessary. But why do we insist upon calling them educational centers rather than training centers?

THE MULTIVERSITY IS NOT AN EDUCATIONAL CENTER, BUT A HIGHLY EFFICIENT INDUSTRY: IT PRODUCES BOMBS, OTHER WAR MACHINES, A FEW TOKEN "PEACEFUL" MACHINES, AND ENORMOUS NUMBERS OF SAFE, HIGHLY SKILLED, AND RESPECTABLE AUTOMATONS TO MEET THE IMMEDIATE NEEDS OF BUSINESS AND GOVERNMENT.

We all know that this is necessary to some extent for the
maintenance of "American know-how"; otherwise the system
would collapse and anarchy would reign, etc. But the forbidden fruit is to ask the devastating question WHY? WHY
ONLY *KNOW-HOW?* Or is it that we wish to produce the
largest population ever known to man of highly skilled idiots?
We may safely say that graduate schools should perform the
function of training for specialized excellence . . . but even
then not exclusively. And if you will recall, we are discussing
the matter of undergraduate freedom to learn. What has occurred when undergraduate education is eradicated; whether
it be for the excuse of "too many students," or "exploding
knowledge," or in the name of political expedience during the
"Cold War"?

WHEN THIS OCCURS IN PUBLIC UNIVERSITIES, THE RESULT
IS ABANDONMENT OF THE AMERICAN DEMOCRATIC EXPERI-
MENT IN WHICH THE RADICAL PROPOSITION OF EDUCATION
FOR ALL IS THE CENTRAL AXIOM. . . .

Dear undergraduate, there is perhaps no other set of questions, in the political realm, of greater importance for you. Let
us return for a moment to the matter of who is responsible for
your freedom to learn. As I said, . . . the Regents have delegated power and responsibility to the Academic Senates of the
eight campuses. Let us just call the Academic Senate the "Faculty," which is the automatic membership of the Senate. At
any rate, there is something terribly wrong here. If we assume
that the faculty is incompetent to effect the necessary changes,
then it would seem of the greatest urgency that the Regents
themselves do something to correct the situation. If the Regents do not act, then we must conclude that they are (1) satisfied; or (2) incompetent; or (3) both. Two things are certain:
(1) as corporate men of power, the Regents are getting precisely what they most desire—enormous numbers of highly
skilled graduates to fill the corporate structure and to keep it
running smoothly; (2) IT IS DEBATABLE, from their own
point of view, whether the Regents would find it practical to
"educate" these skilled people as well as to *train* them. Why?
To put the answer very crudely: the Regents, who run private

corporations, just as the politicians who run public corporations, desire highly skilled, but politically and economically *dumb* "personnel." The politicians have, of course, even made laws to that effect . . . in the form of such legislation as the Hatch Act, which forbids partisan politics in government bureaucracies. Consequently, if the faculty refuses to face the problem of educating undergraduates, but instead is encouraged, and agrees, to make only piecemeal reform which only slightly lessens pressures in some areas while making them more severe in other areas, the Regents might be said to be very happy with such a course of action . . . in fact that is what they are doing. The course/grade/unit system will probably be "adjusted," and the bread and circus will become more intense and dazzling: note the priority in the University building program . . . first you build the Student Union complex, then an auditorium which will be the "largest this side of the Mississippi," and "sometime in the future" will come an undergraduate library. But why do private and public corporate men act this way?

FROM TIME IMMEMORIAL, MEN OF POWER HAVE CONSIDERED IT WISE TO KEEP THEIR CONSTITUENTS AT A LEVEL OF IGNORANCE WHEREBY THE PROCESS OF RULING THEM IS MOST EASILY ACCOMPLISHED.

Or are we to entertain the possibility that the Regents have upset the applecart of history? Have they become revolutionaries? It is true that they recently removed the ban on Communist speakers on campus. Of course, they resisted for fifteen years . . . since the McCarthy era. And during the McCarthy era they were able to force the Academic Senate into adopting a loyalty oath. If you can forgive the faculty of a university for *that,* you can forgive them for anything. Many professors did not forgive the Senate, however, and resigned. The spine of this faculty, close to forty professors, left in disgust; left scars behind which will never heal. Moreover, what the hell difference does it make whether you hear a Communist every year or so. Most of you would laugh at him . . . like laughing at a movement which involves the entire world! If any one of you wisely decided to study a Communist speaker's proposals, to think about them, to read about them seriously, you not only would find it *impossible from the standpoint of time,* but you would also be considered a heretic by your fellow "students." It is probably accurate to say that the removal of the speaker ban on Communists was a great contribution on the symbolic level . . . like a Charter Day Ceremony. Politically, it was very wise.

Speaking of politics, what relation exists between University and the U.S. Government? Aside from providing trained personnel for public corporations (agencies, bureaus, etc.) as in private ones, is there as direct a relation between the University and Government as between the University and the Regents? Yes, it seems that the University, or shall we call a spade a spade—the Regents—it seems that the Regents are snuggled up pretty tightly to the seats of power in Washington (though it is difficult to tell who-hugs-who the hardest in Washington):

> Item—from the *Cal Reporter,* May 13, 1963: According to the Financial Report of 1961-62, the U.S. Government spent about 227 millions on Special Projects. These included 190 millions for Lawrence Radiation Laboratory (U.C.), 76 millions for Los Alamos Radiation Lab (U.C.). The income for the entire University (eight campuses) excluding these special projects was 250 millions.

Let us summarize for a moment. Your learning opportunities are limited to "getting ahead," or acquiring a skill to do so. You are obstructed from the realities of the twentieth-century world-in-revolution. You are left with the conclusion that the Regents are conducting a major love affair with the U.S. Government, both of whom are not particular anxious to see you "get smart" for fear that you might become radical student politicos. In conducting this love affair with the Government, the Regents have left the matter of "educating" the infant-undergraduate to the adolescent faculty, knowing that they cannot do the job properly. The major implication in all of this is that if you wish to remain infants then you can . . . but if you wish to deny your infantile character then you must realize that you can't talk to your adolescent babysitters, the faculty, about your corrupt daddies, the Regents. The reason is simple: the baby-

sitters are afraid of their daddies. No . . . if you really want
to do something, then you must stand up straight, like the
young men and women you really are, and begin to SPEAK
what you feel, to speak loudly, strongly, and to say your highest ideals, your deepest dreams, to pull out all of the stops, to
let go and to tell the world . . . SPEAK TO THE WORLD
AND TELL THEM THAT YOU WANT TO LIVE!!!

Have I sufficiently taken care of your objections? If not,
chances are that what remains is *fear,* and that is *your* problem.
If I have taken care of your objections, then you might be
asking HOW DO YOU START A REBELLION ON THE
CAMPUS? That's a tough one—and you might have to get
tough in order to be heard. You also know that you will need
legitimate demands behind your slogans of FREEDOM
NOW! THE FREEDOM TO KNOW AND TO LEARN!!

DEMANDS?

1. IMMEDIATE COMMITMENT OF THE UNIVERSITY TO THE
   TOTAL ELIMINATION OF THE COURSE/GRADE/UNIT SYS-
   TEM OF UNDERGRADUATE LEARNING: IN THE SOCIAL SCI-
   ENCES AND HUMANITIES.

2. IMMEDIATE DISBANDING OF ALL UNIVERITY DORM AND
   LIVING GROUP RULES WHICH PRESCRIBE HOURS AND
   WHICH PROVIDE FOR A SYSTEM OF STUDENT-IMPOSED
   DISCIPLINE, THEREBY DIVIDING STUDENTS AGAINST
   THEMSELVES.

3. IMMEDIATE NEGOTIATIONS ON THE ESTABLISHMENT OF
   A PERMANENT STUDENT VOICE WHICH IS EFFECTIVE
   (THAT IS, INDEPENDENT) IN RUNNING UNIVERSITY AF-
   FAIRS.

4. IMMEDIATE EFFORTS TO BEGIN RECRUITMENT OF AN
   UNDERGRADUATE TEACHING FACULTY TO HANDLE UN-
   DERGRADUATE LEARNING IN SOCIAL SCIENCES AND HU-
   MANITIES.

5. IMMEDIATE NEGOTIATIONS REGARDING TWO METHODS OF
   UNDERGRADUATE LEARNING WHICH PROVIDE FOR THE
   BASIC FREEDOM REQUIRED IN LEARNING:

> a. A TERMINAL EXAMINATION SYSTEM WHICH WILL BE
>   VOLUNTARY AND AN OPTION WITH "b."
> b. IMMEDIATE CREATION OF UNDERGRADUATE PRO-
>   GRAMS OF A WIDE VARIETY IN WHICH THE STU-
>   DENT WILL BE GIVEN CAREFUL, BUT MINIMAL
>   GUIDANCE, WITHOUT COURSES, GRADES, AND UNITS.

> 6. IMMEDIATE ESTABLISHMENT OF A UNIVERSITY COMMIT-
>   TEE TO DEAL WITH THESE DEMANDS ON THE BERKELEY
>   CAMPUS.

Go to the top. Make your demands to the Regents. If they refuse to give you an audience: start a program of agitation, petitioning, rallies, etc., in which the final resort will be CIVIL DISOBEDIENCE. In the long run there is the possibility that you will find it necessary to perform civil disobedience at a couple of major University public ceremonies. Depending on the resistance, you might consider adding the following two demands:

> 7. RESIGNATION OF CLARK KERR. RESIGNATION OF TOP AD-
>   MINISTRATORS WHO MIGHT EMPLOY SLICK DIVERTING
>   TACTICS.

> 8. RECONSTITUTION OF THE BOARD OF REGENTS, EITHER
>   THROUGH FIRING OR EXPANSION, PERHAPS BOTH. . . .

And if you get this far you will also have witnessed nation-wide publicity which will have exposed Berkeley for the undergraduate sham that it is. Not to say that the public in general will feel that way, what with the press "Red baiting" you, but that students all over the country will read between the lines. By this time you may also be able to call for a mass student strike . . . something which seems unthinkable at present. If a miracle occurs, or two, you might even get to say that you were the seeds of an educational revolution unlike anything which has ever occurred. Remember one thing:

> The task of genius, and man is nothing if not genius, is
> to keep the miracle alive, to live always in the miracle, to
> make the miracle more and more miraculous, to swear

allegiance to nothing, but live only miraculously, think miraculously, to die miraculously—HENRY MILLER

4. *"An End to History"*

Mario Savio expressed the feelings of thousands of Berkeley students, as well as of students in other universities. Because of his ability to articulate both the substance and the emotion of the students' demands, he became the spokesman for the FSM. In the following speech, delivered on the steps of the university administration building, Savio expressed the feelings of the young radicals who have been sitting-in at lunch counters and on highways leading to the World's Fair. And many of those 814 who were arrested at the University followed singer Joan Baez's advice to them: "When you go in, go with love in your hearts."

Last summer I went to Mississippi to join the struggle there for civil rights. This fall I am engaged in another phase of the same struggle, this time in Berkeley. The two battlefields may seem quite different to some observers, but this is not the case. The same rights are at stake in both places—the right to participate as citizens in democratic society and the right to due process of law. Further, it is a struggle against the same enemy. In Mississippi an autocratic and powerful minority rules, through organized violence, to suppress the vast, virtually powerless, majority. In California, the privileged minority manipulates the University bureaucracy to suppress the students' political expression. That "respectable" bureaucracy masks the financial plutocrats; that impersonal bureaucracy is the efficient enemy in a "Brave New World."

In our free speech fight at the University of California, we have come up against what may emerge as the greatest problem of our nation—depersonalized, unresponsive bureaucracy. We

have encountered the organized status quo in Mississippi, but it
is the same in Berkeley. Here we find it impossible usually to
meet with anyone but secretaries. Beyond that, we find function-
aries who cannot make policy but can only hide behind the rules.
We have discovered total lack of response on the part of the
policy makers. To grasp a situation which is truly Kafkaesque,
it is necessary to understand the bureaucratic mentality. And we
have learned quite a bit about it this fall, more outside the classroom than in.

As bureaucrat, an administrator believes that nothing new
happens. He occupies an ahistorical point of view. In September,
to get the attention of this bureaucracy which had issued arbitrary edicts suppressing student political expression and refused
to discuss its action, we held a sit-in on the campus. We sat
around a police car and kept it immobilized for over thirty-two
hours. At last, the administrative bureaucracy agreed to negotiate. But instead, on the following Monday, we discovered that
a committee had been appointed, in accordance with usual regulations, to resolve the dispute. Our attempt to convince any of
the administrators that an event had occurred, that something
new had happened, failed. They saw this simply as something
to be handled by normal university procedures.

The same is true of all bureaucracies. They begin as tools,
means to certain legitimate goals, and they end up feeding their
own existence. The conception that bureaucrats have is that history has in fact come to an end. No events can occur now that
the Second World War is over which can change American society substantially. We proceed by standard procedures as we
are.

The most crucial problems facing the United States today are
the problem of automation and the problem of racial injustice.
Most people who will be put out of jobs by machines will not
accept an end to events, this historical plateau, as the point beyond which no change occurs. Negroes will not accept an end
to history here. All of us must refuse to accept history's final
judgment that in America there is no place in society for people
whose skins are dark. On campus, students are not about to
accept it as fact that the university has ceased evolving and is

in its final state of perfection, that students and faculty are respectively raw material and employees, or that the University is to be autocratically run by unresponsive bureaucrats.

Here is the real contradiction: the bureaucrats hold history as ended. As a result significant parts of the population both on campus and off are dispossessed, and these dispossessed are not about to accept this ahistorical point of view. It is out of this that the conflict has occurred with the university bureaucracy and will continue to occur until that bureaucracy becomes responsive or until it is clear the university cannot function.

The things we are asking for in our civil rights protests have a deceptively quaint ring. We are asking for the due process of law. We are asking for our actions to be judged by committees of our peers. We are asking that regulations ought to be considered as arrived at legitimately only from the consensus of the governed. These phrases are all pretty old, but they are not being taken seriously in America today, nor are they being taken seriously on the Berkeley campus.

I have just come from a meeting with the Dean of Students. She notified us that she was aware of certain violations of university regulations by certain organizations. University friends of SNCC, which I represent, was one of these. We tried to draw from her some statement on these great principles: consent of the governed, jury of one's peers, due process. The best she could do was to evade or to present the administration party line. It is very hard to make any contact with the human being who is behind these organizations.

The university is the place where people begin seriously to question the conditions of their existence and raise the issue of whether they can be committed to the society they have been born into. After a long period of apathy during the fifties, students have begun not only to question but, having arrived at answers, to act on those answers. This is part of a growing understanding among many people in America that history has not ended, that a better society is possible, and that it is worth dying for.

This free speech fight points up a fascinating aspect of contemporary campus life. Students are permitted to talk all they want so long as their speech has no consequences.

One conception of the university, suggested by a classical Christian formulation, is that it be in the world but not of the world. The conception of Clark Kerr, by contrast, is that the university is part and parcel of this particular stage in the history of American society; it stands to serve the need of American industry; it is a factory that turns out a certain product needed by industry or government. Because speech does often have consequences which might alter this perversion of higher education, the university must put itself in a position of censorship. It can permit two kinds of speech: speech which encourages continuation of the status quo, and speech which advocates changes in it so radical as to be irrelevant in the foreseeable future. Someone may advocate radical change in all aspects of American society, and this I am sure he can do with impunity. But if someone advocates sit-ins to bring about changes in discriminatory hiring practices, this can not be permitted because it goes against the status quo of which the university is a part. And that is how the fight began here.

The administration of the Berkeley campus has admitted that external, extra-legal groups have pressured the university not to permit students on campus to organize picket lines, not to permit on campus any speech with consequences. And the bureaucracy went along. Speech with consequences, speech in the area of civil rights, speech which some might regard as illegal, must stop.

Many students here at the university, many people in society, are wandering aimlessly about. Strangers in their own lives, there is no place for them. They are people who have not learned to compromise, who for example have come to the university to learn to question, to grow, to learn—all the standard things that sound like clichés because no one takes them seriously. And they find at one point or other that for them to become part of society, to become lawyers, ministers, businessmen, people in government, that very often they must compromise those principles which were most dear to them. They must suppress the most creative impulses that they have; this is a prior condition for being part of the system. The university is well structured, well tooled, to turn out people with all the sharp edges worn off, the well-rounded person. The university is well equipped to produce that sort of person, and this means that the best among the people who enter must for four years wander aimlessly much of the time questioning why they are on campus at all, doubting whether there is any point in what they are doing, and looking toward a very bleak existence afterward in a game in which all of the rules have been made up, which one cannot really amend.

It is a bleak scene, but it is all a lot of us have to look forward to. Society provides no challenge. American society in the standard conception it has of itself is simply no longer exciting. The most exciting things going on in America today are movements to change America. America is becoming ever more the utopia of sterilized, automated contentment. The "futures" and "careers" for which American students now prepare are for the most part intellectual and moral wastelands. This chrome-plated consumers' paradise would have us grow up to be well-behaved children. But an important minority of men and women coming to the front today have shown that they will die rather than be standardized, replaceable, and irrelevant.

5. *"Freedom and the University"*

Steve Weissman was active in the Free Speech Movement and in SDS. The following excerpts from "Freedom and the University" represent the latest Movement thinking about the University.

A FREE UNIVERSITY

A Free University, like the free society upon which its long-term success depends, is at present only a distant vision. But that vision—based upon the belief that even students have a right to shape the environment in which they live and work—is our most powerful weapon for the subversion of the multiversity. For most students accept the vision of the multiversity. Though alienated, they do not comprehend the source of their alienation. They accept the authoritarian and conformist patterns of the multiversity as natural, inevitable. What right have they to do more than gripe over even the most demeaning and absurd regulation? Are they not being *given* an education? If they don't like it where they are, are they not *free* to be given that education at the multiversity of their choice? Democracy? Most students would be honored to serve on some sandbox administration committee: they wouldn't even realize that their decision-making power was complete only if they made the "right" decisions.

On campus as off, the belief in human dignity, freedom, democracy, and participation in decision-making is in a sorry state. Our first tasks are thus educational:

1.) The Campus Freedom Party. Throughout the country, and especially in the South, activists are organizing political parties to run candidates for student government offices. In most cases, however, they are not running to win, or even with the assumption that putting a good man in a crummy office would change the way in which their university does business. Rather they are running educational campaigns, calling the sandbox by its name, and building constituencies for the abolition of the most obnoxious *in loco parentis* rules, for elimination of compulsory ROTC, to protest the university keeping books for the draft board, for unlimited free speech and political activity, for an end to discriminatory admissions, housing, and hiring, to protest university purchases from and investments in discriminatory corporations, for co-op book stores, and for the idea of eventual student-faculty government. With these platforms student activists raise the vision of student democracy ("rather than student government"), pressure those who do get elected to accept minimal programs leading to that vision, and develop a nucleus to lead action when a direct provocation occurs. After the elections, the parties (or SDS groups which sponsor them) attempt to engage their voters in a year round multi-issue program of radical self-education, work in civil rights or with the poor, anti-war activity, educational reform, and participation in planning the next campaign.

2.) Free Student Unions. One step beyond the political party is the student union. The union focuses not on twice-a-year elections, but on year-round collective bargaining with the administration. It also institutionalizes conflict, the sanction of a student strike, and the notion that students should govern themselves through a mass-participation organization. Berkeley's FSU has so far had only limited success, partially because of the let down after FSM, partially because of the Vietnam protest. Perhaps FSU would now be stronger and more "legitimate" if it had been started during—not after—the free speech controversy. Also, FSU faces a continuing need to expand on the idea of time locals. Union members are organized on smaller units on the basis of their willingness to meet at a certain time, for example there is an 11 A.M. Thursday local. But most union members are not active in time locals, and there is an increasing desire to organize at least some of the time locals on the basis of common political and educational interests and ideologies.

3.) On-campus direct action and demonstrations. Student activitists should make quite clear that they do not expect any great changes to come about through voting: the Regents and the administration, even most of the faculty, think it their right to direct the lives of students. If we are serious about controlling our lives and education, then we must constantly affirm the right to revolt when we are affected by rules and practices over which we have no say.

Compliance with rules should always be received as an unpleasant necessity, never as an obligation. When direct provocations arise, student activists are then prepared to organize massive non-compliance with the regulations in question (like the setting up of the prohibited political tables at Berkeley or sleep-outs against dorm curfews) or against the administration itself. Or, when possible, they can initiate guerrilla campaigns of demonstration, pickets, and sit-ins to call attention to and build opposition against particular injustices.

4.) Organizing around ideas. Radical activitists must continually counterpose their vision of the university and of human society to the liberal ideology which underlies most courses in history, political science, economics, sociology, philosophy and literature. Professors might have all the answers, but to what questions? Moreover, the conventional academic view of human nature and the possibilities of change is probably more pessimistic than that of the activist. One of our most important organizing jobs is to clarify in papers, in classes, and in public forums the bias behind the conventional wisdom and to make explicit our own values. Equally important is the need, especially for graduate students, to define areas of radical research, to go beyond refining established revelation, to pose alternatives to the presently accepted reality. The Vietnam protest offers many such opportunities, as do discussions of the War on Poverty, automation, urban problems, and the social responsibility of scientists.

Full scale counter-curricula have, unfortunately, shown little success in competition with the grade hunger which drives even "free" students back into their regular courses. But efforts should continue with a greater emphasis on demonstrating the validity of a Freedom School methodology. The teach-in also offers possibilities for radical innovation, both with context and with method. And the eagerness to learn evident in past teach-ins should suggest a general policy of integrating radical self-education more closely into protest activities. Fixed counter-courses share with standard university education a certain unreality.

Certainly other programs suggest themselves, but the important thing is to keep our eye on the prize—a new vision for a free university in a free society. Hopefully there will be a greater sharing of experience, and even regional conferences and campaigns to move us closer to our goal. But for most of us, The Movement itself will provide the education, the engagement, and the opportunity for self-realization which the multiversity cannot offer.

6. Dialogue: "How to Make a College"

The "Free University" or "New School" is one answer to the questions raised by students disturbed over the character of the education they are receiving. A number of these schools are operating now throughout the country; a few successfully, in the sense that they have a serious student body, the most not. But successful or not, the fact that they have come into being means that they are responding to needs felt by students to learn differently than they do now about a different order of problems.

Paul Goodman was one of the first writers in America to proselytize for a new form of university education, and a great

*many students in The Movement felt a great attachment to his
ideas. In 1963 he was interviewed in New York by Alvin Duskin,
who was Chairman of Emerson College, at Pacific Grove, California, one of the earliest of the recent attempts to break from
the normal mold of academic life. Emerson was founded in 1960
and went out of existence three years later.*

GOODMAN . . . I wrote *The Community of Scholars* to emphasize the practice of the standard professions and high
scholarship of the Western world. I'm trying to imitate the
medieval university. And that's a very easy thing to do. Just
go and do it on the next block. That's all a medieval university was. You see, I'm thinking of a place that makes a real
doctor and a real lawyer and a real engineer.

DUSKIN You mean undergraduate training that will better prepare a student for enrollment in professional schools?

GOODMAN That's right. Or not necessarily enrolling in professional schools but taking part in society as a learned citizen.
But that importantly includes professional schools. The notion of what it is to be a real lawyer—not so much with a doctor, by the way—but to be a real lawyer, let's say, or a real
architect—this idea has become so foreign to the American
people that they can't imagine what I'm talking about. You
have a guy nowadays studying engineering in order to fill a
niche in some engineering firm. The firm produces stuff on
demand that has nothing to do with real engineering. Because
engineering is supposed to do with utility and social planning.
Social planning, of course, requires a real engineer with professional ability.

So where's your professional? This poor guy can't be a professional because he's been trained to man a machine. You
know, there's a big technological machine operating and he's
grown up thinking that all he can do is man it. And then he'll
argue that that makes him a professional! So it's only the doctors who still have any professionalism left. The lawyers? Not
at all. All they're interested in is the court system, in cases,

certainly not in justice. And in the humanities real professionalism means working as a real editor, a real publisher.
A man who's interested in the advancement of learning, in
raising the cultural tone of the American people. Publishing!
But these guys who are in the publishing business aren't publishers. They're in the grocery business. Except it's books
they're peddling.

DUSKIN   Is there any action we can take to get some professionalism into the existing professions?

GOODMAN   You know what the action is. You want professionalism in city planning? Get Webb and Knapp and the other
promoters out of urban renewal. Then the professionals can
plan some decent neighborhoods. Do you want professionalism in TV and radio? Take the stations away from NBC and
CBS. Then the professionals can do some broadcasting.

You know where the action is, but how will you do it? The
action is a revolution. Really, this is a deep-rooted problem
and you won't solve it without throwing these people out. But
you see, we are helpless. So what else do you want to do? . . .

DUSKIN   . . . let's get back to the problem of how to induce a
group of senior scholars to secede and form their own school.
We see a lot of lawyers getting together and forming new
firms. Doctors get together with other doctors to form independent clinics. It's profitable and convenient for them. But
we don't see groups of teachers getting together to form new
schools. It isn't profitable or convenient for them to give up
their dependence on the existing schools. So it doesn't seem
likely to me that a well-established teacher is going to leave
his university just so he can train a student to be a better
scholar or professional. He'd probably argue that the kind
of thing you're after is available at the existing smaller, more
experimental colleges.

GOODMAN   No. Not really. Not for real careers. Most of the experimental colleges, like the progressive schools—now this is
not an objection to them at all, it's just not my idea, it's not at
all an objection—are interested in making good people.
Happy, integrated, adventurous people. And that's a fine

thing. Who could object to that? But that isn't a medieval university. . . .

DUSKIN . . . But I'm not sure you can so easily create a strong academic scene in a college in which there are only five regular teachers and five part-time teachers. At Emerson there's been a continuous uphill struggle with the people who thought of the college primarily as a school for the art of living, a school in which students had experiences. Now as the school becomes more academic . . .

GOODMAN What is it you mean by "academic," Al? I mean, what do you mean by that? Because it might be what I mean and it might not be what I mean. When I mean professional I don't mean academic in a certain sense.

DUSKIN When I say "academic," I mean using books, using reading and writing for the development of a job in the world. I think we mean pretty much the same thing but I hadn't thought of bringing in a practicing lawyer or a practicing architect as a teacher to undergraduates. But my point is that you can hold up a medieval ideal where the masters bring up the apprentices, but if nobody is actually carrying out this medieval ideal in the real world, then you have to offer some kind of first step so that teachers and students will see that it's possible to start moving in this direction. That is, not just talk about how bad things are, but really move toward something better.

GOODMAN I don't believe that. I think there are a lot of young people who are moving this way even though it's very hard for them and a better school would make it easier. I think there are a lot of young people who are disgusted with society on these grounds rather than on the usual beat grounds. . . .

GOODMAN . . . To be a lawyer is one way of being a man. To be a doctor is a way of being a man. I don't like this being a man and then taking a profession. There is such a thing as being a child or being an adolescent. But a man and a citizen and a productive citizen are one and the same. You cannot be-

come a man unless you are either a lawyer or a carpenter
or a writer. You see, I'm not talking about becoming a man
and then playing a role. To be a lawyer is not a role. To be a
lawyer is a vocation. Man and vocation are the same. Do you
see?

DUSKIN   Wouldn't you say then that the problem of the undergraduate years is, first of all, to make a student for real, taking
over the responsibility for his own work and not just plowing
through a program?

GOODMAN   In this country, yes. Being a student is a vocation at
a certain age. The reason is that in this country—in modern
times—the institutions of society have become emasculated.
Dehumanized. So it's become very difficult for a thirteen- or
fourteen-year-old to latch on to something to do. If you go
back to a more stable society every kid by that age would
have an inkling of where he's going. Partly for family reasons
or partly because he has some special talent that everyone
talks of. They'd tell him: "Gee, you ought to be a lawyer.
Gee, the way you talk." You know. In our society that
scarcely exists. Therefore there gets to be this interregnum
period that could easily be the first few years of college. Where
the problem is to find what it is they want to do. And that's
being a professional student. I think in this country that's true.

DUSKIN   Then what you need, according to the way you set
things up in the book, is teachers who have a vocation other
than teaching. So that the students will get some idea of what
it is to practice a vocation.

GOODMAN   Yes, they should be people who have professional
lives in the world—not in the college. I can't help but see it
that way. There are a few people, there are some people
whose genius is kind of Socratic. That is, they midwife the
kids. . . .
    I'm not terribly impressed by what they call the difficulties
of administration. You know, in a present day European
university many of the problems just don't exist. I'll give you
an example.
    A guy has to take a Ph.D. exam. Not long ago. I think it

was at the University of Vienna. He doesn't know the date on which the professors are going to give him the orals. So he goes around to the professors and they say, "We'll set a date and you'll be notified."

But he says, "I gotta know."

"Well," they say, "go ask the rector."

So he does, but the rector says, "How the devil would I know? I'm just the rector for one year. How would I know? Ask the beadle."

So he goes to the beadle and the beadle looks in his book and says, "They always have it six weeks from yesterday. They'll send you a notice."

Now the beadle is the janitor and of course he knows everything. Do you see? The janitor is the administrator!

Now take admissions. Of course, these are places where students come to. And their professors are great names. People don't just go to get a degree, they go to study with Professor so-and-so. So how is a class chosen? You talk with Professor so-and-so and he says, "Yes, come and I'll teach you," or "No, I don't want you." And then if he's a kindly man he says, "I don't want to teach you but, look, I've talked to you. Why don't you go down to Marburg? You're just the kind of student that so-and-so likes. See, to me you're a pain in the neck." And that's what admissions consist of in these schools. The teachers decide who they'll teach. Who else would they want to teach? Sometimes they don't care. You know, Professor so-and-so will take three unknowns in his class. They seem to want him. But they want *him*. They don't just want History 203b. If they want to study with him, well okay, he's predisposed to like them. . . . something like Black Mountain, . . . was a real community. But it wasn't a community of scholarship, it was a community for living. A student bought into the community. It was what we call an intentional community and the economy was studying.

DUSKIN The cash crop was education.

GOODMAN Yes, the cash crop was education. They wanted to live in the mountains and they supported the community by teaching. What's wrong with that?

DUSKIN   Sure, that's okay. But I'm concerned only with teaching and learning in the most efficient way. I just want a job and I don't want to fool around. But I've found that unless you deal with a set way that students have . . . well, look, say a student comes around—we're talking about America now and there aren't *any* other schools operating the way we do—and this student says, "How do I enroll in the College?" So I say, "Sit down and we'll talk for a while." We talk and then, after a time I say, "You can't take my class. To me you're a pain in the neck. But go down the hall and talk to Jordan. You're just the kind of student he likes."

So what would the kid do? He'd probably go running out of the place because he'd think that if I didn't like him he wouldn't have a chance. And there's no Marburg for him to hike down to. . . .

GOODMAN   What Black Mountain got were rejects from the Ivy League. Perfectly good kids who just couldn't make it in the Yale environment. And kids will gravitate to your school for the same reasons. They want freedom from grading, they want to be able to talk to their teachers, they want the feeling that their teachers have not sold out to the organized system. And yet they're learning something. What's wrong with that?

DUSKIN   Did the teachers and students live together at Black Mountain?

GOODMAN   Some of the students were married and they would get little shacks up the hill. Unmarried students tended to live in little dormitory barracks—they were quite charming. They had every kind of variety. Some of the teachers were married, some were unmarried—that's what caused trouble at the school all the time, of course.

DUSKIN   Sexual rivalries?

GOODMAN   Yes, jealousies continually. Because it was full of parties, wonderful parties. They were very gifted aesthetically and they would make things out of paper that were marvelous. Just for the hell of it. A tremendous effort put in for a day and then it would be all burned up and gone. It was really a good community, it really was. *But,* the other side of it—the sexual rivalries . . .

DUSKIN And the people couldn't put up with it?

GOODMAN Well, the way to handle that is to run a continual group therapy. And they weren't up to that. I suggested it but they weren't up to it.

DUSKIN A continual all-college meeting?

GOODMAN Every time there's trouble have your shock troops come in and instead of trying to calm the trouble—bring it out into the open.

DUSKIN Whenever we've had strong contact we've had conflict.

GOODMAN Yes, but conflict leads to more contact—it works the other way. You know the way Blake says, "My opponent is my friend." And that's true too. If he's a real opponent. But it isn't true that your friend is your opponent.

DUSKIN I would certainly say that it's unwise to have teachers and students living in the same buildings. I've had my fill of that. And I'd like to see Emerson known for academic work rather than its housing arrangements. In the school that you propose in your book you don't say whether or not you think even the students should live together.

GOODMAN I would like the students to live together, but I just don't think the administration should be responsible. You see, I'm often asked when I visit a school—I have some architectural connections—planning connections anyway—so if they're building a new dormitory at a school they ask me, "What about this?" The answer I always give, I look down at the schools in some suburban place and I say, "Why don't you rent or buy six old houses down that block or scattered in this neighborhood and let fifteen kids take them over and live in them? Why do you have to be responsible for the way they live? Really, they've grown up, they can feed their faces. You have a medical staff so in case they get sick you can take care of them. But that you can do as any friend. You would do that even if you had no other connection with them." . . .

My guess . . . is that there is a fantastic demand for more education, but not the way it's usually dished out. And this demand is going to become even stronger as the big schools become even more the same, so that none is a real alternative to any other one.

DUSKIN   How big do you think the dissident group is? I mean the dissenting students who would actually quit and move if there was a reasonable alternative?

GOODMAN   I think the notion that there are just a few such students is wrong. I don't mean pulling out of, say, Stanford to go to Antioch. Because if you do that you might as well have stayed home. You know, the *new* Antioch has come to be more and more like Stanford anyway. But if there were a good alternative, I would say that 5 to 10 percent would be in the market for it.

It is true, of course, that a few of the big schools realize this too. Harvard is starting to do things that make good sense and then there's Michigan State.

DUSKIN   But these schools are simply out of reach for most kids. Telling a kid that he'd get a better education if he happened to be enrolled in an honors course at Michigan State is like telling a Chinese farmer that he'd be better off in Iowa. You'll just get him angry because there's no way for him to get there.

GOODMAN   Yes, and you might say that the big schools are not in the position now to meet the demand for better education. This is certainly true of Harvard. You know the freshman seminar system up there is very good. But the kids—once they get out of it—object to it tremendously.

DUSKIN   What's the objection?

GOODMAN   When they get out of the seminar the rest of Harvard is disappointing. The school is cold to them. Therefore the seminar is wrong. You see, the seminar is so good that it's not fair!

DUSKIN   So instead of drawing the logical conclusion that the seminar should be extended . . .

GOODMAN   They get spiteful and want to abolish it! The poor kids get so confused.

DUSKIN   Then the kids who get to take it haven't demanded it. They've just happened to have wanted to go to Harvard and once they got there they found that the professors had decided that a certain kind of seminar system would be a good thing for their freshman year.

GOODMAN   Yes, and you have a program that builds year by year. You see, a kid has to fall in love with his school. What I mean is he's got to be in love with it and then not fall out of love with it but transfer his love to the real world. And that's why the professionals have to be there, to get him through the transference from concern only with his own life to concern for activity in the real world, the activity of the professionals. Then, you see, your students' love for Emerson becomes a love for law as he grows up. This will get him over the transference from adolescence to being a man because Emerson can be people but the law, whatever it is, is not a person. And this is what our schools just don't do at all. They absolutely fail, utterly fail.

DUSKIN   So the typical graduate's loyalty is to his college's football team and to its buildings. The things that impressed him as an adolescent and which he hasn't outgrown. You might say that that's why Hutchins abolished football at Chicago. And he says somewhere, I think it's Rice who quotes him, that colleges should meet in tents.

Maybe that's how we should think of Emerson. As a big collapsible tent. We could close it down. We could open it again somewhere else.

GOODMAN   Well, what are your alternatives?

DUSKIN   Let's assume that we're going to carry through the plan you proposed in *The Community of Scholars*. Here we sit in this room and within a few months you and I are going to start a college. What would be your plan for action?

GOODMAN   I'd call up people I know, teachers who are old friends of mine, and try to inveigle them in. Then I would get in touch with three students at Columbia, three at Cornell, and maybe a couple at Harvard, and tell them, "Fetch me some students; you all talk so much, now fetch me some students." And they would do it.

DUSKIN   Then it's all personal?

GOODMAN   Well for years I've been Joan of Arcing for these kids. But then the one who could start a school in this way is the one who isn't going to.

DUSKIN   Why not?

GOODMAN   I really have other things to do. But now if such a school were formed and were going in New York, unquestionably I would go there. If these kids from Columbia get three guys to teach them three nights a week, then I'll take the fourth. I'll give them a course in literary theory or something. Who knows what.

DUSKIN   Then in terms of a plan for action . . .

GOODMAN   If a school like this were a going concern, if someone else had done the work, I'd go in. If you had Emerson in this neighborhood I'd teach a course.

DUSKIN   If we close down the College and I rent a place in Hoboken, have the lights turned on, move in the furniture?

GOODMAN   Yes, so long as it's just a question of my showing up at a place two mornings a week and giving a lecture, talking to kids around a coffee table for two hours afterwards . . . sure. You know, if it's a nice club you hang around there when you have the time to hang around. You see, I don't take these things as seriously as you. If your place is pleasant, I'll lounge there. And I like to teach. I like academic clubs with young people.

DUSKIN   Then for someone who is not you, how could he start a college? I mean a man who doesn't have a following of young students in the universities and who doesn't have old friends who are established senior scholars?

GOODMAN   A college like this must be based on personal contacts. But you have them, everyone has. You have to work with the people you know. Otherwise everything is hopeless.

The Vietnam Anti-War Campaign

1. The McComb Anti-War Petition

The McComb, Mississippi, branch of the Freedom Democratic Party issued an anti-war statement in July 1965 which eventually caused the group to be criticized in the U.S. Senate. The statement was sparked by the death in Vietnam of a young Negro soldier who had participated in the 1961 McComb demonstrations.

. . . Here are five reasons why Negroes should not be in any war fighting for America:

1. No Mississippi Negroes should be fighting in Vietnam for the White Man's freedom, until all the Negro People are free in Mississippi.

2. Negro boys should not honor the draft here in Mississippi. Mothers should encourage their sons not to go.

3. We will gain respect and dignity as a race only by forcing the United States Government and the Mississippi Government to come with guns, dogs, and trucks to take our sons away to fight and be killed protecting Mississippi, Alabama, Georgia, and Louisiana.

4. No one has a right to ask us to risk our lives and kill other Colored People in Santo Domingo and Vietnam, so that the White American can get richer. We will be looked upon as traitors by all the Colored People of the world if the Negro people continue to fight and die without a cause.

5. Last week a White soldier from New Jersey was discharged from the Army because he refused to fight in Vietnam and went on a hunger strike. Negro boys can do the same thing. We can write and ask our sons if they know what they are fighting for. If he answers Freedom, tell him that's what we are fighting for here in Mississippi. And if he says Democracy tell him the truth—we don't know anything about Communism, socialism, and all that, but we do know that Negroes have caught hell here under this *American Democracy.*

2. Position on Vietnam: "The U.S. Government Has Deceived Us"

In January 1966 SNCC staffer Julian Bond was denied his seat in the Georgia legislature for openly supporting SNCC's position on the war in Vietnam. Two new murders of Negroes in the South were more than enough to convince any SNCC workers that Negroes must first win freedom at home. SNCC calls the war in Vietnam an effort to "stifle the liberation of Vietnam." This is an excerpt from SNCC's statement.

The Student Nonviolent Coordinating Committee has a right and a responsibility to dissent with United States foreign policy on any issue when it sees fit. The Student Nonviolent Coordinating Committee now states its opposition to United States' involvement in Vietnam on these grounds:

We believe the United States government has been deceptive in its claims of concern for the freedom of the Vietnamese people, just as the government has been deceptive in claiming concern for the freedom of colored people in such other countries as the Dominican Republic, the Congo, South Africa, Rhodesia, and in the United States itself.

We, the Student Nonviolent Coordinating Committee, have been involved in the black people's struggle for liberation and self-determination in this country for the past five years. Our work, particularly in the South, has taught us that the United States government has never guaranteed the freedom of oppressed citizens, and is not yet truly determined to end the rule of terror and oppression within its own borders.

We ourselves have often been victims of violence and confinement executed by United States governmental officials. We recall the numerous persons who have been murdered in the South because of their efforts to secure their civil and human rights, and whose murderers have been allowed to escape penalty for their crimes.

The murder of Samuel Young in Tuskegee, Alabama, is no different than the murder of peasants in Vietnam, for both Young and the Vietnamese sought, and are seeking, to secure the rights guaranteed them by law. In each case, the United States government bears a great part of the responsibility for these deaths.

Samuel Young was murdered because United States law is not being enforced. Vietnamese are murdered because the United States is pursuing an aggressive policy in violation of international law. The United States is no respecter of persons or law when such persons or laws run counter to its needs or desires.

We recall the indifference, suspicion, and outright hostility with which our reports of violence have been met in the past by government officials.

We know that for the most part, elections in this country, in the North as well as the South, are not free. We have seen that the 1965 Voting Rights Act and the 1964 Civil Rights Act have not yet been implemented with full federal power and sincerity.

We question, then, the ability and even the desire of the United States government to guarantee free elections abroad. We maintain that our country's cry of "preserve freedom in the world" is a hypocritical mask behind which it squashes liberation movements which are not bound, and refuse to be bound, by the expediencies of United States Cold War policies.

We are in sympathy with, and support, the men in this country who are unwilling to respond to a military draft which would
compel them to contribute their lives to United States aggression
in Vietnam in the name of "freedom" we find so false in this
country.

We recoil with horror at the inconsistency of a supposedly
"free" society where responsibility to freedom is equated with
the responsibility to lend oneself to military aggression. We take
note of the fact that 16 per cent of the draftees from this country
are Negroes called on to stifle the liberation of Vietnam, to preserve a "democracy" which does not exist for them at home.

We ask, where is the draft for the freedom fight in the United
States?

We therefore encourage those Americans who prefer to use
their energy in building democratic forms within this country.
We believe that work in the civil rights movement and with other
human relations organizations is a valid alternative to the draft.
We urge all Americans to seek this alternative, knowing full
well that it may cost them their lives—as painfully as in Vietnam.

3. *"Attention all Military Personnel"* *

*The Berkeley Vietnam Day Committee was organized in
April 1965 by a small group of unaffiliated radicals to conduct
a massive "teach-in" on the campus of the University of California, May 21–22, 1965. After the success of the teach-in, the
Committee grew in size and began operating on several levels.
"The Vietnam Day Committee is beginning to become a way
of life," wrote Jerry Rubin, one of its founders. The group
picketed President Johnson when he appeared at the twentieth
anniversary of the UN's founding in San Francisco; carried on
demonstrations in front of troop trains in August; participated
in a "congress of unrepresented people" held in an Oakland
park, and organized another teach-in, held on October 15–16,
as part of an international protest against the Vietnam war to be
held on the same days.*

* A leaflet distributed by the Berkeley Vietnam Day Committee.

*The October teach-in brought more attention to the Berkeley
VDC than to any other group of protesters because the Oakland
police refused to allow the marchers to walk through the streets
of the city toward the army terminal the Committee planned to
picket. Another march was scheduled for November 20, and
enough frantic negotiations went on during that period among
the city officials, VDC members, the University of California,
the police departments of Berkeley and Oakland, and the state
government to have settled the war in Vietnam, much less work
out whether or not students were to be allowed the right to parade.*

*"Attention All Military Personnel" was distributed by the
VDC at induction centers and military bases; later it was mailed,
by unknown persons, to soldiers in Vietnam. Circulation of the
leaflet brought denunciations of the VDC and threats by local
officials—never carried out—to prosecute the group for treason.*

You may soon be sent to Vietnam. You have heard about
the war in the news; your officers will give you pep talks about
it. But you probably feel as confused and uncertain as most
Americans do. Many people will tell you to just follow orders
and leave the thinking to others. But you have the right to know
as much about this war as anyone. After all, it's you—not your
Congressman—who might get killed.

WHY ARE WE FIGHTING IN VIETNAM?

We are supposed to be fighting to protect democracy in Vietnam, and yet your own government admits that South Vietnam
is run by a dictatorship. General Ky, the latest military dictator,
is as bad as they come. In a recent interview he said: "People
ask me who my heroes are. I have only one—Hitler. I admire
Hitler because he pulled his country together when it was in a
terrible state" (*London Sunday Mirror,* July 4, 1965).

General Ky doesn't mean much to us; we're not even sure
how to pronounce his name, but the South Vietnamese have
lived under men like him for years. As far as the Vietnamese

are concerned, we are fighting on the side of Hitlerism; and they hope we lose.

WHO IS THE ENEMY?

U.S. military spokesmen have often said that their greatest problem is finding the enemy. The enemy, they say, is everywhere. The old woman feeding her chickens may have a stock of hand grenades in her hut. The little boy who trails after the American soldiers during the day slips out to give information to the guerrillas at night. The washerwoman at the American air base brings a bomb to work one day. It is impossible, say the military, to tell which are the Viet Cong and which are the civilians.

And so, because the whole Vietnamese people seem to be the enemy, the military is taking no chances. They use tear gas—a weapon designed for use against civilians. They order American troops to fire at women and children—because women and children, after all, are firing at American troops. American fighter planes destroy civilian villages with napalm; American B-52s are flattening whole regions. That is why the war in Vietnam is so often called a "dirty war."

When the South Vietnamese people see you in your foreign uniform, they will think of you as *their* enemy. You are the ones bombing their towns. They don't know whether you're a draftee or a volunteer, whether you're for the war or against it; but they're not taking any chances either.

FREE ELECTIONS

The Vietnamese would like to *vote* the foreigners out of their country, but they have been denied the chance. According to the Geneva Agreement of 1954, there were supposed to be elections throughout Vietnam in 1956. But the U.S. government was certain that our man in Vietnam, Premier Diem, would lose. So we decided not to allow any election until we were sure we could win. Diem set up a political police force and put all political opposition—Communist and anti-Communist—in jail. By 1959, it was clear there weren't going to be any elections, and the guerrillas known as the Viet Cong began to fight back. By 1963 our government was fed up with Diem, but still wasn't willing to risk elections. Our CIA helped a group of Vietnamese generals to overthrow Diem and kill him. Since then there have been a series of "better" military dictators. General Ky—the man who admires Hitler—is the latest one.

FIGHTING FOR DEMOCRACY

Your job as a soldier is supposed to be "to win the people of South Vietnam." Win them to what—democracy? No, we keep military dictators in power. What then? The American way of life? But why should they care any more about our way of life than we care about theirs? We can't speak their language or even pronounce their names. We don't know anything about their religion or even what it is. We never even heard of Vietnam until Washington decided to run it.

You are supposed to be fighting "to save the Vietnamese people from Communism." Certainly Communist influence is very strong in the National Liberation Front, the rebel government. Yet most of the people support the NLF. Why? Many of the same people who now lead the NLF led the Vietnamese independence movement against the Japanese during World War II, and then went on to fight against French colonial rule. Most Vietnamese think of the NLF leaders as their country's outstanding patriots. In fact, many anti-Communists have joined the guerrilla forces in the belief that the most important thing is to get rid of foreign domination and military dictators. On the other hand, very few Vietnamese support the official government of General Ky. His army has low morale and a high desertion rate.

THE GUERRILLAS

The newspapers and television have told us again and again what a tough fighter the Vietnamese guerrilla is. Short of ammunition and without any air cover, he can beat forces that outnumber him five or ten to one. Why do they have such high morale? They are not draftees; no draftees ever fight like that. They are not high-paid, professional soldiers. Most of them are peasants who work their fields; they can't even spare the ammunition for target practice.

Their secret is that they know why they are fighting. They didn't hear about Vietnam in the newspapers; they've lived there all their lives. While we were in high school, they were living under the Diem regime and hating it. Now American planes are bombing their towns and strafing their fields; American troops have occupied their country; and if they complain out loud, an American-supported dictator sentences them to jail or the firing squad. Is it any wonder that they fight so fiercely?

CRUSHING THE RESISTANCE

The war in Vietnam is not being fought according to the rules. Prisoners are tortured. Our planes drop incendiary bombs on civilian villages. Our soldiers shoot at women and children. Your officers will tell you that it is all necessary, that we couldn't win the war any other way. *And they are right.* Americans are no more cruel than any other people; American soldiers don't enjoy this kind of war. But if you are going to wage war against an entire people, you have to become cruel.

The ordinary German soldier in occupied Europe wasn't especially cruel, either. But as the resistance movements grew, he *became* cruel. He shot at women and children because they were shooting at him; he never asked himself *why* they were shooting at him. When a certain town became a center of resistance activity, he followed his orders and destroyed the whole town. He knew that SS men were torturing captured resistance fighters, but it wasn't his business to interfere.

FOLLOWING ORDERS

As a soldier you have been trained to obey orders, but as a human being you must take responsibility for your own acts. International and American law recognize that an individual soldier, even if acting under orders, must bear final legal and moral responsibility for what he does. This principle became a part of law after World War II, when the Allied nations, meeting in London, decided that German war criminals must be punished even if they committed war crimes under orders. This principle was the basis of the Nuremberg trials. We believe that the entire war in Vietnam is criminal and immoral. We believe that the atrocities which are necessary to wage this war against the people of Vietnam are inexcusable.

OPPOSE THE WAR

We hope that you too find yourself, as a human being, unable to tolerate this nightmare war, and we hope that you will oppose it. We don't know what kind of risks we are taking in giving you this leaflet; you won't know what risk you will be taking in opposing the war. A growing number of GIs have already refused to fight in Vietnam and have been court-martialed. They have shown great courage. We believe that they, together with other courageous men who will join them, will have influence far out of proportion to their numbers.

There may be many other things you can do; since you are in the service, you know better than civilians what sorts of opposition are possible. But whatever you do, keep your eyes open. Draw your own conclusions from the things you see, read, and hear. At orientation sessions, don't be afraid to ask questions, and if you're not satisfied with the answers, keep asking. Take every chance you get to talk to your fellow soldiers about the war.

You may feel the war is wrong, and still decide not to face a court-martial. You may then find yourself in Vietnam under orders. You might be forced to do some fighting—but don't do any more than you have to. Good luck.

4. *"Liberalism and the Corporate State"*

More than twenty thousand people, most of them young, participated in the November 27, 1965, March on Washington, sponsored by SANE and less militant than the SDS march in April 1965. The speech made by Carl Oglesby, President of SDS, is one of the most accurate reflections of the "new radical" viewpoint on the war in Vietnam. There was some apprehension that Oglesby would "go too far," but his speech won the assembled crowd's loudest approval. The speech is reproduced here as Oglesby delivered it, and therefore differs in minor ways from the text distributed in advance.

Seven months ago at the April March on Washington, Paul Potter, then President of Students for a Democratic Society, stood in approximately this spot and said that we must name the system that creates and sustains the war in Vietnam—name it, describe it, analyze it, understand it, and change it.

Today I will try to name it—to suggest an analysis which, to be quite frank, may disturb some of you—and to suggest what changing it may require of us.

We are here again to protest against a growing war. Since it is a very bad war, we acquire the habit of thinking that it must be caused by very bad men. But we only conceal reality, I think, to denounce on such grounds the menacing coalition of industrial and military power, or the brutality of the blitzkrieg we are waging against Vietnam, or the ominous signs around us that heresy may soon no longer be permitted. We must simply observe, and quite plainly say, that this coalition, this blitzkrieg, and this demand for acquiescence are creatures, all of them, of a government that since 1932 has considered itself to be fundamentally *liberal*.

The original commitment in Vietnam was made by President Truman, a mainstream liberal. It was seconded by President Eisenhower, a moderate liberal. It was intensified by the late President Kennedy, a flaming liberal. Think of the men who now engineer that war—those who study the maps, give the commands, push the buttons, and tally the dead: Bundy, McNamara, Rusk, Lodge, Goldberg, the President himself.

They are not moral monsters.

They are all honorable men.

They are all liberals.

But so, I'm sure, are many of us who are here today in protest. To understand the war, then, it seems necessary to take a closer look at this American liberalism. Maybe we are in for some surprises. Maybe we have here two quite different liberalisms: one authentically humanist, the other not so human at all.

Not long ago, I considered myself a liberal. And if someone had asked me what I meant by that, I'd perhaps have quoted Thomas Jefferson or Thomas Paine, who first made plain our nation's unprovisional commitment to human rights. But what do

you think would happen if these two heroes could sit down now
for a chat with President Johnson and McGeorge Bundy?

They would surely talk of the Vietnam war. Our dead revolutionaries would soon wonder why their country was fighting
against what appeared to be a revolution. The living liberals
would hotly deny that it is one: there are troops coming in from
outside, the rebels get arms from other countries, most of the
people are not on their side, and they practice terror against
their own. Therefore, *not* a revolution.

What would our dead revolutionaries answer? They might say:
"What fools and bandits, sirs, you make then of us. Outside
help? Do you remember Lafayette? Or the three thousand British freighters the French navy sank for our side? Or the arms and
men we got from France and Spain? And what's this about terror? Did you never hear what we did to our own loyalists? Or
about the thousands of rich American Tories who fled for their
lives to Canada? And as for popular support, do you not know
that we had less than one third of our people with us? That, in
fact, the colony of New York recruited more troops for the British than for the revolution? Should we give it all back?"

Revolutions do not take place in velvet boxes. They never
have. It is only the poets who make them lovely. What the National Liberation Front is fighting in Vietnam is a complex and
vicious war. This war is also a revolution, as honest a revolution
as you can find anywhere in history. And this is a fact which all
our intricate official denials will never change.

But it doesn't make any difference to our leaders anyway.
Their aim in Vietnam is really much simpler than this implies.
It is to safeguard what they take to be American interests around
the world against revolution or revolutionary change, which they
always call Communism—as if that were that. In the case of
Vietnam, this interest is, first, the principle that revolution shall
not be tolerated anywhere, and second, that South Vietnam shall
never sell its rice to China—or even to North Vietnam.

There is simply no such thing now, for us, as a just revolution
—never mind that for two thirds of the world's people the twentieth century might as well be the Stone Age; never mind the terrible poverty and hopelessness that are the basic facts of life for

most modern men; and never mind that for these millions there is now an increasingly perceptible relationship between their sorrow and our contentment.

Can we understand why the Negroes of Watts rebelled? Then why do we need a devil theory to explain the rebellion of the South Vietnamese? Can we understand the oppression in Mississippi, or the anguish that our Northern ghettos make epidemic? Then why can't we see that our proper human struggle is not with Communism or revolutionaries, but with the social desperation that drives good men to violence, both here and abroad?

To be sure, we have been most generous with our aid, and in Western Europe, a mature industrial society, that aid worked. But there are always political and financial strings. And we have never shown ourselves capable of allowing others to make those traumatic institutional changes that are often the prerequisites of progress in colonial societies. For all our official feeling for the millions who are enslaved to what we so self-righteously call the yoke of Communist tyranny, we make no real effort at all to crack through the much more vicious right-wing tyrannies that our businessmen traffic with and our nation profits from every day. And for all our cries about the international red conspiracy to take over the world, we take only pride in our six thousand military bases on foreign soil.

We gave Rhodesia a grave look just now—but we keep on buying her chromium, which is cheap because black slave labor mines it.

We deplore the racism of Verwoerd's fascist South Africa— but our banks make big loans to that country and our private technology makes it a nuclear power.

We are saddened and puzzled by random back-page stories of revolt in this or that Latin American state—but are convinced by a few pretty photos in the Sunday supplement that things are getting better, that the world is coming our way, that change from disorder can be orderly, that our benevolence will pacify the distressed, that our might will intimidate the angry.

Optimists, may I suggest that these are quite unlikely fantasies? They are fantasies because we have lost that mysterious social desire for human equity that from time to time has given us genuine moral drive. We have become a nation of young, bright-eyed, hard-hearted, slim-waisted, bullet-headed make-out artists. A nation—may I say it?—of beardless liberals.

You say I am being hard? Only think.

This country, with its thirty-some years of liberalism, can send two hundred thousand young men to Vietnam to kill and die in the most dubious of wars, but it cannot get a hundred voter registrars to go into Mississippi.

What do you make of it?

The financial burden of the war obliges us to cut millions from an already pathetic War on Poverty budget. But in almost the same breath, Congress appropriates $140 million for the Lockheed and Boeing companies to compete with each other on the supersonic transport project—that Disneyland creation that will cost us all about $2 billion before it's done.

What do you make of it?

Many of us have been earnestly resisting for some years now the idea of putting atomic weapons into West German hands, an action that would perpetuate the division of Europe and thus the Cold War. Now just this week we find out that, with the meagerest of security systems, West Germany has had nuclear weapons in her hands for the past six years.

What do you make of it?

Some will make of it that I overdraw the matter. Many will ask: What about the other side? To be sure, there is the bitter ugliness of Czechoslovakia, Poland, those infamous Russian tanks in the streets of Budapest. But my anger only rises to hear some say that sorrow cancels sorrow, or that *this* one's shame deposits in *that* one's account the right to shamefulness.

And others will make of it that I sound mighty anti-American. To these, I say: Don't blame *me* for *that!* Blame those who mouthed my liberal values and broke my American heart.

Just who might they be, by the way? Let's take a brief factual inventory of the latter-day Cold War.

In 1953 our Central Intelligence Agency managed to overthrow Mossadegh in Iran, the complaint being his neutralism in the Cold War and his plans to nationalize the country's oil resources to improve his people's lives. Most evil aims, most evil man. In his place we put in General Zahedi, a World War II

Nazi collaborator. New arrangements on Iran's oil gave twenty-five-year leases on 40 percent of it to three United States firms, one of which was Gulf Oil. The CIA's leader for this coup was Kermit Roosevelt. In 1960 Kermit Roosevelt became a vice-president of Gulf Oil.

In 1954 the democratically elected Arbenz of Guatemala wanted to nationalize a portion of United Fruit Company's plantations in his country, land he needed badly for a modest program of agrarian reform. His government was overthrown in a CIA-supported right-wing coup. The following year, General Walter Bedell Smith, director of the CIA when the Guatemala venture was being planned, joined the board of directors of the United Fruit Company.

Comes 1960 and Castro cries we are about to invade Cuba. The Administration sneers "poppycock," and we Americans believe it. Comes 1961 and the invasion. Comes with it the awful realization that the United States government had lied.

Comes 1962 and the missile crisis, and our Administration stands prepared to fight global atomic war on the curious principle that another state does not have the right to its own foreign policy.

Comes 1963 and British Guiana, where Cheddi Jagan wants independence from England and a labor law modeled on the Wagner Act. And Jay Lovestone, the AFL-CIO foreign policy chief, acting, as always, quite independently of labor's rank and file, arranges with our government to finance an eleven-week dock strike that brings Jagan down, ensuring that the state will remain *British* Guiana, and that any workingman who wants a wage better than fifty cents a day is a dupe of Communism.

Comes 1964. Two weeks after Under Secretary Thomas Mann announces that we have abandoned the *Alianza's* principle of no aid to tyrants, Brazil's Goulart is overthrown by the vicious right-winger Ademar Barros, supported by a show of American gunboats at Rio de Janeiro. Within twenty-four hours the new head of state, Mazzilli, receives a congratulatory wire from our President.

Comes 1965. The Dominican Republic. Rebellion in the streets. We scurry to the spot with twenty thousand neutral Marines and our neutral peacemakers—like Ellsworth Bunker, Jr., Ambassador to the Organization of American States. Most of us know that our neutral Marines fought openly on the side of the junta, a fact that the Administration still denies. But how many also know that what was at stake was our new Caribbean sugar bowl? That this same neutral peacemaking Bunker is a board member and stock owner of the National Sugar Refining Company, a firm his father founded in the good old days, and one which has a major interest in maintaining the status quo in the Dominican Republic? Or that the President's close personal friend and advisor, our new Supreme Court Justice Abe Fortas, has sat for the past nineteen years on the board of the Sucrest Company, which imports black-strap molasses from the Dominican Republic? Or that the rhetorician of corporate liberalism and the late President Kennedy's close friend, Adolf Berle, was chairman of that same board? Or that our roving ambassador Averell Harriman's brother Roland is on the board of National Sugar? Or that our former Ambassador to the Dominican Republic, Joseph Farland, is a board member of the South Puerto Rico Sugar Co., which owns 275,000 acres of rich land in the Dominican Republic and is the largest employer on the island—at about one dollar a day?

Neutralists! God save the hungry people of the world from such neutralists!

We do not say these men are evil. We say, rather, that good men can be divided from their compassion by the institutional system that inherits us all. Generation in and out, we are put to use. People become instruments. Generals do not hear the screams of the bombed; sugar executives do not see the misery of the cane cutters: for to do so is to be that much *less* the general, that much *less* the executive.

The foregoing facts of recent history describe one main aspect of the estate of Western liberalism. Where is our American humanism here? What went wrong?

Let's stare our situation coldly in the face. All of us are born to the colossus of history, our American corporate system—in many ways an awesome organism. There is one fact that describes it: with about 5 percent of the world's people, we consume about half the world's goods. We take a richness that is in good part not our own, and we put it in our pockets, our garages, our split-levels, our bellies, and our futures.

On the *face* of it, it is a crime that so few should have so much at the expense of so many. Where is the moral imagination so abused as to call this just? Perhaps many of us feel a bit uneasy in our sleep. We are not, after all, a cruel people. And perhaps we don't really need this super-dominance that deforms others. But what can we do? The investments are made. The financial ties are established. The plants abroad are built. Our system *exists*. One is swept up into it. How intolerable—to be born moral, but addicted to a stolen and maybe surplus luxury. Our goodness threatens to become counterfeit before our eyes—unless we change. But change threatens us with uncertainty—at least.

Our problem, then, is to justify this system and give its theft another name—to make kind and moral what is neither, to perform some alchemy with language that will make this injustice seem to be a most magnanimous gift.

A hard problem. But the Western democracies, in the heyday of their colonial expansionism, produced a hero worthy of the task.

Its name was free enterprise, and its partner was an *illiberal liberalism* that said to the poor and the dispossessed: What we acquire of your resources we repay in civilization. The white man's burden. But this was too poetic. So a much more hard-headed theory was produced. This theory said that colonial status is in fact a *boon* to the colonized. We give them technology and bring them into modern times.

But this deceived no one but ourselves. We were delighted with this new theory. The poor saw in it merely an admission that their claims were irrefutable. They stood up to us, without gratitude. We were shocked—but also confused, for the poor seemed again to be right. How long is it going to be the case, we wondered, that the poor will be right and the rich will be wrong?

Liberalism faced a crisis. In the face of the collapse of the European empires, how could it continue to hold together our twin need for richness and righteousness? How can we continue to sack the ports of Asia and still dream of Jesus?

The challenge was met with a most ingenious solution: the ideology of anti-Communism. This was the bind: we cannot call revolution bad, because we started that way ourselves, and because it is all too easy to see why the dispossessed should rebel. So we will call revolution *Communism*. And we will reserve for ourselves the right to say what Communism means. We take note of revolution's enormities, wrenching them where necessary from their historical context and often exaggerating them, and say: Behold, Communism is a bloodbath. We take note of those reactionaries who stole the revolution, and say: Behold, Communism is a betrayal of the people. We take note of the revolution's need to consolidate itself, and say: Behold, Communism is a tyranny.

It has been all these things, and it will be these things again, and we will never be at a loss for those tales of atrocity that comfort us so in our self-righteousness. Nuns will be raped and bureaucrats will be disemboweled. Indeed, revolution is a *fury*. For it is a letting loose of outrages pent up sometimes over centuries. But the more brutal and longer-lasting the suppression of this energy, all the more ferocious will be its explosive release.

Far from helping Americans deal with this truth, the anti-Communist ideology merely tries to disguise it so that things may stay the way they are. Thus, it depicts our presence in other lands not as a coercion, but a protection. It allows us even to say that the napalm in Vietnam is only another aspect of our humanitarian love—like those exorcisms in the Middle Ages that so often killed the patient. So we say to the Vietnamese peasant, the Cuban intellectual, the Peruvian worker: "You are better dead than red. If it hurts or if you don't understand why—sorry about that."

This is the action of *corporate liberalism*. It performs for the corporate state a function quite like what the Church once performed for the feudal state. It seeks to justify its burdens and protect it from change. As the Church exaggerated this office in the Inquisition, so with liberalism in the McCarthy time—which, if it was a reactionary phenomenon, was still made possible by our anti-Communist corporate liberalism.

Let me then speak directly to humanist liberals. If my facts are wrong, I will soon be corrected. But if they are right, then you may face a crisis of conscience. Corporatism or humanism; which? For it has come to that. Will you let your dreams be used? Will you be grudging apologists for the corporate state? Or will you help try to change it—not in the name of this or that blueprint or ism, but in the name of simple human decency and democracy and the vision that wise and brave men saw in the time of our own Revolution?

And if your commitment to human value is unconditional, then disabuse yourselves of the notion that statements will bring change, if only the right statements can be written, or that interviews with the mighty will bring change if only the mighty can be reached, or that marches will bring change if only we can make them massive enough, or that policy proposals will bring change if only we can make them responsible enough.

We are dealing now with a colossus that does not want to be changed. It will not change itself. It will not cooperate with those who want to change it. Those allies of ours in the government— are they really our allies? If they *are,* then they don't need advice, they need *constituencies;* they don't need study groups, they need a *movement.* And if they are *not,* then all the more reason for building that movement with a most relentless conviction.

There are people in this country today who are trying to build that movement, who aim at nothing less than a humanist reformation. And the humanist liberals must understand that it is this movement with which their own best hopes are most in tune. We radicals know the same history that you liberals know, and we can understand your occasional cynicism, exasperation, and even distrust. But we ask you to put these aside and help us risk a leap. Help us find enough time for the enormous work that needs doing here. Help us build. Help us shake the future in the name of plain human hope.

Ideology, Communism, and Coalition

1. "Up From Irrelevance" and "Reply"

One of the most significant debates about The Movement's future took place in an exchange among the editors of Studies *on the Left in its Spring 1965 issue (Vol. 5, No. 2). Tom Hayden, Norm Fruchter, and Alan Cheuse debated with James Weinstein, Stanley Aronowitz, Lee Baxandall, Eugene D. Genovese, and Helen Kramer over how the new radicals ought to build a movement. The debate grew from the proposal made in an earlier* Studies *editorial about the need for a radical center which could serve as the basis for building a new radical ideology.*

Up From Irrelevance

In the past *Studies* concentrated on the broad contours of American social structure and history; now it focuses on specific problems of social revolution in this country. This makes the magazine identify with "insurgent forces": people in the civil rights movement, community unions, trade unions, student organizations, radical intellectuals and artists. Our last editorial, "After the Elections," tried to analyze the few possibilities for change open to these new insurgents. Our editorial board agreed on a description of this society as "the most flexible of totalitarianisms," in which nearly all human activity is paralyzed in dependence on welfare-capitalism and the Cold War. There was disagreement among the editors, however, when we faced the question of finding a way to effectively confront this society and to change it.

Since this problem, which has split radicals in the past, still causes bafflement and conflict, it seemed to me that the editors should focus on exploring dilemmas instead of proposing organizational formulas. However, most members of the *Studies* board favored an organizational call of some sort: a unification of the new movements; a coalition of the old and new left; a new Socialist Party; or at least a common and guiding radical ideology. The editorial concluded by calling ambiguously for a "radical center" that could serve as a communications and coordinating agency linking the new insurgents with the traditional left. While this new center should be built around the insights and needs of the new radicals, the editorial argued, it should make a basic place for the older radicals who now are lodged in single-issue groups (traditional civil rights, educational reform, peace activity) where their radicalism is subdued and isolated from the new movements.

This seemed to me an artificial attempt to order the chaos of the contemporary Left; as such, it short-circuits an important discussion that began in *Studies* with last summer's focus on the issues of community organizing.

Proposing a "radical center" assumes there is a sufficiently large radical movement in need of coordination; or, at least it assumes that a "radical center" could forge existing materials into such a movement. But, as *Studies* also pointed out, the new movements are in their infancy. From Washington, it may look as though the Freedom Democratic Party is organized; from McComb, it is clear that only the beginnings have been made. The movement is even less developed in other reaches of the Black Belt, and no movement at all is current in the major Southern and Northern cities. Work among poor whites is negligible. New organizing campaigns among youth and industrial workers are just being conceived. Only this year are students becoming an intimate and profound force, both in community organizing and on campuses; but again, the student movement is just beginning to become massive. Assuming these movements must and will expand, as I think events indicate, it seems rather early to pull them into a national center. The critical work still remains at the *base,* and only an overemphasis on the *image* of a national movement can make one believe it exists. We ought not to fall into the trap of confusing widespread outbursts with a solid movement. Behind the sit-ins, teach-ins, freedom votes, wildcat strikes and other protests which are beginning to shake society; behind the "new unrest" reported everywhere from *Life* to the *National Guardian,* is the persistent reality of human inertia which still is stronger than the few energies now being released.

Moreover, I think the development of a radical movement depends on what force can be freed by the current civil rights movement. The civil rights issue is pivotal because it is exposing the limits of American economics and politics; it is beginning to arouse the interest of poor people; it is forcing a realignment of people within labor, liberal, religious and left groups; it is the problem which moves and educates the effective students. But I doubt that these tendencies can change into the strands of a wider movement, a movement with a total program for change, in the near future. This is partly because the first task for most organizations will be to clear up whatever racial problems can be cleared up without taking on the whole country. The more important point, in explaining why an independent radicalism is stymied, is that the radical and moderate wings of the civil rights movement are mutually dependent. Martin Luther King needs SNCC to do basic organizing; SNCC needs King to support the FDP; both need the NAACP to support national legislation. Thus, while people in SNCC, SDS, FDP, and even CORE and SCLC form a loose "left" in the movement, with their emphasis on poverty and community organization, this "left" is partially dependent on the more conservative establishment that reaches all the way into the national government. Certainly it is desirable to loosen this conservative grip. But for this to take place, there must be something to break *toward:* other people in the society who together can make up an alternative community to the establishment. But such people are not available at the present time in sufficient numbers and strength and, unless they are, it is hollow to call for a "radical center."

If this is true, it is irrelevant also to "choose" between the political alternatives which usually are presented to radicals: working within the Democratic Party for realignment versus independent political action. The new movements which give us hope *are* realigning the Democratic Party even though they often work outside the Party and their values go far beyond those of the Democratic leadership. The new movements are neither fully dependent nor independent; at present, they are creating tensions in both directions. The FDP is the most obvious case in point. At Atlantic City it sought entry into the national Democratic Party, not because the Freedom Democrats believed in political realignment, but because the current situation permitted no more radical stance. This situation, which is subject to change, is made up of: 1) the political weight of the radical-democratic sharecroppers in the FDP against the more conservative "teachers and preachers" who are allied with the national NAACP and the Johnson Administration; 2) how effectively FDP organizers can expand the Party's base in the rural areas; 3) whether there are similar power groups, North or South, which the FDP can connect with instead of the national Democratic Party; 4) the ability and desire of the Administration to meet the needs of the FDP.

How much can a single movement in one state liberate itself from the national power centers which can guarantee its survival and short-term gains? This depends on whether the support for the FDP comes from Democratic machines and liberal reformers in the North, or whether the sharecroppers can expect to join up with other people around the country who have the same needs. If the FDP cannot depend on strength from local people's movements elsewhere, then its most democratic qualities will be held back as the price of acceptance within a "realigned" Democratic Party—a Party, however, which will be committed still to elite domination of politics, industry and war.

This means that, instead of assuming that a viable radicalism is present, an assumption which leads to the idea that a "radical center" is needed, we instead ought to focus on the obstacles to a radical movement in the first place. To an overwhelming degree American society has controlled its internal class, radical and psychological strains. With social controls ranging from terrorism to welfare, the country has moved far in the direction of "one-dimensional society" Herbert Marcuse describes. Almost everyone develops a vested interest of some kind in the American system as a whole, and within the system there are virtually no legitimate places from which to launch a total opposition movement. Politically, any group looking for a radical alternative to liberal-left politics seems to be either isolated and destroyed, or swallowed into an uncomfortable coalition with the leadership of labor, civil rights and religious organizations.

Some radicals now accept this situation by claiming it is impossible to go "outside" the system. Bayard Rustin, for example, argues that poor people are incapable of leading a revolutionary movement. ("Rousseau was not a cotton-picker," he told an Antioch audience recently.) From this, he goes on to embrace the idea that a coalition of organizational leaders, pressured by the discontent of their rank-and-file, is needed to carry through a program of new liberal social legislation. *Studies,* along with the new movements, suspects the wisdom of this approach. Our suspicion begins with the belief that welfare-state reforms, conducted within the private, selfish control of the economy, are ineffective because they are not conceived by the poor people they are designed for. Instead, they mangle and manipulate the poor while relaxing most of the middle class into the comfortable sense that everything is being managed well. But this criticism itself indicates why there is no present radical alternative: the welfare state effectively satisfies or contains its subject population. Rustin can invent a clear strategy because he chooses to move with, and in fact rationalize, the main trends in this society: he even argues that ending poverty would be good for big business. But anyone wishing to counter these dominant trends, as the new left is trying to do, is facing a mystery when they look for a workable strategy. What we seek to make viable, against the grain of an affluent and coercive society, is a thoroughly democratic revolution, in which the most oppressed aspire to govern and decide, begin to practice their aspiration, and finally carry it to fulfillment by transforming decision-making everywhere. The emphasis in the movement on "letting the people decide," on decentralized decision-making, on refusing alliances with top leaders, stems from the need to create a personal and group identity that can survive both the temptations and the crippling effects of this society. Power in America is abdicated by individuals to top-down organizational units, and it is in the recovery of this power that the movement becomes distinct from the rest of the country, and a new kind of man emerges.

This kind of man cannot be purchased because his needs cannot be translated into cash; he cannot be manipulated because it is precisely against manipulation that he has defined his rebellion. Should it be possible to create this new identity on a large scale, then the movement can avoid two key dangers. The first of these is dependency on fixed leaders, who inevitably develop interests in maintaining the organization (or themselves) and lose touch with the immediate aspirations of the rank-and-file. The second danger is that the rank-and-file will not understand or commit themselves to the long-range goals of the movement. What results from these tendencies is the present structure of all liberal and left organizations: they are shells.

What we should try to do, on the contrary, is assume that we have failed so far to discover the relationships and the forms that will free individuals to think and work as radicals, and build a movement where "everybody is a leader." Not until then will a "center" reflect anything radical and deep in society.

In the course of discussing new movements, much is being said in criticism and defense of the "traditional left." The *Studies* editorial called for the inclusion of the older radicals in a coalition with the new movements. My own feeling is that too many traditional leftists are still engulfed by the Communist-anti-Communist debate; adhere to overly bureaucratic conceptions of organizing; or are limited fundamentally by their job and family situations, to be considered mainstays of a new movement. The many people who are exceptions to this general picture should concentrate on organizing the millions of people who never experienced the history of the American left, instead of attempting to reconstruct their old-left colleagues.

Perhaps these comments are too harsh; most of the *Studies* editors are probably more sympathetic to these views than I have been able to convey. Nevertheless, there are differences. A "radical center" is an overly administrative concept, a false way of making the insubstantial substantial. It is a way of sliding over the frightening possibility that American radicalism may be baseless and doomed, that the imperial arrogance of this country will be safely rooted until a thermonuclear war destroys it. It is also a way of sliding over the richest possibility we have, that of beginning to slowly organize people. In the effort to open up this possibility for a new identity and a new movement, we are going to drift and experiment for sometime to come.

Tom Hayden
Norm Fruchter
Alan Cheuse

Reply

We agree with Tom Hayden that the problem of finding an effective way to "confront this society and change it" has split radicals and continues to baffle them. But while we attempt to confront this problem, Hayden skips over it and focuses on the problems of organizing the poor. Our proposal was not to solve the problem with new "organizational formulas," but to begin the search for effective strategies to challenge and change this society. Our goals are the same as Hayden's. We agree on the need to build a movement that is fully conscious of the need to transcend the values and priority systems of America's present rulers. We disagree on the need for radicals to discuss and work out the necessary theories and strategy of social change.

Underlying this disagreement is a difference over the nature of potential radical constituencies, and a confusion between the problem of organizing the poor and that of working toward a coalition of radical constituencies capable of becoming an effective political force on the left. Hayden's concern is with the former; ours is with the latter. We focus on different problems, but there is nothing inherently contradictory or mutually exclusive in our two approaches. Stated simply (hopefully not over-simply), Hayden's theory has two parts: 1) the poor, both in the rural South and the Northern ghettos, are the only potentially radical mass constituencies (because they are most cheated by this society and least corrupted by involvement in its institutions); 2) the poor cannot be organized along traditional liberal or old left lines (because these are bureaucratic, exclusive, and hierarchical and only serve to further alienate the already most alienated people in our society). Hayden spends a great deal of time on the second question, but he simply assumes the first. Our argument with him is over the assumption. We agree with much of what he says about organizing the poor.

There are several aspects of Hayden's position that do not seem to us to hold up under examination. He assumes that work among the urban poor and Southern rural Negroes is politically relevant, but he sets up a model which can only lead to defeat or insignificance. Assuming that the poor can be fully organized and will become fully conscious of the need for radical politics, by themselves they must remain impotent. There are not enough of them, nor do they command sufficient resources to constitute a political force that can win power. Hayden concedes that students are also a potential radical base, but his view of the radical student is essentially as an organizer of the poor. He presents no prospective for organizing a mass radical student movement, and explicitly denies or ignores the existence of other possible components of a radical coalition. Yet if a significant movement is to be built it must be around a coalition large enough, at least in theory, to contest for political power. Every group of potential allies should be explored. Programs of action should be developed to facilitate connections between the various components—including the poor—when they become sufficiently conscious to engage in explicitly political action. Such a coalition needs a common view of the existing society, common programmatic demands (or at least complementary ones), a common vision of a new form of social organization designed to satisfy human needs. We feel it is necessary to begin the theoretical work on which such a movement can be based.

Of course it may be that other groups or classes cannot develop mass radical consciousness (it may also be impossible to build this among the poor). If that is so then a meaningful radical politics will be impossible, and radicals will be well advised to retire from politics or join the mainstream as the loyal opposition to our liberal totalitarianism. But before this is done we believe radicals have the responsibility to explore the possibilities for the development of mass radical consciousness and to attempt its organization among several other groups in the society.

We see two general types of potential constituencies that

should be analyzed and explored as potential components in a
new radical coalition, or ideological center. First are class or social groupings: students, industrial workers, urban poor whites
and working poor, the aged. Recent protests and demonstrations
about the purposes and organization of universities and the surge
of activity against further American intervention in Vietnam
have made clear the possibility of a mass radical movement
among students. The great increase in the student population
that will continue to take place in the immediate future suggests
an increasing potential for such radical activity. Among industrial workers, despite ever higher wages, questions of job control
and job security have led to wildcat strikes, as in the automobile
industry last fall, and to the displacement of entrenched leaders
in two basic old CIO unions, the Steelworkers and the International Union of Electrical Workers. The obstacles to radical organization among these workers are immense, given the tight
structure and control that exists in most union locals in the
basic industries; but discontent is widespread, the conditions of
work continue to worsen and security will diminish steadily with
the continued spread of automation. Urban poor whites and
working poor, unlike the organized industrial workers, have been
excluded from even the monetary benefits of the welfare state.
The conditions under which they work are worse, and politically
they are even more powerless. The aged are another surplus, and
therefore excluded, group in the Great Society. As living costs,
particularly medical care, go up, their real income goes down.
One of the responses to automation is earlier retirement, but the
retired are neither financially nor socially prepared for their lives
of leisure. We do not know that all, or any, of these groups will
be sources of radical consciousness. Certainly they will not be if
left to chance. But we believe the conditions under which each
group works and lives require radical changes if the individuals
involved are to fulfill themselves as human beings. None of these
social groups have control over their own lives. Even where, as
in the trade unions, the leadership of a group is included in the
consensus, the rank and file are almost as powerless as the poor.
Although most receive more money, all are excluded from decision-making, are manipulated by elites they are unable to defeat.
Hayden argues that these groups are not potentially radical be-

cause they share in the material rewards of this society. But they do not differ substantially from the poor in the degree to which they control their own destinies. Hayden is right to argue that they *are* less alienated and are psychologically incorporated into the dominant society by a rising standard of living. But if the poor are capable of organizing politically and developing their own pressures and leadership, there is no reason to assume that they, too, cannot be granted material rewards. Certainly our society is wealthy enough to be able to make such concessions if threatened. Hayden's defense against this is to organize around the concept of participatory democracy; if this works for the poor, however, there is no reason why it should not work for other social groups. Before such groups are abandoned to continued manipulation and use as producers or consumers in our welfare state, we should at least examine the possibilities for organizing them and developing a radical consciousness among them.

The second type of constituencies are those built around issues or areas of social concern: the peace movement, housing and urban renewal movements, school and parent associations. These movements cut across class lines to some extent. They have at least a theoretical possibility for radicalization in that the solution of most of the problems they confront will require deepgoing changes in the nature and priorities of existing American society. This will also require a change in the nature of these movements, or, at least, in the strategy of radicals within them. If the peace movement, for example, is to develop a radical consciousness of its own, and to serve to radicalize others, it must be reoriented around a root opposition to the imperial role of the United States in world affairs and an explicit rejection of the underlying assumptions of our intervention against all popular revolutions. Radicals cannot be concerned with arguments about the most effective way to defeat Communism, or agree that intervention is necessary (no matter how painful) if the absence of it might lead to a new Communist government. In the other movements radicals should examine the kinds of changes that will be needed to solve the problems of housing, schools, etc., and seek to develop programs and activity that increase people's awareness of the relatedness of each issue to an over-all reorganization of society. Again, this may not be fully possible. As sufficient pressures around issues develop the "great society" may solve particular problems. But this has always happened to some extent; the value of such activity beyond the immediate victories is in the degree it serves to build a vision of a better society and an understanding that change can be achieved by concerted social action.

When we spoke of the need for a new radical center we did not have in mind an organizational short circuit of the new experiments with community organization. Our use of the term was ideological, not organizational; what we sought was discussion, analysis, examination of all these social movements with a view to finding common programs, a common attitude toward existing American social organization, a common vision of a new society, and a long-range strategy for putting together a coalition that might have some political relevance. We do not believe this can be done by limiting ourselves to the problems of organizing or working within communities of Northern poor and Southern rural Negroes, even if that work is now the most advanced and has the greatest potential for rapid development. If it develops fully in the absence of other movements it will lead nowhere.

Beyond that, there are other movements developing and they already suffer from the lack of such a strategy. In the absence of a new radical ideology and center the student and peace movements remain unable to free themselves of the ideological and organizational influences of the old left, with its archaic concerns about Stalinism and anti-Stalinism. Or, worse, they remain under the influence of the liberal ideologies of the Johnson Administration.

As Hayden points out, the radical and moderate civil rights organizations are mutually dependent, and within the over-all picture King sometimes aligns with the left forces. But King (not to mention the NAACP) does not share SNCC's perspective on the Freedom Democratic Party and the development of a radical independent political movement in the South. King is committed to the Administration and to the integration of Negroes into the existing Democratic Party structures in the South. King's strategy is carefully worked out in consultation with high Administration liberals, and it is King who becomes the publicly acknowledged leader when he moves into situations created by SNCC. He gives the political content to SNCC's groundwork, whatever SNCC's intention, although there is often compromise and operational unity. Yet Northern whites, both liberal and radical, are unaware of the differences and support both thinking they are supporting the same thing. Because there are no independent radical connections in the North, SNCC has no way of making public its differences or attempting to rally independent support, both financial and political, for its position. In a way this experience is analogous to the role of the left in organizing the CIO in the 1930s. Then, too, the left were the militant organizers; then, too, the ideological content was provided by leaders with connections in the Administration (John L. Lewis and Sidney Hillman). The difference is that the left in the 1930s had no strategy of opposition to absorption in the liberal consensus, whereas some in SNCC do. But while SNCC's rivals receive vast political and organizational support, SNCC, because of the absence of a general consciousness of the content of the struggle, can rely only on general appeals to sentiment, or on private appeals based on strategic considerations. Unlike King, they are part of no ideological community from which they can get support and with which they can work out and coordinate strategy.

The discussion in our editorial about unaffiliated radicals also relates to this point, and was not understood by Hayden. Many former old leftists reject the approaches, and especially the bureaucratic forms of organization and the sterile debates over Stalinism versus social democracy, of such old left sects as the Socialist Party, the Communist Party and the Socialist Workers Party. To some extent, of course, these people still think and act in the old ways, even though they reject the organizations of the old left and the context of old left politics. This is precisely why they share, in common with the new movements, a need for a new radical center. Such people are now either without direction, except that which they give themselves, or follow vaguely the old styles and tactics. They often serve as the militant organizers of activity in the peace movement, in the reform movements within the Democratic Party, in PTAs, in tenants' organizations, in trade union locals, but almost invariably the ideological content and political impact of such activity is determined by others—by the "big names" who are pushed into action by these radicals, or by the liberal leadership of the organizations in which they are active.

The new left's diversity and decentralization is one of its greatest strengths and should be supported and aided in every way. Those who, consciously or not, adopt a "Leninist" concept of political organization offer structural or administrative solutions for political and ideological problems. Such an approach, however necessary or appropriate under the conditions that existed in Czarist Russia or Kuomintang China, can only inhibit the search for new political forms, can only stifle the kind of initiative and experimentation in the development of radical consciousness and program which is the strength of SNCC in Mississippi and some of the ghetto projects in the North. We do not propose "democratic centralism" or highly disciplined structures when we assert the need for a radical center. In this sense, the experience of radical organizations in the United States since the early 1920s is useless. Organizationally one must go back to the old Socialist Party of Debs to find any meaningful precedents. The great success of pre-1919 Socialism depended on its democratic and decentralized character. Local Socialist organizations then had their own press, developed their own programs, adopted different tactics. This often led to serious debates and to factional antagonisms, but these remained within the confines of the Party because of general agreement on the nature of American capitalism and on the desirability of basic social reorganization, so that workers and farmers might control the conditions under which they worked and lived. This changed and ended after 1919 when the "Leninist" concept of party organization began to stifle the kind of free development and local participation that Hayden defends. In defending something that we also appreciate, he misconstrues our proposal.

James Weinstein
Stanley Aronowitz
Lee Baxandall
Eugene D. Genovese
Helen Kramer

2. *"New Styles in 'Leftism'"* *

Dissent magazine began publishing in 1954 as a quarterly; it became a bi-monthly in 1966. Its editors are of the anti-Communist radical generation of the thirties, the very group from which the "new radicals" are so estranged. Irving Howe, editor of Dissent, *has been one of the most outspoken critics of the new radicals. In April 1965 he gave a lecture, "New Styles in 'Leftism,'" which then appeared in the Summer 1965 issue of* Dissent. *The edited version printed here contains two of the most important sections of the article: an analysis of the group Howe characterizes as "Ideologues and Desperadoes" and what he describes as the "Cultural Style" of some new radicals. His criticisms have created a great deal of discussion. Howe takes the New Radicals seriously and believes they are entitled to a serious and detailed analysis of their position from representatives of other viewpoints.*

I propose to describe a political style or outlook before it has become hardened into an ideology or the property of an organization. This outlook is visible along limited portions of the political scene; for the sake of exposition I will make it seem more precise and structured than it really is. . . .

II. IDEOLOGUES AND DESPERADOES

A) Ideologues, white

The disintegration of American radicalism these last few decades left a good many ideologues emotionally unemployed: people accustomed to grand theorizing who have had their theories shot out from under them; people still looking for some belated evidence that they were "right" all along; people with unex-

* This text consists of a somewhat condensed and edited version of a lecture given at a New York *Dissent* forum in April 1965. I have left it pretty much in its original outline-plus-notes form.—I. H.

pended social energy and idealism of a sort, who desperately needed new arenas in which to function.

(1) *The Remains of Stalinism.* The American Communist Party was broken first by McCarthyite and government persecution, and second by an inner crisis following Khrushchev's revelations and the Hungarian Revolution. Those who left out of disillusionment were heartsick people, their convictions and sometimes their lives shattered. But those who left the party or its supporting organizations because they feared government attack were often people who kept, semi-privately, their earlier convictions. Many of them had a good deal of political experience; some remained significantly placed in the network of what might be called conscience organizations. Naturally enough, they continued to keep in touch with one another, forming a kind of reserve apparatus based on common opinions, feelings, memories. As soon as some ferment began a few years ago in the civil rights movement and the peace groups, these people were present, ready and eager; they needed no directives from the CP to which, in any case, they no longer (or may never have) belonged; they were quite capable of working on their own *as if they were working together,* through a variety of groups and periodicals like *The National Guardian.* Organizational Stalinism declined, but a good part of its heritage remained: people who could offer political advice, raise money, write leaflets, sit patiently at meetings, put up in a pleasant New York apartment visitors from a distant state, who, by chance, had been recommended by an old friend.

2) *True Believers.* On the far left there remains a scatter of groups still convinced that Marxism-Leninism, in one or another version, is "correct." What has failed them, however, is the historical motor provided by Marxist theory: the proletariat, which has not shown the "revolutionary potential" or fulfilled the "historical mission" to which it was assigned. Though the veteran Marxists cannot, for fear of shattering their whole structure of belief, give up the *idea* of the proletariat, they can hardly act, day by day, as if the American working class were indeed satisfying Marxist expectations or were the actual center of revolutionary ferment. Thus, in somewhat schizoid fashion, they have clung to their traditional faith in the proletariat as the revolu-

tionary class, while in practice searching for a new embodiment of it which might provide the social energy they desire. And in the Negro movement they seem to have found it.

That this movement, with great creative flair, has worked out an indigenous strategy of its own; that it has developed nonviolent resistance into an enormously powerful weapon; that the Negro clergy, in apparent disregard of Leninist formulas, plays a leading and often militant role—all this does not sit well with the old Marxists. They must therefore develop new theories, by means of which the Negroes become the vanguard of the working class or perhaps the "true" (not yet "bought-off") working class. And, clustering around the Negro movement, they contribute a mite of wisdom here and there: scoffing at nonviolence, employing the shibboleth of "militancy" as if it were a magical device for satisfying the needs of the Negro poor, etc. They are experienced in "deepening the struggle," usually other people's struggles: which means to scorn the leadership of Dr. King without considering that the "revolutionary" course they propose for the Negro movement could, if adopted, lead it into a *cul de sac* of isolation, exhaustion and heroic blood. Understandably, they find allies in Negro nationalists who want not so much to deepen as to divert the struggle, and among young militants who dislike the idea that Negroes might, if successful in their struggle, come to share some of the American affluence and thus become "middle-class."

3) *Authoritarian Leftists.* In figures like Isaac Deutscher and Paul Sweezey we find the true intellectual progenitors of at least part of the "new leftism"; the influence they exert has been indirect, since they are not involved in immediate struggles, but it has nevertheless been there.

Sweezey's *Monthly Review* is the main spokesman in this country for the view that authoritarianism is inherent or necessary in the so-called socialist countries; that what makes them "socialist" is simply the nationalization of the means of production; that democracy, while perhaps desirable in some long-range calculation, is not crucial for judging the socialist character of a society; that the claim that workers must be in a position to exercise political power if the state can in any sense be called "theirs," is a utopian fallacy. At times this technological determinism, put to the service of brutal dictatorship, has been given a more subtle reading by Sweezey: namely, that when the conditions supposedly causing the Communist dictatorship—economic backwardness and international insecurity—have been overcome, the Soviet regime would in some unspecified way democratize itself. In November 1957, after the Khrushchev revelations, *Monthly Review* printed a notably frank editorial:

> The conditions which produced the [Soviet] dictatorship have been overcome . . . Our theory is being put to the crucial test of practise. And so far—let us face it frankly—there is precious little evidence to confirm it. In all that has happened since Stalin's death we can find nothing to indicate that the Communist Party or any of its competing factions, has changed in the slightest degree its view of the proper relation between the people and their leadership . . . there is apparently no thought that the Soviet people will ever grow up enough to decide for itself who knows best and hence who should make and administer the policies which determine its fate.

And finally from Sweezey: "forty years is too long for a dictatorship to remain temporary"—surely the understatement of the Christian Era!

One might suppose that if "our theory is being put to the crucial test" and there "is precious little evidence to confirm it," honest men would proceed to look for another theory, provided, that is, they continued to believe that freedom is desirable.

Eight years have passed since the above passage appeared in *Monthly Review,* the "precious little evidence" remains precious little, and Sweezey, once apparently dismayed over the lack of democracy in Russia, has moved not to Titoism or "revisionism." No, he has moved toward Maoist China, where presumably one does not have to worry about "the proper relation between the people and their leadership. . . ." Writing in December 1964 the *MR* editors declared with satisfaction that "there could be no question of the moral ascendency of Peking over Moscow in the underdeveloped world." They agreed with the Chinese that Khrushchev's fall was "a good thing" and they wrote further:

> The Chinese possession of a nuclear potential does not increase the danger of nuclear war. Quite the contrary. The Chinese have solemnly pledged never to be the first to use nuclear weapons . . . and their revolutionary record of devotion to the cause of socialism and progress entitles them to full trust and confidence.

The logic is clear: begin with theoretical inquiry and concern over the perpetuation of dictatorship in Russia and end with "full trust and confidence" in China, where the dictatorship is more severe.

There is an aphorism by a recent Polish writer: "The dispensing of injustice is always in the right hands." And so is its defense.

B) Ideologues, Negro

1) *Black nationalism.* Here is a creed that speaks or appears to speak totally against compromise, against negotiating with "the white power structure," against the falsities of white liberals, indeed, against anything but an indulgence of verbal violence. Shortly before his tragic murder Malcolm X spoke at a Trotskyist-sponsored meeting and listening to him, I felt, as did others, that he was in a state of internal struggle, reaching out for an ideology he did not yet have. For the Negroes in his audience he offered the relief of articulating subterranean feelings of hatred, contempt, defiance, feelings that did not have to be held in check because there was a tacit compact that the talk about violence would remain talk. Malcolm declared that he would go, not unarmed, to Mississippi, *if* the Negroes there would ask him to come: a condition that could only leave him safely North, since the last thing the Negroes of Mississippi needed or wanted was Malcolm's military aid. For both the Negroes and whites in the audience there was an apparent feeling that Malcolm and Malcolm alone among the Negro spokesmen was authentic because . . . well, because finally he spoke for nothing but his rage, for no proposal, no plan, no program, just a sheer outpouring of anger and pain. And that they could understand. The formidable sterility of his speech, so impressive in its relation to a deep personal suffering, touched something in their hearts. For

Malcolm, intransigent in words and nihilistic in reality, never invoked the possibility or temptations of immediate struggle; he never posed the problems, confusions and risks of maneuver, compromise, retreat. Brilliantly Malcolm spoke for a rejection so complete it transformed him into an apolitical spectator, or in the language his admirers are more inclined to use than I am, a pure "cop-out."

2) *Caricature.* If, nevertheless, there was something about Malcolm which commands our respect, that is because we know his life-struggle, his rise from the depths, his conquest of thought and speech. LeRoi Jones, by contrast, stands as a burlesque double of whatever is significant in Malcolm.

In his success as both a New School lecturer and prophet of "guerrilla warfare" in the U.S.; in his badgering of white liberal audiences; in his orgies of verbal violence committed, to be sure, not in Selma, Alabama, but Sheridan Square, New York; in his fantasies of an international race war in which the whites will be slaughtered, Jones speaks for a contemporary sensibility. But he speaks for it in a special way: as a distinctively American success, the pop-art guerrilla warrior.

He speaks at that center of revolutionary upsurge, the Village Vanguard. He explains that the murder of Negroes in the South does not arouse the kind of horror and indignation that the murder of white civil rights workers does. *He is absolutely right,* the point cannot be made too often. But Jones cannot stop there: it would be too sensible, too humane, and it would not yield pages in the *Village Voice.* Instead, responding to a question, "What about Goodman and Schwerner, the two white boys killed in Mississippi, don't you care about them?" Jones continues, as quoted in the *Voice:*

> "Absolutely not," rapped out Jones. "Those boys were just artifacts, artifacts, man. They weren't real. If they want to assuage their leaking consciences, that's their business. I won't mourn for them. I have my own dead to mourn for."

Is this not exactly the attitude Jones had a moment earlier condemned in regard to killings in the South, but the same attitude in reverse? And is it really impossible for the human heart to mourn for *both* Negro and white victims? Not, to be sure, for ordinary whites, since they, we all know, are "white devils"; but at least for those who have given their lives in the struggle?

The essential point about Jones' racist buffoonery has been made by George Dennison in a recent review of Jones' plays:

> Just as he mis-labels the victims *black,* he mis-labels the authority *white.* Certainly he knows, or should know, that the authority which in fact pertains is not the authority of race . . . but an authority of property and arms; and certainly he knows, or should know, that the life-destroying evil inheres in the nature of the authority, not in the color of those who wield it. But if Jones wanted change, he would speak change. He speaks, instead, for the greatest possible rejection, a rejection so absolute, so confined to fantasy, that it amounts to nothing more than hands-off-the-status-quo. . . . Point by point his is an upside down version of the most genteel, middle-class, liberal position. And I think that the liberals see him as one of their own, albeit a Dropout. He addresses every word to them and is confined to their systems of values because he is in the business of denying no other values but those. That spurious anger, so resonant with career, can be trusted not to upset the apple-cart.

3) *Desperadoes, white.* In effect, I have already described this group, so let me here confine myself to a few remarks about one of its central battle cries, "alienation."

The trouble with the current use of alienation as a mode of social analysis is that it explains almost everything, and thereby almost nothing. The term has become impossibly loose (like those other handy tags, "the Establishment" and "the Power Structure"). As used by Marx, alienation had a rather precise reference: it pointed to the condition of the worker in the capitalist productive process, a condition in which "the worker's deed becomes an alien power . . . forcing him to develop some specialized dexterity at the cost of a world of productive impulses." This kind of analysis focuses upon the place of the proletarian within the social structure, and not upon the sediment of malaise among those outside it.

Since Marx wrote, the term has acquired an impossible load of signification. During most of the bourgeois era, the European intellectuals grew increasingly estranged from the social community because the very ideals that had animated the bourgeois revolution were now being violated by bourgeois society; their "alienation" was prompted not by Bohemian wilfullness but by a loyalty to Liberty, Fraternity, Equality, or to an induced vision of pre-industrial society which, by a twist of history, came pretty much to resemble Liberty, Fraternity, Equality. Just as it was the triumph of capitalism which largely caused this sense of estrangement, so it was the expansion of capitalism which allowed the intellectuals enough freedom to release it. During the greater part of the bourgeois era, intellectuals preferred alienation from the community to alienation from themselves. Precisely this choice made possible their boldness and strength, precisely this "lack of roots" gave them their speculative power.

By now the term "alienation" frequently carries with it a curious reversal of moral and emotional stress. For where intellectuals had once used it as a banner of pride and self-assertion, today it tends to become a complaint, a token of self-pity, a rationale for a degree of estrangement from the society which connotes not an active rebellion against—nor even any active relation to—it, but rather a justification for marginality and withdrawal.

Somewhere amid the current talk about "alienation" an important reality *is* being touched upon or pointed to. There *is,* in our society, a profound estrangement from the sources of selfhood, the possibilities of human growth and social cohesion. But simply to proclaim this estrangement can be a way of preserving it. Alienation is not some metaphysical equivalent of the bubonic plague which constitutes an irrevocable doom; it is the powerlessness deriving from human failure to act. It is neither a substitute for thought, nor a dissolvent of human will, nor even a roadblock in the way of useful work. To enter into the society which in part causes this estrangement and by establishing bonds with other men to transform the society, is one way of partially overcoming alienation. Each time the civil rights movement brings previously mute Negroes into active political life, each time a trade union extends its power of decision within a factory, the boundaries of alienation are shrunk.

Meanwhile, there is truth in Harold Rosenberg's remark that

> The sentiment of diminution of personality ["alienation"] is an historical hypothesis upon which writers have constructed a set of literary conventions by this time richly equipped with theatrical machinery and symbolic allusions. . . . By all evidence, the hollow-man tradition has completely captured our "serious" prose [and some of our serious youth]. . . . Once vanguardist, this tradition . . . has lately come to dominate popular literature and feeling. The individual's emptiness and inability to act have become an irrefrangible cliche, untiringly supported by an immense phalanx of latecomers to modernism. In this manifestation, the notion of the void has lost its critical edge and is thoroughly reactionary.

4) *Desperadoes, Negro.* A new kind of young Negro militant has appeared in the last few years, and he is a figure far more authentic and impressive than any of those I have thus far mentioned. He is fed up with white promises. He is proud to be estranged from white society. He has strong, if vague, "nationalist" inclinations. He is desperate—impatient with the tactics of gradualism, nonviolence and passive resistance. He sees few, if any, allies upon whom he can count; few, if any, positive forces in society that might stir people into action. In effect, he decides that he must "go it alone," scornful of the white liberal and labor groups, as well as of those Negro leaders who choose to work with them. He seeks to substitute for a stagnant history his own desire and sacrifice.

Let me suggest a very limited comparison. This kind of young Negro militant, though not of course interested in any kind of individual terrorism, acts out of social motives somewhat like those of the late-nineteenth-century Russian terrorists, who also tried to substitute their intransigent will for the sluggishness of history. And the consequences may be similar: the best cadres exhausted in isolation and defeat.

Such a response may well be the inevitable result of an abrupt and painful coming-to-awareness on the part of young Negro

militants who had previously suppressed their suffering simply in
order to survive but now feel somewhat freer to release it. Their
devotion is beyond doubt, as their heroism is beyond praise; yet
what I'm here tempted to call kamikaze radicalism, or what
Bayard Rustin calls the "no win" outlook, can become self-
defeating in political life. . . .

III. THE "NEW LEFTIST"—A SKETCH

A) Cultural Style

The "new leftist" appears, at times, as a figure embodying a
style of speech, dress, work and culture. Often, especially if
white, the son of the middle class—and sometimes the son of
middle-class parents nursing radical memories—he asserts his
rebellion against the deceit and hollowness of American society.
Very good; there is plenty to rebel against. But in the course of
his rebellion he tends to reject not merely the middle-class ethos
but a good many other things he too hastily associates with it:
the intellectual heritage of the West, the tradition of liberalism
at its most serious, the commitment to democracy as an indispensable part of civilized life. He tends to think of style as the
very substance of his revolt, and while he may, on one side of
himself, engage in valuable activities in behalf of civil rights,
student freedom, etc., he nevertheless tacitly accepts the "given-
ness" of American society, has little hope or expectation of
changing it, and thereby, in effect, settles for a mode of personal
differentiation.

Primarily that means the wish to shock, the wish to assault
the sensibilities of a world he cannot overcome. If he cannot
change it, then at least he can outrage it. He searches in the
limited repertoire of sensation and shock: for sick comics who
will say "fuck" in nightclubs; for drugs that will vault him beyond the perimeters of the suburbs; for varieties, perversities,
and publicities of sex so as perhaps to create an inner, private
revolution that will accompany—or replace?—the outer, public
revolution.

But "the new leftist" is frequently trapped in a symbiotic relationship with the very middle class he rejects, dependent upon it
for his self-definition: quite as the professional anti-Communist
of a few years ago was caught up with the Communist Party

which, had it not existed, he would have had to invent—as indeed at times he did invent. So that for all its humor and charm, the style of the "new leftist" tends to become a rigid anti-style, dependent for its survival on the enemy it is supposed to panic. To *épater le bourgeois*—in this case, perhaps, to *épater le père* —is to acquiesce in a basic assumption of at least the more sophisticated segments of the middle class: that values can be inferred from, or are resident in, the externals of dress, appearance, furnishings and hair-dos.

Shock as he will, disaffiliate as he may choose, the "new leftist" discovers after a while that nothing has greatly changed. The relations of power remain as before, the Man still hovers over the scene, the "power structure" is unshaken. A few old ladies in California may grow indignant, a DA occasionally arrest someone, a *Village Voice* reporter arrange an interview; but surely that is all small change. And soon the "new leftist" must recognize that even he has not been greatly transformed. For in his personal manner he is acting out the dilemmas of a utopian community, and just as Brook Farm had to remain subject to the laws of the market despite its internal ethic of cooperation, so must he remain subject to the impress of the dominant institutions despite his desire to be totally different.

Victimized by a lack of the historical sense, the "new leftist" does not realize that the desire to shock and create sensations has itself a long and largely disastrous history. The notion, as Meyer Schapiro has remarked, that opium is the revolution of the people has been luring powerless intellectuals and semi-intellectuals for a long time. But the damnable thing is that for an almost equally long time the more sophisticated and urban sectors of the middle class have refused to be shocked. They know the repertoire of sensationalism quite as well as the "new leftist"; and if he is to succeed in shocking them or even himself, he must keep raising the ante. The very rebel who believes himself devoted to an absolute of freedom and looks with contempt upon any mode of compromise, is thereby caught up in the compulsiveness of his escalation: a compulsiveness inherently bad enough, but rendered still more difficult, and sometimes pathetic, by the fact that, alas, each year he gets a year older.

Let me amend this somewhat. To say that the urban middle class has become jaded and can no longer be shocked, is not quite correct. No; a kind of complicity is set up between the outraged and/or amused urban middle class and the rebels of sensation. Their mutual dependency requires that each shock, to provide the pleasures of indignation, must be a little stronger (like a larger dose . . .) than the previous one. For the point is not so much that the urban middle class can no longer be shocked as that it positively yearns for and comes to depend upon the titillating assaults of its cultural enemies. So that when a new sensation (be it literary violence, sexual fashion, intellectual outrage, high-toned pornography, or sadistic denunciation) is provided by the shock troops of culture, the sophisticated middle class responds with outrage, resistance and anger—*for upon these initial responses its pleasure depends*. But then, a little later, it rolls over like a happy puppy on its back, moaning, "Oh, baby, *épater* me again, harder this time, tell me what a sterile impotent louse I am and how you are so tough and virile, how you're planning to murder me, *épater* me again, baby. . . ."

Thus a fire-eating character like LeRoi Jones becomes an adjunct of middle-class amusement and, to take an enormous leap upward in talent and seriousness, a writer like Norman Mailer becomes enmeshed in his public conduct with popular journalism and publicity.

The whole problem was anticipated many years ago by Trotsky when, writing about the Russian poet Yesenin, he remarked that the poet thought to frighten the bourgeoisie by making scenes but as it turned out, the bourgeoisie was delighted, it adored scenes.

One thing alone will not delight the bourgeoisie: a decrease in income, a loss in social power, a threat to its property.

There is another sense in which cultural style dominates the behavior of the "new leftists." Some of them display a tendency to regard political—and perhaps all of—life as a Hemingway-esque contest in courage and rectitude. People are constantly being tested for endurance, bravery, resistance to temptation, and if found inadequate, are denounced for having "copped out." Personal endurance thus becomes the substance of, and perhaps even a replacement for, political ideas.

Now this can be a valid and serious way of looking at things, especially in extreme situations: which is, of course, what Hemingway had in mind. Among civil rights workers in the Deep South such a vision of life reflects the ordeal they must constantly face; they *are* under extreme pressure and their courage *is* constantly being tested. Yet their situation cannot be taken as a model for the political life of the country as a whole. If one wants to do more than create a tiny group of the heroic, the tested and the martyred, their style of work will not suffice. If one wants to build a movement in which not everyone need give "the whole of their lives," then the suspicion and hostility such an outlook is bound to engender toward the somewhat less active and somewhat less committed can only be damaging. For in effect, if not intent, it is a strategy of exclusion, leaving no place for anyone but the vanguard of the scarred.

It is, at times, a strategy of exclusion in a still more troubling sense: it reduces differences of opinion to grades of moral rectitude. If, for example, you think Martin Luther King or Bayard Rustin was wrong in regard to certain tactical matters; if you disagree with what Rustin proposed at the Democratic National Convention and what King did in Selma, then you call into question their loyalty and commitment: you may even charge them with "copping-out" or "fooling with the power structure." This approach makes it impossible to build a movement and, in the long run, even to maintain a sect. . . .

C) Politics and Freedom

The "new leftists" feel little attachment to Russia. Precisely as it has turned away from the more extreme and terroristic version of totalitarianism, so have they begun to find it unsatisfactory as a model: too Victorian, even "bourgeois." Nor are they interested in distinguishing among kinds of anti-Communism, whether of the right or left.

When they turn to politics, they have little concern for precise or complex thought. (By contrast, the more reflective among the younger radicals, such as some leaders of Students for a Democratic Society, have made a serious effort to develop their intellectual and political views; they understand the sterility to which a mere "activism" can lead, in fact, the way it must sooner or later undermine the possibilities even for activity.) A few years ago the "new leftists" were likely to be drawn to Communist China, which then seemed bolder than Khrushchev's Russia. But though the Mao regime has kept the loyalty of a small group of students, most of the "new leftists" seem to find it too grim and repressive. They tend to look for their new heroes and models among the leaders of underdeveloped countries. Figures like Lumumba, Nasser, Sukarno, Babu and above all Castro attract them, suggesting the possibility of a politics not yet bureaucratized and rationalized. But meanwhile they neglect to notice, or do not care, that totalitarian and authoritarian dictatorship can set in even before a society has become fully modernized. They have been drawn to charismatic figures like Lumumba and Castro out of a distaste for the mania of industrial production which the Soviet Union shares with the United States; but they fail to see that such leaders of the underdeveloped countries, who in their eyes represent spontaneity and anarchic freedom, are themselves—perhaps unavoidably—infused with the same mania for industrial production.

Let me specify a few more of the characteristic attitudes among the "new leftists":

1) *An extreme, sometimes unwarranted, hostility toward liberalism.* . . .

2) *An impatience with the problems that concerned an older generation of radicals.* . . .

3) *A vicarious indulgence in violence, often merely theoretic and thereby all the more irresponsible.* . . .

4) *An unconsidered enmity toward something vaguely called the Establishment.* . . .

5) *An equally unreflective belief in "the decline of the West".* . . .

6) *A crude, unqualified anti-Americanism, drawing from every possible source, even if one contradicts another: the aristocratic bias of Eliot and Ortega, Communist propaganda, the speculations of Tocqueville, the resentment of post-war Europe, etc.*

7) *An increasing identification with that sector of the "third*

world" in which "radical" nationalism and Communist authori-
tarianism merge. . . .

The authoritarians find political tendencies and representative
men with whom to identify in the Communist world; but so do
we. We identify with the people who have died for freedom, like
Imre Nagy, or who rot in prison, like Djilas. We identify with
the "revisionists," those political *maranoes* who, forced to em-
ploy Communist jargon, yet spoke out for a socialism democratic in character and distinct from both Communism and capitalism. As it happens, our friends in the Communist world are
not in power; but since when has that mattered to socialists?

In 1957, at the height of the Polish ferment, the young philos-
opher Leszek Kolakowski wrote a brief article entitled "What Is
Socialism?" It consisted of a series of epigrammatic sentences
describing what socialism is not (at the moment perhaps the
more immediate concern), but tacitly indicating as well what
socialism should be. The article was banned by the Gomulka
regime but copies reached Western periodicals. Here are a few
sentences:

> Socialism is not
> A society in which a person who has committed a crime
> sits at home waiting for the police.
> A society in which one person is unhappy because he says
> what he thinks, and another happy because he does not say
> what is in his mind.
> A society in which a person lives better because he does
> not think at all.
> A state whose neighbors curse geography.
> A state which wants all its citizens to have the same opin-
> ions in philosophy, foreign policy, economics, literature
> and ethics.
> A state whose government defines its citizens' rights, but
> whose citizens do not define the government's rights.
> A state in which there is private ownership of the means of
> production.
> A state which considers itself solidly socialist because it
> has liquidated private ownership of the means of produc-
> tion.

A state which always knows the will of the people before it asks them.

A state in which the philosophers and writers always say the same as the generals and ministers, but always after them.

A state in which the returns of parliamentary elections are always predictable.

A state which does not like to see its citizens read back numbers of newspapers.

These negatives imply a positive, and that positive is the greatest lesson of contemporary history: the unity of socialism and democracy. To preserve democracy as a political mode without extending it into every crevice of social and economic life is to make it increasingly sterile, formal, ceremonial. To nationalize an economy without enlarging democratic freedoms is to create a new kind of social exploitation. Radicals may properly and fraternally disagree about many other things; but upon this single axiom, this conviction wrung from the tragedy of our age, politics must rest.

3. "From Protest to Politics: The Future of the Civil Rights Movement"

Bayard Rustin's article "From Protest to Politics," which appeared originally in the February 1965 Commentary *has become the classic statement of the belief that the civil rights movement needs to shift its focus. Rustin, who has been associated closely with A. Philip Randolph and Martin Luther King, was the organizer of the 1963 March on Washington and the 1964 School Boycott in New York. In this article, he calls for the creation of a coalition of "Negroes, trade unionists, liberals and religious groups" as an essential requirement of further progress in The Movement. This article was directed, in effect, against the black nationalists and those sections of SNCC and SDS which reject the concept of working inside the present political system.*

I

The decade spanned by the 1954 Supreme Court decision on school desegregation and the Civil Rights Act of 1964 will undoubtedly be recorded as the period in which the legal foundations of racism in America were destroyed. To be sure, pockets of resistance remain; but it would be hard to quarrel with the assertion that the elaborate legal structure of segregation and discrimination, particularly in relation to public accommodations, has virtually collapsed. On the other hand, without making light of the human sacrifices involved in the direct-action tactics (sit-ins, Freedom Rides, and the rest) that were so instrumental to this achievement, we must recognize that in desegregating public accommodations, we affected institutions which are relatively peripheral both to the American socioeconomic order and to the fundamental conditions of life of the Negro people. In a highly industrialized, twentieth-century civilization, we hit Jim Crow precisely where it was most anachronistic, dispensable, and vulnerable—in hotels, lunch counters, terminals, libraries, swimming pools, and the like. For in these forms, Jim Crow does impede the flow of commerce in the broadest sense: it is a nuisance in a society on the move (and on the make). Not surprisingly, therefore, it was the most mobility-conscious and relatively liberated groups in the Negro community—lower-middle-class college students—who launched the attack that brought down this imposing but hollow structure.

The term "classical" appears especially apt for this phase of the civil rights movement. But in the few years that have passed since the first flush of sit-ins, several developments have taken place that have complicated matters enormously. One is the shifting focus of the movement in the South, symbolized by Birmingham; another is the spread of the revolution to the North; and the third, common to the other two, is the expansion of the movement's base in the Negro community. To attempt to disentangle these three strands is to do violence to reality. David Danzig's perceptive article, "The Meaning of Negro Strategy,"* correctly saw in the Birmingham events the victory of the con-

* *Commentary,* February 1964.

cept of collective struggle over individual achievement as the
road to Negro freedom. And Birmingham remains the un-
matched symbol of grass-roots protest involving all strata of the
black community. It was also in this most industrialized of
Southern cities that the single-issue demands of the movement's
classical stage gave way to the "package deal." No longer were
Negroes satisfied with integrating lunch counters. They now
sought advances in employment, housing, school integration, police protection, and so forth.

Thus, the movement in the South began to attack areas of
discrimination which were not so remote from the Northern experience as were Jim Crow lunch counters. At the same time,
the interrelationship of these apparently distinct areas became
increasingly evident. What is the value of winning access to public accommodations for those who lack money to use them? The
minute the movement faced this question, it was compelled to
expand its vision beyond race relations to economic relations,
including the role of education in modern society. And what also
became clear is that all these interrelated problems, by their very
nature, are not soluble by private, voluntary efforts but require
government action—or politics. Already Southern demonstrators had recognized that the most effective way to strike at the
police brutality they suffered from was by getting rid of the local
sheriff—and that meant political action, which in turn meant,
and still means, political action within the Democratic Party
where the only meaningful primary contests in the South are
fought.

And so, in Mississippi, thanks largely to the leadership of Bob
Moses, a turn toward political action has been taken. More than
voter registration is involved here. A conscious bid for *political
power* is being made, and in the course of that effort a tactical
shift is being effected: direct-action techniques are being subor-
dinated to a strategy calling for the building of community institutions or power bases. Clearly, the implications of this shift
reach far beyond Mississippi. What began as a protest movement is being challenged to translate itself into a political movement. Is this the right course? And if it is, can the transformation be accomplished?

II

The very decade which has witnessed the decline of legal Jim Crow has also seen the rise of *de facto* segregation in our most fundamental socioeconomic institutions. More Negroes are unemployed today than in 1954, and the unemployment gap between the races is wider. The median income of Negroes has dropped from 57 percent to 54 percent of that of whites. A higher percentage of Negro workers is now concentrated in jobs vulnerable to automation than was the case ten years ago. More Negroes attend *de facto* segregated schools today than when the Supreme Court handed down its famous decision; while school integration proceeds at a snail's pace in the South, the number of Northern schools with an excessive proportion of minority youth proliferates. And behind this is the continuing growth of racial slums, spreading over our central cities and trapping Negro youth in a milieu which, whatever its legal definition, sows an unimaginable demoralization. Again, legal niceties aside, a resident of a racial ghetto lives in segregated housing, and more Negroes fall into this category than ever before.

These are the facts of life which generate frustration in the Negro community and challenge the civil rights movement. At issue, after all, is not *civil rights,* strictly speaking, but social and economic conditions. Last summer's riots were not race riots; they were outbursts of class aggression in a society where class and color definitions are converging disastrously. How can the (perhaps misnamed) civil rights movement deal with this problem?

Before trying to answer, let me first insist that the task of the movement is vastly complicated by the failure of many whites of good will to understand the nature of our problem. There is a widespread assumption that the removal of artificial racial barriers should result in the automatic integration of the Negro into all aspects of American life. This myth is fostered by facile analogies with the experience of various ethnic immigrant groups, particularly the Jews. But the analogies with the Jews do not hold for three simple but profound reasons. First, Jews have a long history as a literate people, a resource which has afforded them opportunities to advance in the academic and professional worlds, to achieve intellectual status even in the midst of economic hardship, and to evolve sustaining value systems in the context of ghetto life. Negroes, for the greater part of their presence in this country, were forbidden by law to read or write. Second, Jews have a long history of family stability, the importance of which in terms of aspiration and self-image is obvious. The Negro family structure was totally destroyed by slavery and with it the possibility of cultural transmission (the right of Negroes to marry and rear children is barely a century old). Third, Jews are white and have the *option* of relinquishing their cultural-religious identity, intermarrying, passing, etc. Negroes, or at least the overwhelming majority of them, do not have this option. There is also a fourth, vulgar reason. If the Jewish and Negro communities are not comparable in terms of education, family structure, and color, it is also true that their respective economic roles bear little resemblance.

This matter of economic role brings us to the greater problem —the fact that we are moving into an era in which the natural functioning of the market does not by itself ensure every man with will and ambition a place in the productive process. The immigrant who came to this country during the late nineteenth and early twentieth centuries entered a society which was expanding territorially and/or economically. It was then possible to start at the bottom, as an unskilled or semi-skilled worker, and move up the ladder, acquiring new skills along the way. Especially was this true when industrial unionism was burgeoning, giving new dignity and higher wages to organized workers. Today the situation has changed. We are not expanding territorially, the western frontier is settled, labor organizing has leveled off, our rate of economic growth has been stagnant for a decade. And we are in the midst of a technological revolution which is altering the fundamental structure of the labor force, destroying unskilled and semi-skilled jobs—jobs in which Negroes are disproportionately concentrated.

Whatever the pace of this technological revolution may be, the *direction* is clear: the lower rungs of the economic ladder are being lopped off. This means that an individual will no longer be able to start at the bottom and work his way up; he will have to start in the middle or on top, and hold on tight. It will not even be enough to have certain specific skills, for many skilled jobs are also vulnerable to automation. A broad educational background, permitting vocational adaptability and flexibility, seems more imperative than ever. We live in a society where, as Secretary of Labor Willard Wirtz puts it, machines have the equivalent of a high school diploma. Yet the average educational attainment of American Negroes is 8.2 years.

Negroes, of course, are not the only people being affected by these developments. It is reported that there are now 50 percent fewer unskilled and semi-skilled jobs than there are high school dropouts. Almost one third of the twenty-six million young people entering the labor market in the 1960s will be dropouts. But the percentage of Negro dropouts nationally is 57 percent, and in New York City, among Negroes 25 years of age or over, it is 68 percent. They are without a future.

To what extent can the kind of self-help campaign recently prescribed by Eric Hoffer in the *New York Times Magazine* cope with such a situation? I would advise those who think that self-help is the answer to familiarize themselves with the long history of such efforts in the Negro community, and to consider why so many foundered on the shoals of ghetto life. It goes without saying that any effort to combat demoralization and apathy is desirable, but we must understand that demoralization in the Negro community is largely a common-sense response to an objective reality. Negro youths have no need of statistics to perceive, fairly accurately, what their odds are in American society. Indeed, from the point of view of motivation, some of the healthiest Negro youngsters I know are juvenile delinquents: vigorously pursuing the American Dream of material acquisition and status, yet finding the conventional means of attaining it blocked off, they do not yield to defeatism but resort to illegal (and often ingenious) methods. They are not alien to American culture. They are, in Gunnar Myrdal's phrase, "exaggerated Americans." To want a Cadillac is not un-American; to push a cart in the garment center is. If Negroes are to be persuaded that the conventional path (school, work, etc.) is superior, we had better provide evidence which is now sorely lacking. It is a double cruelty to harangue Negro youth about education and training when we do not know what jobs will be available for them.

When a Negro youth can reasonably foresee a future free of slums, when the prospect of gainful employment is realistic, we will see motivation and self-help in abundant enough quantities.

Meanwhile, there is an ironic similarity between the self-help advocated by many liberals and the doctrines of the Black Muslims. Professional sociologists, psychiatrists, and social workers have expressed amazement at the Muslims' success in transforming prostitutes and dope addicts into respectable citizens. But every prostitute the Muslims convert to a model of Calvinist virtue is replaced by the ghetto with two more. Dedicated as they are to maintenance of the ghetto, the Muslims are powerless to effect substantial moral reform. So too with every other group or program which is not aimed at the destruction of slums, their causes and effects. Self-help efforts, directly or indirectly, must be geared to mobilizing people into power units capable of effecting social change. That is, their goal must be genuine self-help, not merely self-improvement. Obviously, where self-improvement activities succeed in imparting to their participants a feeling of some control over their environment, those involved may find their appetites for change whetted; they may move into the political arena.

III

Let me sum up what I have thus far been trying to say: the civil rights movement is evolving from a protest movement into a full-fledged *social movement*—an evolution calling its very name into question. It is now concerned not merely with removing the barriers to full *opportunity* but with achieving the fact of *equality*. From sit-ins and Freedom Rides we have gone into rent strikes, boycotts, community organization, and political action. As a consequence of this natural evolution, the Negro today finds himself stymied by obstacles of far greater magnitude than the legal barriers he was attacking before: automation, urban decay, *de facto* school segregation. These are problems which, while conditioned by Jim Crow, do not vanish upon its demise. They are more deeply rooted in our socioeconomic order; they are the result of the total society's failure to meet not only the Negro's needs, but human needs generally.

These propositions have won increasing recognition and acceptance, but with a curious twist. They have formed the common premise of two apparently contradictory lines of thought which simultaneously nourish and antagonize each other. On the one hand, there is the reasoning of the *New York Times* moderate who says that the problems are so enormous and complicated that Negro militancy is a futile irritation, and that the need is for "intelligent moderation." Thus, during the first New York school boycott, the *Times* editorialized that Negro demands, while abstractly just, would necessitate massive reforms, the funds for which could not realistically be anticipated; therefore the just demands were also foolish demands and would only antagonize white people. Moderates of this stripe are often correct in perceiving the difficulty or impossibility of racial progress in the context of present social and economic policies. But they accept the context as fixed. They ignore (or perhaps see all too well) the potentialities inherent in linking Negro demands to broader pressures for radical revision of existing policies. They apparently see nothing strange in the fact that in the last twenty-five years we have spent nearly a trillion dollars fighting or preparing for wars, yet throw up our hands before the need for overhauling our schools, clearing the slums, and really abolishing poverty. My quarrel with these moderates is that they do not even envision radical changes; their admonitions of moderation are, for all practical purposes, admonitions to the Negro to adjust to the status quo, and are therefore immoral.

The more effectively the moderates argue their case, the more they convince Negroes that American society will not or cannot be reorganized for full racial equality. Michael Harrington has said that a successful war on poverty might well require the expenditure of a $100 billion. Where, the Negro wonders, are the forces now in motion to compel such a commitment? If the voices of the moderates were raised in an insistence upon a reallocation of national resources at levels that could not be confused with tokenism (that is, if the moderates stopped being moderates), Negroes would have greater grounds for hope. Meanwhile, the Negro movement cannot escape a sense of isolation.

It is precisely this sense of isolation that gives rise to the second line of thought I want to examine—the tendency within the civil rights movement which, despite its militancy, pursues what I call a "no-win" policy. Sharing with many moderates a recognition of the magnitude of the obstacles to freedom, spokesmen for this tendency survey the American scene and find no forces prepared to move toward radical solutions. From this they conclude that the only viable strategy is shock; above all, the hypocrisy of white liberals must be exposed. These spokesmen are often described as the radicals of the movement, but they are really its moralists. They seek to change white hearts—by traumatizing them. Frequently abetted by white self-flagellants, they may gleefully applaud (though not really agreeing with) Malcolm X because, while they admit he has no program, they think he can frighten white people into doing the right thing. To believe this, of course, you must be convinced, even if unconsciously, that at the core of the white man's heart lies a buried affection for Negroes—a proposition one may be permitted to doubt. But in any case, hearts are not relevant to the issue; neither racial affinities nor racial hostilities are rooted there. It is institutions—social, political, and economic institutions—which are the ultimate molders of collective sentiments. Let these institutions be reconstructed *today,* and let the ineluctable gradualism of history govern the formation of a new psychology.

My quarrel with the "no-win" tendency in the civil rights movement (and the reason I have so designated it) parallels my quarrel with the moderates outside the movement. As the latter lack the vision or will for fundamental change, the former lack a realistic strategy for achieving it. For such a strategy they substitute militancy. But militancy is a matter of posture and volume and not of effect.

I believe that the Negro's struggle for equality in America is essentially revolutionary. While most Negroes—in their hearts —unquestionably seek only to enjoy the fruits of American society as it now exists, their quest cannot *objectively* be satisfied within the framework of existing political and economic relations. The young Negro who would demonstrate his way into the labor market may be motivated by a thoroughly bourgeois ambition and thoroughly "capitalist" considerations, but he will end up having to favor a great expansion of the public sector of the economy. At any rate, that is the position the movement will be forced to take as it looks at the number of jobs being generated by the private economy, and if it is to remain true to the masses of Negroes.

The revolutionary character of the Negro's struggle is manifest in the fact that this struggle may have done more to democratize life for whites than for Negroes. Clearly, it was the sit-in movement of young Southern Negroes which, as it galvanized white students, banished the ugliest features of McCarthyism from the American campus and resurrected political debate. It was not until Negroes assaulted *de facto* school segregation in the urban centers that the issue of quality education for *all* children stirred into motion. Finally, it seems reasonably clear that the civil rights movement, directly and through the resurgence of social conscience it kindled, did more to initiate the War on Poverty than any other single force.

It will be—it has been—argued that these by-products of the Negro struggle are not revolutionary. But the term revolutionary, as I am using it, does not connote violence; it refers to the qualitative transformation of fundamental institutions, more or less rapidly, to the point where the social and economic structure which they comprised can no longer be said to be the same. The Negro struggle has hardly run its course; and it will not stop moving until it has been utterly defeated or won substantial equality. But I fail to see how the movement can be victorious in the absence of radical programs for full employment, abolition of slums, the reconstruction of our educational system, new definitions of work and leisure. Adding up the cost of such programs, we can only conclude that we are talking about a refashioning of our political economy. It has been estimated, for example, that the price of replacing New York City's slums with public housing would be $17 billion. Again, a multibillion-dollar federal public-works program, dwarfing the currently proposed $2-billion program, is required to reabsorb unskilled and semi-skilled workers into the labor market—and this must be done if Negro workers in these categories are to be employed. "Preferential treatment" cannot help them.

I am not trying here to delineate a total program, only to suggest the scope of economic reforms which are most immediately related to the plight of the Negro community. One could speculate on their political implications—whether, for example, they do not indicate the obsolescence of state government and the superiority of regional structures as viable units of planning. Such speculations aside, it is clear that Negro needs cannot be satisfied unless we go beyond what has so far been placed on the agenda. How are these radical objectives to be achieved? The answer is simple, deceptively so: *through political power.*

There is a strong moralistic strain in the civil rights movement which would remind us that power corrupts, forgetting that the absence of power also corrupts. But this is not the view I want to debate here, for it is waning. Our problem is posed by those who accept the need for political power but do not understand the nature of the object and therefore lack sound strategies for achieving it; they tend to confuse political institutions with lunch counters.

A handful of Negroes, acting alone, could integrate a lunch counter by strategically locating their bodies so as *directly* to interrupt the operation of the proprietor's will; their numbers were relatively unimportant. In politics, however, such a confrontation is difficult because the interests involved are merely *represented.* In the execution of a political decision a direct confrontation may ensue (as when federal marshals escorted James Meredith into the University of Mississippi—to turn from an example of nonviolent coercion to one of force backed up with the threat of violence). But in arriving at a political decision, numbers and organizations are crucial, especially for the economically disenfranchised. (Needless to say, I am assuming that the forms of political democracy exist in America, however imperfectly, that they are valued, and that elitist or putschist conceptions of exercising power are beyond the pale of discussion for the civil rights movement.)

Neither that movement nor the country's twenty million black people can win political power alone. We need allies. The future of the Negro struggle depends on whether the contradictions of this society can be resolved by a coalition of progressive forces which becomes the *effective* political majority in the United States. I speak of the coalition which staged the March on Washington, passed the Civil Rights Act, and laid the basis for the

Johnson landslide—Negroes, trade unionists, liberals, and religious groups.

There are those who argue that a coalition strategy would force the Negro to surrender his political independence to white liberals, that he would be neutralized, deprived of his cutting edge, absorbed into the Establishment. Some who take this position urged last year that votes be withheld from the Johnson-Humphrey ticket as a demonstration of the Negro's political power. Curiously enough, these people who sought to demonstrate power through the non-exercise of it, also point to the Negro "swing vote" in crucial urban areas as the source of the Negro's independent political power. But here they are closer to being right: the urban Negro vote will grow in importance in the coming years. If there is anything positive in the spread of the ghetto, it is the potential political power base thus created, and to realize this potential is one of the most challenging and urgent tasks before the civil rights movement. If the movement can wrest leadership of the ghetto vote from the machines, it will have acquired an organized constituency such as other major groups in our society now have.

But we must also remember that the effectiveness of a swing vote depends solely on "other" votes. It derives its power from them. In that sense, it can never be "independent," but must opt for one candidate or the other, even if by default. Thus coalitions are inescapable, however tentative they may be. And this is the case in all but those few situations in which Negroes running on an independent ticket might conceivably win. "Independence," in other words, is not a value in itself. The issue is which coalition to join and how to make it responsive to your program. Necessarily there will be compromise. But the difference between expediency and morality in politics is the difference between selling out a principle and making smaller concessions to win larger ones. The leader who shrinks from this task reveals not his purity but his lack of political sense.

The task of molding a political movement out of the March on Washington coalition is not simple, but no alternatives have been advanced. We need to choose our allies on the basis of common political objectives. It has become fashionable in some no-win Negro circles to decry the white liberal as the main enemy (his hypocrisy is what sustains racism); by virtue of this reverse recitation of the reactionary's litany (liberalism leads to socialism, which leads to Communism) the Negro is left in majestic isolation, except for a tiny band of fervent white initiates. But the objective fact is that *Eastland and Goldwater* are the main enemies—they and the opponents of civil rights, of the War on Poverty, of medicare, of social security, of federal aid to education, of unions, and so forth. The labor movement, despite its obvious faults, has been the largest single organized force in this country pushing for progressive social legislation. And where the Negro-labor-liberal axis is weak, as in the farm belt, it was the religious groups that were most influential in rallying support for the Civil Rights Bill.

The durability of the coalition was interestingly tested during the election. I do not believe that the Johnson landslide proved the "white backlash" to be a myth. It proved, rather, that economic interests are more fundamental than prejudice: the backlashers decided that loss of social security was, after all, too high a price to pay for a slap at the Negro. This lesson was a valuable first step in re-educating such people, and it must be kept alive, for the civil rights movement will be advanced only to the degree that social and economic welfare gets to be inextricably entangled with civil rights.

The 1964 elections marked a turning point in American politics. The Democratic landslide was not merely the result of a negative reaction to Goldwaterism; it was also the expression of a majority liberal consensus. The near unanimity with which Negro voters joined in that expression was, I am convinced, a vindication of the July 25th statement by Negro leaders calling for a strategic turn toward political action and a temporary curtailment of mass demonstrations. Despite the controversy surrounding the statement, the instinctive response it met with in the community is suggested by the fact that demonstrations were down 75 percent as compared with the same period in 1963. But should so high a percentage of Negro voters have gone to Johnson, or should they have held back to narrow his margin of victory and thus give greater visibility to our swing vote? How has our loyalty changed things? Certainly the Negro vote had higher visibility in 1960, when a switch of only 7 percent from the Republican column of 1956 elected President Kennedy. But the slimness of Kennedy's victory—of his "mandate"—dictated a go-slow approach on civil rights, at least until the Birmingham upheaval.

Although Johnson's popular majority was so large that he could have won without such overwhelming Negro support, that support was important from several angles. Beyond adding to Johnson's total national margin, it was specifically responsible for his victories in Virginia, Florida, Tennessee, and Arkansas. Goldwater took only those states where fewer than 45 percent of eligible Negroes were registered. That Johnson would have won those states had Negro voting rights been enforced is a lesson not likely to be lost on a man who would have been happy with a unanimous electoral college. In any case, the 1.6 million Southern Negroes who voted have had a shattering impact on the Southern political party structure, as illustrated in the changed composition of the Southern Congressional delegation. The "backlash" gave the Republicans five House seats in Alabama, one in Georgia, and one in Mississippi. But on the Democratic side, seven segregationists were defeated while all nine Southerners who voted for the Civil Rights Act were re-elected. It may be premature to predict a Southern Democratic Party of Negroes and white moderates and a Republican Party of refugee racists and economic conservatives, but there certainly is a strong tendency toward such a realignment; and an additional 3.6 million Negroes of voting age in the eleven Southern states are still to be heard from. Even the *tendency* toward disintegration of the Democratic Party's racist wing defines a new context for Presidential and liberal strategy in the Congressional battles ahead. Thus the Negro vote (North as well as South), while not *decisive* in the Presidential race, was enormously effective. It was a dramatic element of a historic mandate which contains vast possibilities and dangers that will fundamentally affect the future course of the civil rights movement.

The liberal Congressional sweep raises hope for an assault on the seniority system, Rule Twenty-two, and other citadels of Dixiecrat-Republican power. The overwhelming of this conservative coalition should also mean progress on much bottle-necked legislation of profound interest to the movement (e.g., bills by Senators Clark and Nelson on planning, manpower, and employment). Moreover, the irrelevance of the South to John-son's victory gives the President more freedom to act than his predecessor had and more leverage to the movement to pressure for executive action in Mississippi and other racist strongholds.

None of this *guarantees* vigorous executive or legislative ac-tion, for the other side of the Johnson landslide is that it has a Gaullist quality. Goldwater's capture of the Republican Party forced into the Democratic camp many disparate elements which do not belong there, Big Business being the major exam-ple. Johnson, who wants to be President "of all the people," may try to keep his new coalition together by sticking close to the political center. But if he decides to do this, it is unlikely that even his political genius will be able to hold together a coalition so inherently unstable and rife with contradictions. It must come apart. Should it do so while Johnson is pursuing a centrist course, then the mandate will have been wastefully dissipated. However, if the mandate is seized upon to set fundamental changes in motion, then the basis can be laid for a new mandate, a new coalition including hitherto inert and dispossessed strata of the population.

Here is where the cutting edge of the civil rights movement can be applied. We must see to it that the reorganization of the "consensus party" proceeds along lines which will make it an effective vehicle for social reconstruction, a role it cannot play so long as it furnishes Southern racism with its national political power. (One of Barry Goldwater's few attractive ideas was that the Dixiecrats belong with him in the same party.) And nowhere has the civil rights movement's political cutting edge been more magnificently demonstrated than at Atlantic City, where the Mississippi Freedom Democratic Party not only secured recog-nition as a bona fide component of the national party, but in the process routed the representatives of the most rabid racists—the white Mississippi and Alabama delegations. While I still believe that the FDP made a tactical error in spurning the compromise, there is no question that they launched a political revolution whose logic is the displacement of Dixiecrat power. They launched that revolution within a major political institution and as part of a coalitional effort.

The role of the civil rights movement in the reorganization of American political life is programmatic as well as strategic. We are challenged now to broaden our social vision, to develop functional programs with concrete objectives. We need to propose alternatives to technological unemployment, urban decay, and the rest. We need to be calling for public works and training, for national economic planning, for federal aid to education, for attractive public housing—all this on a sufficiently massive scale to make a difference. We need to protest the notion that our integration into American life, so long delayed, must now proceed in an atmosphere of competitive scarcity instead of in the security of abundance which technology makes possible. We cannot claim to have answers to all the complex problems of modern society. That is too much to ask of a movement still battling barbarism in Mississippi. But we can agitate the right questions by probing at the contradictions which still stand in the way of the "Great Society." The questions having been asked, motion must begin in the larger society, for there is a limit to what Negroes can do alone.

4. *"Coalition Politics or Nonviolent Revolution?"*

Staughton Lynd, who teaches history at Yale University and is an editor of Studies on the Left, *is a vigorous defender of the new radical viewpoint. In company with Tom Hayden of SDS and Herbert Aptheker of the Communist Party, Lynd recently journeyed to North Vietnam on an unofficial and unauthorized mission to talk with North Vietnamese leaders.*

In "Coalition Politics or Nonviolent Revolution?," which appeared in the June-July 1965 Liberation *Lynd attacks Bayard Rustin's advocacy of developing a liberal-left coalition inside the Democratic Party and other liberal organizations.*

Bayard Rustin's "From Protest to Politics: The Future of the Civil Rights Movement," an article which appeared in *Commentary* magazine for February 1965, has been widely criticized in radical publications. . . .

The gist of the radical critique of Rustin might be summarized as follows:

1.) Rustin writes that "the objective fact is that *Eastland and Goldwater* are the main enemies." In so doing he exaggerates the liberalism of the Johnson coalition, even asserting that Big Business, forced into the Democratic Party by Goldwater, "does not belong there."

2.) Not only does Rustin urge that direct action be abandoned for politics, he argues also that independent political action is only rarely appropriate. The accurate perception that Negroes need white allies leads him to the conclusion that one must choose between existing aggregations of political forces: "The issue is which coalition to join and how to make it responsive to your program."

3.) Thus, by exaggerating the Johnson coalition's capacity to solve fundamental social problems and by underestimating the need for independent action by Negroes, Rustin arrives at a stance which (in Radosh's words) "leads to a dissolution of the old Rights movement, as well as assuring that any new Movement will not develop in a more radical fashion." The effect of his advice would be to assimilate Negro protest to the Establishment just as labor protest was coöpted at the end of the 1930s, in each case leaving the poorest, least organized parts of the population out in the cold. . . .

Fully to appraise Rustin's *Commentary* article, one must see it as the second in a series of three Rustin actions during the past year. First was his attempt to get the credentials committee offer of token seating accepted by the Mississippi Freedom Democratic Party delegates at Atlantic City (August 1964). Second was the article (February 1965). Third was the effort to undermine and stop the March on Washington against the war in Vietnam (March-April 1965). In this perspective, the most basic criticisms of his article should be these: 1.) The coalition he advocates turns out to mean implicit acceptance of Administration foreign policy, to be coalition with the marines; 2.) The style of politics he advocates turns out to mean a kind of elitism which Bayard has been fighting all his life, in which rank-and-file persons would cease to act on their own behalf and be (in the words of "From Protest to Politics") "merely represented."

In opposing the March on Washington against the war in Vietnam, Bayard Rustin has permitted himself to drift into that posture which once evoked epithets such as "labor lieutenant of capitalism." Exaggerated as such labels may have been, they designated something real. There were in Europe and there are now in America pacifists and socialists who always support their own government in its international confrontations when push comes to shove. Such Americans insist on condemning Washington and Moscow "equally," but end up supporting the U.S. government which "after all" and "on the whole" stands on the side of "freedom." They specialize in advising revolutionary movements overseas to be nonviolent, forgetting that American arms and aggression play a major role (as in Vietnam) in driving peaceful protest toward insurrection. They cultivate the concept that the President is a man of peace misled by his advisors, who if only one could reach him, would surely turn on the military-industrial complex and overcome. Theirs is the stance of telling Washington what *they* would do were *they* in power. If there is to be protest, so they say, let it be decorous protest which (as Norman Thomas said in his April 22nd letter to the *Times*) "goes off well," i.e., poses no serious embarrassment to the good man in the White House.

The basic error in this analysis seems to me the assumption that there now exists what Michael Harrington calls *"de facto coexistence"* between the United States and world revolution. Rustin and Harrington confine their analysis to domestic problems, as if believing that foreign affairs are frozen and can be forgotten. But as Harrington conceded in *Partisan Review:* " 'escalation' of the Vietnamese—or any other—crisis would . . . end talk of the War on Poverty, and of the Great Society." That escalation has occurred.

Coalitionism, then, is pro-Americanism. It is what Sidney Lens has called "two-and-a-half campism." It is a posture which subordinates foreign to domestic politics, which mutes criticism of American imperialism so as to keep open its channels to the

White House, which tacitly assumes that no major war will occur. But war is occurring in Vietnam, major enough for the innocent people which it has killed. How can one reconcile virtual silence on Vietnam with the screams of Vietnamese women and children?

Coalitionism is also elitism. Its assumption is that major political decisions are made by deals between the representatives of the interests included in the coalition. Negro protest, according to the Rustin formula, should now take on the role of such an interest. And men like Rustin will become the national spokesmen who sell the line agreed on behind doors to the faithful followers waiting in the street.

This was the meaning of Atlantic City. What was at stake, as it seemed to the SNCC people there, was not so much the question, Should the compromise be accepted? as the question, Are plain people from Mississippi competent to decide? Rustin, Martin Luther King and Roy Wilkins answered the latter question: No. The decision, they insisted, involved "national considerations." In some sense the destiny of America rested in the hands of those who made this decision. Hence it should be made wisely, by the leaders, and put over to the delegates from Mississippi.

But what those delegates and their SNCC associates learned at Atlantic City was simply no longer to trust these "national civil rights leaders." They learned, as Mrs. Hamer put it on her return, that hypocrisy exists all over America. They learned, so Robert Parris told the *National Guardian* dinner in November, that the destiny of America was *not* in their hands, that they should seek their own objectives, "let the chips fall where they may."

So as some sank deeper into the coils of coalitionism, SNCC people have joined with Students for a Democratic Society this winter in laying a new emphasis on "participatory democracy." Democracy, they say, means ordinary people making decisions for themselves. It means the staff of an organization making decisions rather than an executive committee, it means the organization itself working itself out of a job so that new popular organizations take over Freedom parties, Freedom schools.

All this Bayard Rustin used to believe. Direct action is inseparable from the idea that everyone involved in a movement has some ultimate responsibility and initiative. Decentralization was the hallmark of the early *Liberation,* which Bayard helped to found. Participatory democrats, as they move from direct action into politics, insist that direct action must continue along with politics, that there come into being a new politics which forces the representative back to his people, and politics back to life.

There is very little point in criticizing the coalition strategy suggested by Rustin unless one has an alternative to offer.

THE NONVIOLENT ALTERNATIVE

I think the time has come to begin to think of "nonviolent revolution" as the only long-run alternative to coalition with the marines. The civil rights movement, so often called a revolution, is thus far no more a revolution than the trade union movement of the 1930s. Presumably the definition of a revolution is that the direction of society's affairs shifts from one group to another, and that the economic foundation of political power is transformed so as to make this shift permanent. A revolution in this sense—and not merely public works planning by an Administration whose power rests on private ownership and lack of planning—seems to me required both to prevent war and to satisfy the needs of the other America. But is talk of revolution merely what Rustin calls moral gesturing?

So long as revolution is pictured as a violent insurrection it seems to me both distasteful and unreal. The traditional alternative, the Social Democratic vision of electing more and more radical legislators until power passes peacefully to the Left, seems equally illusory. However, the events of the past year— the creation of the Mississippi Freedom Democratic Party and the protest against the war in Vietnam—suggest a third strategy. One can now begin to envision a series of nonviolent protests which would from the beginning question the legitimacy of the Administration's authority where it has gone beyond constitutional and moral limits, and might, if its insane foreign policy continues, culminate in the decision of hundreds of thousands of people to recognize the authority of alternative institutions of their own making.

Robert Parris has sketched out such a scenario as a possibility in Mississippi. What, he has asked, if Mississippi Freedom Democratic Party voters elected not only legislators but public officials as well? What if the Negroes of Neshoba County, Mississippi, began to obey the instructions of the Freedom Sheriff rather than Sheriff Rainey? What if the Freedom Sheriff empaneled a Freedom Grand Jury which indicted Sheriff Rainey for murder?

The value of these imaginings is that they break up the concept of "revolution" as a monolithic, unitary event, and remind us that revolution begins as the decision of individuals to say, No, and take a first step. Even the most violent revolutions involved a larger component of nonviolent civil disobedience than is often recognized. Masses of poor men who defy constituted authority typically lack weapons, and succeed only when they convince the government's soldiers not to fire on them but to join them. Thus Trotsky presents the crux of the Russian Revolution as an encounter between mounted Cossacks and unarmed poor people rioting for bread; when the soldiers decided to join the rioters, the revolution was essentially won. Saint-Éxupéry, writing of the Spanish Civil War, describes two peasants, one in the Nationalist Army and one in the Republican, whose units were stationed on opposite slopes of a valley and who as night fell hurled to each other across the great distance single words which sought to persuade: "Liberty," "Brotherhood." This is how real revolutions, as distinct from plots and insurrections, succeed or fail. Camus was wrong in presenting revolution and rebellion as mutually exclusive: no popular revolution is possible which is not composed of hundreds of smaller rebellions. Thus the American Civil War, our closest approach to revolution, began with solitary decisions to defy Congress and the Supreme Court and to succor fugitive slaves.

Needless to say all this makes sense only if our situation is desperate. I think it is desperate. If it was desperate in Mississippi when perhaps two dozen people were murdered over a period of five years, what is it in Vietnam where a hundred thousand lives have needlessly been thrown away since 1954? If there are, in Camus' phrase, "limits" inherent in human nature to permissible government policy, what more can we do after what we have done in Vietnam? If Vietnam is permissible, can anything be forbidden? And how many more secret undebated Presidential decisions will it take to convince us that a constitutional crisis exists in America, that we have moved into a twilight zone between democratically delegated authority and something accurately called "fascism"? When the President sent troops into the Dominican Republic he called in Congressmen to tell them, he explained, before they read about it in the newspapers. As the *New York Times* has pointed out, government management of the news, characteristic of previous temporary crises such as the U-2 and Bay of Pigs affairs, has in connection with Vietnam become settled public policy over a period of months and years. I believe we should have seen that America could not endlessly practice Seven Days in May in underdeveloped countries all over the world, making and unmaking governments at the behest of generals and CIA agents, without these habits crossing the Rubicon between foreign and domestic politics to become our political style at home as well. I think the situation is desperate.

Yet nonviolence offers rational hope which can forestall desperation issuing in apathy or senseless violence. The situation of the Administration is more desperate than ours, and its present policy is the blind lashing-out of the cornered and frustrated, who see no orderly method to achieve their goals. On the other hand, few as we are our aspirations run along the grain of the hopes and strivings of the majority of mankind. International public opinion constitutes some check even on an Administration which has determined to go it alone without friends. When suffragettes were over and over again imprisoned and mishandled on the streets of Washington during World War I, public opinion was aroused, some high government officials resigned, and women's suffrage was enacted into law. If students chained themselves to the Capitol this summer in wave after wave of massive civil disobedience, even the Johnson Administration would be constrained in its choice of means.

A CONTINENTAL CONGRESS

What then is to be done? Let me offer an imagined scenario, comparable to Parris' for Mississippi, which without presuming

to define a "position" or lay down a "line" may help our thinking converge toward common action.

Suppose (I take this idea from Tom Hayden) there were convened in Washington this summer a new continental congress.
The congresses of 1774 and 1775 came about on the initiative
of committees of correspondence of the individual colonies. The
continental congress of 1965 might stem from the initiative of
the community union in a Northern ghetto, or the Freedom
Party of a Southern state. Suppose, at any rate, that such a call
goes out, saying in effect: This is a desperate situation; our government no longer represents us; let us come together at Washington to consult on what needs to be done.

Already there are in Washington, Freedom Democratic Con-
gresswomen who are, in a sense, tribunes of all the unrepresented people in America. As the actions of the Administration
systematically exclude Congress from effective decision-making,
the category of the unrepresented comes to include not only
those (like 95 percent of adult Mississippi Negroes) who cannot
vote, but the rest of the American people who no longer have decision-makers that represent them. Although Mrs. Hamer and
Mrs. Gray have held no "freedom legislative hearings" and introduced no "freedom bills," their presence is a symbol of the determination of the American excluded to have some say in what
their government does.

The continental congress goes one step further. The act of
convening it would stem from a conviction that even the victory
of Mrs. Hamer and her colleagues would have little significance
if the Congress which they joined no longer had effective power.
The continental congress would be the coming-together of
project and community union representatives who, were they
one day to be elected to Congress, might refuse to go on the
ground that Congress has given up its power.

Just as the American Colonists organized Provincial Conventions and a Continental Congress to take the place of the colonial legislatures and the British Parliament, so the continental
congress of 1965 would seriously and responsibly begin to debate the policies of the United States. The discussions which
have failed to take place in the Senate about Vietnam would

take place here. Resolutions would be adopted and the form of treaties ratified; emissaries of the congress could seek to make direct contact with the people of other countries. In effect the continental congress would begin to govern.

The transfer of allegiance would apply, to begin with, only to specific acts. Those refusing to pay taxes might pay them to the continental congress. Those refusing to serve in the army might volunteer their labor to community projects under congress sponsorship. Some, with or without the explicit authorization of a congress majority, might initiate systematic civil disobedience in their own communities or in Washington (just so in 1774 Massachusetts moved out ahead of the Continental Congress and began to organize its own government and to prepare for war). Professors might organize a committee to hold foreign policy hearings, since the Senate Committee on Foreign Relations has failed to do so. Men of spiritual authority from all over the world might be convened as a parallel Supreme Court, to assess guilt and responsibility for the horror of Vietnam.

The pressures on American policy-makers suggest an iron drift toward more and more blatant repression at home and abroad. Yet even if this is so, all is not lost. Six months ago the air-conditioned nightmare seemed secure and invulnerable. Liberals congratulated themselves that America had turned its last corner, integrating the Negro into the happy permanent societal consensus. This was an illusion. America's situation was less secure, Johnson was less rational, the American people were less brainwashed, than they seemed six months ago. Now we know: whom the gods would destroy they first make mad; but also: we can overcome.

At the April 17th march in Washington it was unbearably moving to watch the sea of banners and signs move out from the Sylvan Theater toward the Capitol as Joan Baez, Judy Collins and others sang "We Shall Overcome." Still more poignant was the perception—and I checked my reaction with many many others who felt as I did—that as the crowd moved down the Mall toward the seat of government, its path delimited on each side by rows of chartered buses so that there was nowhere to go but forward, toward the waiting policemen, it seemed that the great mass of people would simply flow on through and over the marble buildings, that our forward movement was irresistibly strong, that even had some been shot or arrested nothing could have stopped that crowd from taking possession of its government. Perhaps next time we should keep going, occupying for a time the rooms from which orders issue and sending to the people of Vietnam and the Dominican Republic the profound apologies which are due; or quietly waiting on the Capitol steps until those who make policy for us, and who like ourselves are trapped by fear and pride, consent to enter into dialogue with us and with mankind.

*O*nly limitations of space have prevented us from including in this appendix material from the many groups and individuals who have contributed to the new radicalism. Paul Sweezey and Leo Huberman have published *Monthly Review* for more than fifteen years, keeping alive an orthodox Marxist analysis of world events. Dave Dellinger, David McReynolds, and the *Liberation* staff have provided a consistent tone for the peace movement, and *Liberation's* pages have been filled with debate about The Movement's nature and future. *New Politics, Dissent,* and *New America* have kept alive for the new radicals the tradition of democratic socialism. *The Worker* and *People's World* have presented the Communist view of the news and the times. *The National Guardian* has offered a broad coverage of the old and new left. Magazines like *The Realist,* edited by Paul Krassner, offer an honest, audacious iconoclasm new in the 1960s. Finally, I. F. Stone publishes a weekly that is trusted by almost the entire left. He is one of The Movement's few heroes.

The Catholic Worker has influenced many young radicals and has provided some of the true saints of American life. The Committee for Non-Violent Action (CNVA) has reminded all of us, through its acts of moral witness, that we are not doing all that we can to achieve the peace and justice we believe in. Groups as far apart as the Northern Student Movement, which is close to the SDS, and the Spartacist, "the revolutionary tendency expelled from the Socialist Workers Party," are also part of The Movement's spectrum. Trends or fads of behavior, like the Sexual Freedom League and the "Psychedelic Left," interested in experiences that result from hallucinogenic drugs like LSD, have contributed to the over-all sense of freedom that many in The Movement now feel. The new horizons are personal and political, and it is difficult to weigh the contribution of Allen Ginsberg or Lenny Bruce to the spirit of the new radicalism, but we believe that it is important.

We could not offer more than a sparse sample of the rich literature that has developed around The Movement in the past six years. We had to omit important documents like Hal Draper's "Defense of the New Radicals," which appeared in *New Politics,* and Michael Harrington's analysis of the Communist problem in The Movement. We apologize for these omissions and hope that this book will serve to stimulate the reader into finding out more of what the best young people in America are thinking and writing.

Chronology of Events

The following events were selected out of thousands to provide the reader with a rough chronological guide to the development of The Movement.

1954

May The Supreme Court finds school segregation unconstitutional on grounds that "separate but equal" is inherently unequal. The Court orders desegregation of the public school system "with all deliberate speed." Border areas comply, including Washington, D.C., but the Deep South plans massive resistance.

1956

Revelations about Stalin at the 20th Communist Party Congress. Revolts occur in Poland and Hungary, and the latter is crushed by Soviet tanks. England, France, and Israel invade Egypt.

1956-1958

A new literary left appears in Europe, including Polish revisionists, French existentialists, and Oxford Marxists. In the U.S. "beat" literature appears: Allen Ginsberg publishes "Howl" and Jack Kerouac writes *On the Road.*

1957

President Eisenhower orders federal troops to Arkansas to enforce integration of Little Rock Central High School in defiance of Governor Orval Faubus.

1958

Winter–Spring Student activity begins in contrast to the quiet and apathetic McCarthy 1950s. At the University of Wisconsin a lively Socialist Club educates and agitates; at the University of California SLATE is organized to run independent candidates for progressive student governments.

1959

January 1 Fidel Castro's guerrillas overthrow the Cuban dictatorship of Fulgencio Batista.

Summer The Student Peace Union (SPU) is organized in Chicago by people active in the Socialist Party.

October An eighteen-year-old University of California student stages a one-man vigil on the steps of Sproul Hall to protest compulsory ROTC (Reserve Officers Training Corps) in a state-supported university; 150 students there demonstrate in December, 1960; one student receives a failing grade in ROTC course for picketing in uniform; the Regents vote in June 1963 to abolish compulsory ROTC.

1960

February Lunch counter sit-ins led by Negro students begin at Greensboro, N.C., spread to a score of Southern cities. Woolworth stores are picketed throughout the country, mainly by students, because the Southern branches of the store segregate their lunch counters.

A hundred Bay Area Students (from San Francisco State College and the University of California at Berkeley) march from San Francisco to San Quentin to protest the execution of Caryl Chessman; Chessman is executed despite the efforts of students and liberals.

March *New University Thought* is published by graduate students at the University of Chicago.

March–April Fifty-six are killed in Sharpeville, South Africa, when South African police fire on twenty thousand demonstrators protesting the pass law. Riots are set off throughout South Africa, resulting in further restrictive legislation by the dominant white government.

April   Fair Play for Cuba Committee is founded. A *New York Times* advertisement challenging U.S. press and government views is signed by such artists and writers as Jean-Paul Sartre, James Baldwin, Norman Mailer, and Kenneth Tynan.

Student Nonviolent Coordinating Committee (SNCC) is organized at Raleigh, North Carolina.

In England, thousands join the march from Aldermaston to London sponsored by the Committee for Nuclear Disarmament. In October 1960 the Labour Party adopts a platform of unilateral nuclear disarmament over the protests of party leaders Gaitskell and Brown. The platform is later reversed. The Aldermaston Marches continue during the next few years.

April–May   Students demonstrate in South Korea and Turkey against repressive political regimes; their activities form the backbone for opposition which topples Premiers Rhee and Mendes and establishes representative forms of government. In Korea the parliamentary democracy is destroyed the following year by an anti-Communist military junta, with the support of the U.S. government.

May   HUAC is picketed by eight thousand in San Francisco; sixty-eight are arrested as police drive students down City Hall steps with water hoses. Students at many campuses form a nation-wide campaign to abolish HUAC.

June   What is now Students for a Democratic Society (SDS) is formed in New York City from the old Student League for Industrial Democracy.

Summer   Thousands of students visit Cuba. Many join the Fair Play for Cuba Committee or organize chapters on their campuses.

Sit-ins continue.

Fall   C. Wright Mills publishes *Listen Yankee*. U.S.–Cuban relations dominate the news.

1961

January   The U.S. breaks diplomatic relations with Cuba; student demonstrations calling for restoration of relations are organized at several campuses.

The W.E.B. DuBois Clubs are formed in San Francisco as local educational action groups.

February   The State Department bans general travel to Cuba.

Congolese nationalist leader Patrice Lumumba is murdered after being captured by U.S., British, Belgian, and French-supported reactionaries; demonstrations occur throughout the world, and American Negroes create violence in the UN gallery.

March   President Kennedy announces the Peace Corps which draws, initially, some students who had been active in the civil rights struggle.

April   The Eichmann trial opens in Jerusalem; he is convicted of the mass murder of German Jews and hanged by the Israeli government; The controversy begins over the bureaucrat who is "just doing my job," as Eichmann claims he is the "wrong man." In 1963, Rolf Hochhuth publishes the controversial play *The Deputy*, critical of Pope Pius XII and all others who were guilty by silence.

The U.S. sponsors an invasion of Cuba at Playa Givon, in the Bay of Pigs; Castro's forces defeat the landing force. Students protest from coast-to-coast. The Fair Play for Cuba Committee is investigated by Senator Eastland's Internal Security Subcommittee.

May   Freedom Riders, sponsored by the Congress of Racial Equality (CORE), leave Washington, D.C., for New Orleans in integrated buses, successfully, to test segregation of interstate carriers; many riders are beaten and arrested.

June   Students at the University of Texas sponsor "stand-in" demonstrations to protest segregation in Austin movie houses; their actions are supported by national student organizations, who picket the movie chain in cities across the country.

August   SNCC opens a voter registration campaign in Pike County, Mississippi.

September   Robert Williams flees Monroe, N.C., after the U.S. charges him with kidnaping; he requests and receives asylum in Cuba, where he broadcasts "Radio Free Dixie"; William is suspended as chairman of the county chapter of NAACP for advocating that Negroes arm themselves and practice self-defense.

SNCC's voter registration activity and a sit-in at McComb bring white violence. Negro Herbert Lee is murdered by white E. H. Hurst; Hurst is acquitted in Liberty, Mississippi.

A Moscow journal assails Russian poet Yevgeny Yevtushenko for a poem denouncing Soviet anti-Semitism; a literary controversy begins in the Soviet Union; Yevtushenko is cheered by a crowd in Moscow. It is the beginning of a new critical era in U.S.S.R. as the "Red cats" enjoy temporary popularity with Russian youth.

October Moralist-comedian Lenny Bruce is arrested in a San Francisco night club for saying "cocksucker"; he is later acquitted in a trial that brings him to the attention of the nation. In his act, his records, and his many courtroom appearances—for obscenity or narcotics charges, almost all of them resulting in acquittals on appeal—Bruce attempts to expose many of the hypocrisies of U.S. law and society.

November Students all over the country hold vigils opposing the Soviet resumption of nuclear testing.

Dagmar Wilson organizes Women Strike for Peace, a grassroots group, and calls a demonstration in Washington, D.C., for an end to nuclear testing. The organization is later subpoenaed by HUAC, and Mrs. Wilson refuses to disclaim Communists in the WSP membership; the House Committee's prestige is weakened.

Three thousand New York City College students boycott classes to protest an administration ban on Communist speakers.

1962

January Two hundred and fifty Negro students in New Orleans arrested in demonstrations at Southern University; school officials close the university.

February Student Peace Union sponsors a March on Washington, D.C., for peace; five thousand students attempt to talk with Administration officials.

May Graduate students at the University of California at Berkeley publish *Root and Branch;* in the tradition of other campus magazines, it folds after two issues.

May Members of the Committee for Non-Violent Action (CNVA) sail their ship from San Francisco toward Christmas Island, site of a scheduled nuclear test, to protest the resumption of nuclear testing; they are intercepted by the Coast Guard. Linked closely with British pacifists, like Lord Bertrand Russell, CNVA members periodically commit acts of moral witness which result in their arrest, such as climbing the fence of army installations.

June　SDS meets at Port Huron, Michigan, and issues a sixty-three-page pamphlet to guide radicals in their political action.

Summer　Students participate in civil rights drive, North and South. More than one thousand are arrested for demonstrating in Albany, Georgia.

A large U.S. delegation attends the Helsinki Youth Festival.

September　National Student Association passes resolutions opposing nuclear testing and the McCarran Act.

In Hazard, Kentucky, a Miners' Movement is begun by unemployed miners battling for their rights against the coal companies and the officials who hold political offices throughout the Appalachia region; led by Berman Gibson, this group receives national support, and a Committee for Miners is established. SDS members and other Movement people go to Hazard to help the miners.

October　James Meredith becomes the first Negro to be admitted to the University of Mississippi, and, against violence, enters.

The U.S. demands that the Soviet Union withdraw its missiles from Cuba; demonstrations opposing the U.S. blockade of Cuba are organized around the country; ten thousand rally at the UN.

November　Michigan State University refuses to renew the contract of Professor Samuel Shapiro, a vocal critic of U.S. Cuban policy.

Harvard Professor H. Stuart Hughes runs for the U.S. Senate from Massachusetts. He receives only a small vote despite a great deal of campaigning by Movement people.

1963

March　SNCC sponsors its Mississippi Delta Project of voter registration and community organizing in cooperation with other civil rights groups; formed into the Council of Federated Organizations (COFO)

April　White mailman William Moore murdered while walking for civil rights in the South; SNCC and CORE staff resume his walk, are arrested at the Alabama border.

Harvard University dismisses Dr. Timothy Leary and Professor Richard Alpert for testing hallucinogenic drugs on undergraduates. Leary founds the International Foundation for Internal Freedom in Mexico, which he abandons because of harassment from the Mexican government. LSD and other hallucinogens attain wide popularity among students and many Movement youth. Campaigns to legalize marijuana grow throughout the country. The "Psychedelic Left" emerges as an underground aesthetic: Ken Kesey and Allen Ginsberg are its writers, Bob Dylan and the Beatles its musicians.

Pope John XXIII issues encyclical *"Pacem in Terris,"* reflecting his belief that the Church must promote social reform, and calling for peace throughout the world. His Easter message is applauded by Kennedy and Khrushchev. In August the U.S., U.S.S.R., and Great Britain sign a nuclear test ban treaty, banning all but underground tests.

May Demonstrations by Negro workers and unemployed in Birmingham led by Martin Luther King, Jr., become uncontrollable riots.

Three Indiana University students, members of the Young Socialist Alliance (YSA), are indicted under a state sedition law in Bloomington; they are convicted, but finally acquitted in apellate court.

July Progressive Labor (PL) organizes a student trip to Cuba; on return some are subpoenaed by HUAC.

SNCC sponsors folk festival in Mississippi Delta.

September Six Negro children die in Birmingham; four killed when the Sixteenth St. Baptist Church is dynamited, two shot in the aftermath; these incidents climax a summer of violence in Alabama and the South.

Jesse Gray leads rent strikes in New York; Harlem families refuse to pay rent to slumlords and picket City Hall to enforce the housing code; civil court upholds tenants' right to withhold rent because of hazardous conditions. Rent Strikes are organized with some success in Newark and San Francisco.

Bob Dylan writes "Blowing in the Wind," a song about the civil rights movement; he begins a trend of pop and folk songs with social significance. Folksinger Joan Baez declares she will not pay Federal income tax.

November Student groups organize in support of unemployed miners at Hazard, Ky.

"Conspiracy" and "insurrection" charges convict civil rights workers in southwest Georgia.

SNCC and COFO sponsor "Freedom Vote" for Governor of

Mississippi; eighty thousand Negroes vote for an integrated ticket.

November 22   President Kennedy is assassinated in Dallas; his alleged assassin, Lee Harvey Oswald, is in turn murdered.

December   SDS approves community organizing projects in large Northern cities: Economic Research and Action Project (ERAP); begun in August 1963 under a grant from the United Auto Workers, ERAP plans to organize the poor along the lines of SNCC in the South.

1964

February   CORE sponsors a school boycott in New York City to protest *de facto* segregation; half a million students stay home; the city makes some concessions—bus plans and other integration devices.

President Johnson announces a War on Poverty; the program is the result, in part, of Michael Harrington's *The Other America.*

Southern Students Organizing Committee (SSOC) formed in Atlanta for white students to work for civil rights.

Sit-in demonstrators at San Francisco's Sheraton Palace Hotel succeed in desegregating hiring practices in all large San Francisco hotels; 167 are arrested.

The San Francisco New School is opened to provide "radical education"; the school is taken over by SDS in June 1965.

March   Malcolm X breaks with Elijah Muhammed and the Chicago Black Muslims; he enters the political arena by announcing plans for a black nationalist party and challenging the nonviolent assumptions of civil rights organizations. Malcolm is assassinated in February 1965, allegedly by agents of Elijah Muhammed.

April–May   Four hundred students from twenty-one New England colleges meet at a Yale symposium to discuss the role of radicals in the U.S.; every socialist group participates. From the Yale Symposium, Progressive Labor and other militant groups form the May 2nd Movement at New Haven to organize student protest around the war in Vietnam.

Spring   Minister crushed to death at a Cleveland construction site as demonstrators protest racial discrimination in the building trades. Increasingly, churches join the civil rights movement as activists; the National Council of Churches opens offices in the Mississippi Delta.

April More than one thousand are arrested in San Francisco for sit-ins at auto dealers; all dealers agree to hire more Negro salesmen; at subsequent trials the students are given very stiff sentences.

The Progressive Labor Movement (PLM), a pro-China group that split from the Communist Party in 1962, forms the Progressive Labor Party; PLers advocate revolution and openly and proudly admit they are Communists.

Despite a court injunction, Brooklyn CORE attempts to block traffic en route to the opening of the New York World's Fair; previously, CORE workers had sat-in on New York's Triborough Bridge to dramatize to suburban commuters the *de facto* segregation in the city.

May Student Committee for Travel to Cuba, run by PL, announces plans for another trip to Cuba.

June The National Council of Churches and SNCC sponsor orientation sessions in Oxford, Ohio, for the Summer Project, an integrated invasion of Mississippi by volunteer Northern students directed by Bob Moses; the tasks of the volunteers are: to run freedom schools, help build up the Mississippi Freedom Democratic Party, register Negro voters.

Andrew Goodman, James Chaney, and Michael Schwerner, all SNCC workers, are murdered by Mississippi law enforcement officers and others.

Summer Negroes riot in Harlem; William Epton of the Harlem Progressive Labor Party is charged with criminal anarchy. Riots also erupt in Philadelphia, Rochester, and several smaller cities.

U.S. escalates the war in Vietnam. Forty-seven May 2nd Movement students arrested at New York rally.

MFDP challenges the legitimacy of the "illegally elected" regular Mississippi delegation at the Democratic National Convention in Atlantic City; liberal Democrats offer a compromise to the MFDP, which is refused.

The W.E.B. DuBois Clubs become a national organization.

September University of California at Berkeley sets limits on student political activity; many campus organizations defy ban;

police arrest a CORE member, but police car is surrounded by thousands in a spontaneous 32-hour demonstration.

October   Free Speech Movement (FSM) founded.

December   More than eight hundred students arrested at the University of California administration building for sitting-in; Teaching Assistants strike; U.C. paralyzed for several days; U.C. President Clark Kerr agrees to FSM demands. Free Speech Movements founded at other universities.

New York's Mobilization for Youth, a government anti-poverty agency, is attacked for "harboring subversives." In fact, Mobilization's best staff workers were young radicals.

1965

January   MFDP challenges the all-white Mississippi representatives to the House. The challenge fails to get the required number of votes.

February   U.S. planes bomb targets in North Vietnam.

March   Led by Martin Luther King, Jr., thousands of blacks and whites march from Selma to Montgomery, Alabama, after days of violence; the march leads to the passage of the Voting Rights Bill.

SDS sponsors demonstrations against U.S. business support of *apartheid* in South Africa; arrests are made at the picket of the Chase Manhattan bank in New York, which has large investments in South Africa.

A teach-in on Vietnam attracts three thousand students and faculty at the University of Michigan. Teach-ins are held at hundreds of colleges in the U.S. and abroad. In May 1965 national teach-ins are held; the State Department sends representatives to defend U.S. policy.

SDS sponsors a twenty-five thousand-man March on Washington to protest the war in Vietnam.

University of California teach-in on Vietnam weekend attracts over twelve thousand to hear speakers.

U.S. troops invade the Dominican Republic "to prevent a Communist takeover"; protest demonstrations are held throughout the country by radicals and liberals.

June   SNCC Public Relations Director Julian Bond is elected to

Georgia State Legislature. He is subsequently refused his seat because he endorses SNCC's opposition to the war in Vietnam.

Free University of New York (FUNY) founded; more than twenty courses (that range from politics to sex) attract over two hundred students.

Summer   A SNCC-sponsored Negro political party is organized in the Black Belt Lowndes County, Alabama.

The Child Development Group of Mississippi (CDGM) begins Project Headstart in Mississippi, a federal anti-poverty program for six thousand deprived Negro children throughout the state; Senator Stennis attempts to destroy the program by charging CDGM is subsidizing civil rights organizations; the program is cleared in Senate hearings in October.

Negroes in the Watts district of Los Angeles riot, burn, and loot for more than three days; more than thirty are killed. Martin Luther King states that the civil rights movement has failed to bring any relief to the mass of black people in America.

In Chicago demonstrations against *de facto* segregation in the schools attract thousands; comedian Dick Gregory, who aided SNCC projects in 1963 and 1964, was arrested along with others.

Berkeley Vietnam Day Committee members attempt to stop a troop train to dramatize their opposition to the war in Vietnam.

SDS announces a militant anti-draft program but later modifies this; in the fall of 1965, draft card burnings by students bring retaliation from the Selective Service Commission in the form of 1A classifications for those who persist.

Farm workers organize a partially successful grape strike in the Delano, California, area; pushed by strike leader Cesar Chavez, other unions cooperate in refusing to load scab-picked grapes onto carriers; Movement people begin to go to Delano to aid the strikers.

September   Under DuBois Club leadership the New Left School is founded in Los Angeles to educate for socialism.

National Student Association passes a resolution calling for the U.S. to cease offensive action and negotiate with the National Liberation Front in Vietnam; since 1962 NSA has emphasized the students' role in politics and in the community.

October   International Days of Protest sponsored by the National Committee to End the War in Vietnam; one hundred thousand people march or attend rallies throughout the nation.

November   Bettina Aptheker is elected a delegate to the convention to write a constitution for student government at the University of California at Berkeley; she has announced shortly before that she is a Communist Party member.

Norman Morrison, Roger LaPorte, and Alice Herz immolate themselves to force Americans to act to stop the war in Vietnam.

A Berkeley VDC plan to march fifteen thousand to the Oakland Army Terminal is blocked by Oakland Police; the march finally takes place without incident.

The New Jersey gubernatorial election is won by the Democrat who backed the right of Rutgers history professor and *Studies on the Left* editor Eugene Genovese openly to support a Viet Cong victory at a teach-in.

December   SANE sponsors a forty thousand-man March on Washington.

Students and some faculty at St. John's University, a Catholic school, strike for academic freedom.

A pacifist, drafted and undergoing basic training in California, is tried by a court-martial for "disobeying an order"; he is sentenced to three years at hard labor. Other servicemen refuse to bear arms because they oppose the war in Vietnam.

ABOUT THE AUTHORS

PAUL JACOBS is on the staff of the Center for the Study of Democratic Institutions and is associated with the Center for the Study of Law and Society at the University of California, Berkeley. His most recent book, *Is Curly Jewish?*, was published in 1965.

SAUL LANDAU has been an editor of *Studies on the Left* since 1959. He has written *A Minstrel Show*, currently being performed in San Francisco, and is writing a novel about the Cuban Revolution based on his experiences in Cuba in 1960-1961.